FutureSight

A PSYCHIC ODYSSEY

Also by Barry Neil Kaufman

Son-Rise

To Love Is To Be Happy With

Giant Steps

A Miracle To Believe In

The Book Of Wows And Ughs

Happiness Is A Choice

Son-Rise: The Miracle Continues

A Sacred Dying

Out-Smarting Your Karma
and Other PreOrdained Conditions

FutureSight

Barry Neil Kaufman

EPIC CENTURY PUBLISHERS

FutureSight copyright © 1998
by Barry Neil Kaufman

Published by Epic Century Publishers,
a division of Epic Communications Corporation,
2080 South Undermountain Road, Sheffield, MA 01257-9643

Originally published under the title *A Sense Of Warning* (Copyright © 1983)
by Barry Neil Kaufman

First published by Delacorte Press
Second publication by Dell
Third publication by Fawcett Crest (Ballantine Books/Random House)

Cover design and illustration by Lightbourne Images, copyright © 1998

Library of Congress Catalog Card Number: 95-067843
ISBN 1-887254-00-5

Printed in the United States of America

"I am larger than I thought.
I did not think I held so much goodness."

—Walt Whitman

"The most incomprehensible thing about
the universe is that it is comprehensible."

—Albert Einstein

"I can't believe that!" said Alice.
"...can't believe in impossible things."
"I daresay you haven't had much practice,"
said the Queen. "When I was your age,
I always did it for half-an-hour a day. Why,
sometimes I've believed as many as six
impossible things before breakfast."

—*Alice in Wonderland*
by Lewis Carroll

Author's Note

Time makes fools and heroes of us all. There are no replays of the past—only recollections in the present moment which keep changing and evolving. When we commit our stories to paper, we freeze them. But that frozen moment is no more reliable to tell a whole adventure than a series of photographs can accurately portray the events of some-one's life.

Although I have freely altered portions of this story and modified the presentation of those participating in order to maintain the privacy of all involved, the underlying fiber of the journey remains intact. As I look back now, decades later, and try to understand the causes of what happened, I find no simple answers. What did come from this experi-ence was a compelling opportunity for my wife and me to confront some of life's wondrous mysteries and learn to trust ourselves. Never again would we ignore that voice within.

This early experience became the impetus for us to con-tinue to challenge with passion and awe the limitations of unexplored perceptions and self-defeating beliefs. In the years that followed these events, we developed many addi-tional new perspectives which contributed to a body of understanding and knowledge that enabled our family sub-sequently to facilitate the healing of our son caught in the grip of a seemingly incurable illness. The challenge this child presented forever altered the course of our lives. As a result, we have gone on to work with and help people from all around the world and write about those experiences.

I can still remember the first time I began to celebrate my life, rather than mourn it; the first time I made friends with an ache or pain in my body, rather than fight it like an enemy; the first time I looked inside myself for answers and knowledge, rather than scurry around the countryside for some elusive truth etched in marble. Many things can turn our lives around: births, deaths, loves, losses, unexpected events, other people. Although, at the time, I neither fully understood nor foresaw the ultimate impact of what appeared to be a chance meeting, my life changed irrevocably as the result of my encounter with a stranger and the bizarre, unnerving and recurring series of premonitions that followed.

Often, thoughts and feelings about people and events come to us for no apparent reason. Many parents have noted "intuitive" feelings about danger to their children. Other people have reported hearing the voice of a friend or loved one in trouble although they were hundreds or thousands of miles away. Some of us know what others are going to say before the words leave their mouths. How often has a friend or acquaintance called us on the telephone at the very same moment we were thinking about them? And yet, the majority of these experiences are dismissed as hunches, daydreams or coincidences. When do we decide to heed that little voice inside of each of us that tells us to recheck a locked door or pause before entering a darkened room or be cautious when walking a street we've walked a hundred times before?

Years ago a newspaper article documented the action of a businessman who refused to board an aircraft when he "sensed" it would crash. He actually stopped at the doorway to the plane and turned around. Four hours later, that same jetliner did, indeed, crash. Had others on the plane had the same premonition and ignored it?

Our culture champions the left side of the brain, where

logic and science have become reigning deities. But the more primitive, more intuitive, and, perhaps, more knowing center lies on the other side. Most of us began to abandon the right-brain function after infancy. How could we trust what we couldn't explain? The natural ability to grasp our environment instantaneously and move uninhibitedly from a reliable center faded and, for some of us, atrophied. We no longer consulted some inner fiber to test the validity of our actions and thoughts. Our guidance came from external, rather than internal, sources.

We have noticed among the people we now teach and counsel that the more loving and accepting they are of themselves, the more aware and trusting they become of that little voice within. Precognition, or the ability to sense events before their occurrence, could develop naturally in a person who becomes more in harmony and balance with himself and his environment.

However, sometimes we can open the doorway to "futuresight" before we have developed the understanding and skills to deal effectively with such awareness. This was the case as my wife and I began walking this path. Nevertheless, what we learned inspired us to develop a much deeper level of self-trust as we confronted new and seemingly unpredictable challenges in our lives.

This book invites you on a journey into the right side of your brain, where intuition ultimately proves to be a clearer "god" than logic.

This story will be told from the vantage point of Peter Halsted. He will act as my surrogate.

1

"If you never know what you're looking for, Peter, how are you going to know when you find it?" Jamie had asked that morning, hours before my first encounter with Luke.

"Jesus, Jamie, you always do it in the morning. Do you lie awake at night trying to figure out which question to trip me with?" I pressed my fingers against my temples and moved them in a slow, circular rhythm. "It's seven-thirty in the morning, and all I want to do is just make it through the day."

Though Jamie approached me with her hand extended, she stopped her own motion. "I'm sorry, honey, I didn't—"

"That's what everyone says," I snapped, then closed my eyes, sighed, and shook my head. "I'm sorry, too. It's not you, Jamie. It's me," I said, unable to look directly at her as I backed away and left.

"If you never know what you're looking for, how are you going to know when you find it?" Her question haunted me all morning. Would I ever know? How would I decide when I found "it"? And would "it" help? Would "it" make a difference? I wondered how long Jamie could endure our arguments, our fights, or, more appropriately, my arguments, my fury, my discomfort. Had I always been this way?

Everything seemed so muddled. I still wanted to scream sometimes as I had twenty years before at little Denny Morton, who had killed a kitten with a rock just for the sport of it. When a car crushed Jessica Simon's head and the entire eighth grade attended her funeral, the anger I felt about Denny Morton and his rock surfaced again, but this time I had no one to scream at.

I dragged their memories into early adulthood along with the memory of Malcolm Green, a dear friend, who had abandoned a six-year friendship with me when he became a black studies advocate and had some internal compulsion to cleanse himself of all his politically incorrect relationships which included me. I remember becoming nauseated when I saw a dead American soldier without any legs in a photograph on the front page of the *New York Post*. Nothing made any sense. More than anything else, I had wanted to find a reason to stop feeling so confused and so damned vulnerable.

As an undergraduate I had hoped to find some relief in courses on ethics, metaphysics and evolution. I even interviewed members of the Newman Club, brushed up on my studies of the Catholic Church, and attended services at a Unitarian church, all to no avail. A visit to the Hillel Club on campus, a course in Yoga and three weeks in a Zen Buddhist temple did not give me a handle on my pain. In the end, I surfaced without any comprehensible answers. I wondered whether something was wrong with me, whether some deep, dark, unknowable fault had perverted permanently my ability to understand.

While most of my peers dove into their professions, I slipped sideways into mine, a fact that supported my perception of myself as out of step. My mother had saved all my sketches and paintings since second grade, validating some as masterpieces by framing them. "My Peter," she'd tell her friends, "he could take any face and make it beautiful." Maybe it had been her enthusiasm or that of the art teacher in high school who had tried to persuade me unsuccessfully to go to the Rhode Island School of Design, or that of Angela Vecchio, my first real fling in the eleventh grade, who called me Michelangelo Halsted every time we bedded down together, or a visit to the Whitney when I was depressed, that influenced my decision to use my hands as a tool for survival. What else could I do? Nevertheless, once committed, I created grandiose goals and pursued them obsessively.

At twenty-four, I started my own design and graphics studio. An apparent success. At twenty-five, I fell in love and married. Another apparent success. Then the loss of my mother and a dear friend within a year of each other almost completely destroyed my sense of purpose again. Denny Morton, Jessica Simon and other phantoms fell from cobwebbed attics. Returning to the university at night, I entered a doctoral psychology program. After three years, impatient and disappointed, I withdrew from formal enrollment to plot my own course of independent study. I remained a part-time student in homage to my own continued dissatisfaction . . . a dissatisfaction that had begun to intrude seriously on my marriage as well as my business. My impulse to find a pathway through my growing discomfort led to an intensive therapeutic relationship in which both the psychologist and I, unfortunately, shared the same confusions. No answers. No relief.

Some people shed their pasts like old clothing, but my past followed me like a four o'clock shadow on a sunny day. My early-morning argument with Jamie, random thoughts about my sister, and my recently developing paranoia about having a brain tumor created the background melody against which I tried to focus on a current conversation with two of my employees. Although I wanted to be alone, I brought Dominick, my studio manager, and Colleen, one of our senior designers, into Central Park to review the morning meetings and the workload for the remainder of the day.

"Don't forget the dye transfers for Harley this afternoon," I said. "And Kenny has to be notified about the Western retouching job for tonight." I waited until Dominick made his notes, then continued. "I'll handle, uh . . ."

Blank. I lost my thought. The second pulsating migraine of the day began to take its toll. I rubbed my head.

"Listen, you've been under a lot of pressure," Dominick interjected. "Why don't you take the rest of the day and..."

"That's it," I interrupted, smiling weakly. "The blueprints for the Hall of Justice building will be in today. I'll lay out sections for pure graphics, others for illustration."

"I can do that," Colleen insisted. "Dom's right, you've been..."

"I know how I've been," I said softly. Jagged, vibrating lines began to distort my vision. I slipped my hand into my pocket, then remembered I had left the pillbox on the desk. I couldn't bear going back to the office now. "Okay, Colleen, if I'm not back by two, you handle it."

She nodded enthusiastically. Colleen had been with me since the beginning, when my company consisted of a single sublet room. I had hired her right out of school. At first, she considered my idealism naive, almost foolish; she had learned different rules for survival in the streets of Spanish Harlem. But when I thrived, heaping success upon success, she found in herself a renewed ability to care. Then it all turned sour . . . not for her, but for me. What had happened? The headaches that had started three years before continued to get worse. Within the last two months, my studio lost two out of its five major clients because of my inconsistent involvement.

"I will also get some of the crew to work on logos for the hospital," Colleen declared. I didn't answer immediately. "What's the matter? You don't trust me?"

"You know better than that," I said. "I appreciate your help, but I'm not a basket case . . . not yet." I laughed for the first time in days. Even Dominick and Colleen found release in my macabre humor as they chuckled. "I'll also work on the logos while I take a walk in the park," I continued, "just to show you I still have it."

"One more thing," Dominick posed uncomfortably.

"What about Sam?"

"I'll take care of Sam."

"That's what you said last week, Peter. Do you know how many times I've had to have somebody redo his errors?"

I nodded, trying to concentrate and ignore the pain that now extended from my forehead to the back of my neck. "He'll come around, Dom."

"We carried Bob during his divorce and then he quit anyway. We subsidized Donna when she became pregnant. And now Sam and his drinking problem. C'mon, Pete, this is a business, not a psychiatric clinic. It's your money, but you're throwing it away."

"Hey, if you ever get sick, if you break one of those precious hands and can't draw for a while, should I dump you?" No answer. "Let me handle Sam, okay?"

"No more questions," Dominick mumbled self-consciously.

I had won the debate, but I knew Dominick had been right. But how could I fire Sam, crippled and flawed, without firing myself? The walls around Sam's pain had crumbled while mine remained reasonably intact. I couldn't let myself be so exposed, so vulnerable.

"Listen, Colleen," I added, staring into her dark almond shaped eyes. "There are layouts on my board from last night. The two with the check marks have to be finished. Okay?"

She smiled, giving her copper-colored skin a slightly rose cast, reflecting the delicate marriage of her Native American and Hispanic heritages. "Consider it done. Anything else?" I shook my head. "Peter, lean on us. You taught us well. We'll handle it."

"I . . ." The sentence faded before it cleared my throat. Her warmth had disarmed me. "I appreciate the mothering, but we're all allowed an off day. Give me two hours in the park and I will return renewed." Fat chance without my pills, I thought, tapping my pencil and then pulling out a pad from my breast pocket. A portable office. The basic tools of an illustrator and art director. Cliché. Almost a joke. One pencil, one pad. And yet these simple instruments had become my rosary beads, my connection to a familiar, sometimes comforting ritual of expression. "See, I'm all prepared to catch some sun and do some work."

After they left, I wandered past the ice-skating rink and climbed a series of steps leading to a large hill formed out of black granite. I leaned against a large boulder at the base of the huge mound. I withdrew a pencil, opened the pad and stared at the page. The intensity of my headache increased. Still trying to ignore the pain, I concentrated on the images drifting across the silent screen somewhere inside my head. Water. Green leaves. A woman laughing. A toothpaste tube dancing the Charleston. Mud pies. Clouds with hangers holding long underwear. "Damn," I muttered. I rubbed my forehead in a futile attempt to loosen the grip of the migraine. My eyes drifted back to the blank page. I waited. This time nothing came. Determined to break the conceptual constipation, I sketched a dog urinating on a hydrant several yards in front of me, then made several quick superimposed impressions of a jogger bouncing like a kangaroo along a distant path. I put a cross through the drawing and threw my pencil in the field. As it hit the ground, I heard a voice say, "There are many ways to plant a flower."

Turning, I became aware of a man sitting on the rocks above me. The glare of the sun bleached the hard edges of his form, making him a portly silhouette squatting on a ledge.

"On a river, we either paddle with the current or against it," the man said, as if speaking to an audience, though he faced an empty field.

I scanned the rocks, then the areas on either side of the man. Not a soul in sight. The sun irritated my eyes as I squinted at the figure.

"Excuse me," I called, "but are you talking to me?"

The man bent his head. "I talk to those who want to listen."

"Ah, ha." I sighed, chuckling. A New York crazy. One of those self-appointed lobbyists or crusaders who expound their views like dazed evangelists to any passing pedestrian or driver who would stop. I tipped my head, wanting to be polite, to at least acknowledge the stranger's existence, before turning my back to him.

The man spoke again—his voice soft, his diction surprisingly polished. "There is a time for each of us to hear what we were born to hear. But, sometimes, we busy ourselves with other things like headaches. Do you want help with your headache?"

I turned around, cocked my head and stared at the figure on the rocks, aghast. How could this stranger possibly know? I almost blurted out the question directly but felt ridiculous. I cupped my hands over my eyes protectively as a shield against the sun. Although my vision blurred from the glare, somehow I couldn't take my concentration off the lone figure. "But, sometimes, we busy ourselves with other things like headaches." I thought uncomfortably about my psychotherapist, who had once accused me of using pain, physical pain, as a way to retreat from my problems and personal disappointments.

"Can I help you?" the man asked in response to my continued scrutiny.

The familiarity, the implicit intimacy, in the stranger's voice unnerved me. Hadn't Colleen asked a similar question just minutes ago? Hadn't Jamie also made the same offer? Turning self-consciously, I proceeded to move away from the rocks, walking briskly across the field. I didn't understand my impulse to flee, but I didn't deny it. Eyes glued to the ground, I watched the grass bend under the weight of my feet. When I spotted the pencil I had thrown,

I stopped to pick it up, then looked back over my shoulder. The man's distinct form remained silhouetted against the sky. I'm running, I thought. Why the hell am I running? I fingered the edge of the pencil nervously, remembering the story in the morning newspaper about a man who had been knifed by a perfect stranger the day before in Central Park. Instant paranoia.

Nevertheless, I forced myself to turn and retrace my steps back to the hill.

Armed with pad and pencil, I climbed the rocky slope to the top. "Excuse me again," I said cautiously, "but do you mind if I sketch you?"

The man nodded his consent as he stared out across the field. His profile, childlike and ageless, creased into a smile from beneath his full beard. "I'm here for you," he said.

"Well, uh, great," I replied, noticing the thinness of my own voice. I couldn't quite get myself to stand in front of him, so I stood off to one side. The pencil line re-created the imposing perimeter of the man's massive skull. Atop his head the soft hair yielded to a perfect tonsure. With his legs tucked neatly underneath his short but ample form, he looked like a medieval monk despite the incongruity of his polo shirt, wrapped skin-tight around his large girth. Holding a cigarette and sipping from a can of cream soda, the man belched. Several minutes of silence followed that sound.

"Do you come here often?" I asked, trying to fill the void.

"Actually . . . no. I come here only when I know to."

"I see. Well, that's the best reason there is . . . I guess." I guided the pencil to form the man's legs and rendered his sneakers impressionistically. "My office is only ten blocks from here. This is my backyard, so to speak. Uh, my name's Peter . . . Peter Halsted."

"I'm Luke."

"Tell me," I said, attempting to appear nonchalant, "how did you know I had a headache?"

Luke inhaled on his cigarette, gulped a mouthful of soda, and smiled. "Sometimes we wear our conditions on our faces much like we wear our clothing on our bodies. I simply asked you what was apparent on your face."

I felt a rushing in my head. Did I look so desperate? And did I want help? From this man? From this chubby, adolescent-looking stranger loitering in the park? That seemed ludicrous, yet I asked another question.

"What do you do, Luke?"

"Some call what I do teaching. But how do you teach people what they already know?"

"And how do you help people with headaches?" I asked pointedly.

The little man stroked his beard thoughtfully. "By helping them to be happier."

"And how is that accomplished?"

"By letting go! I mean, I don't do it, of course; people do it for themselves. All I do is talk a lot and," he chuckled, "ask some questions."

"Oh, I see," I said, but I didn't see at all. The man's answers intrigued and frustrated me. I wanted to pin him down, confine him, and fit him into some easily digestible category. Only after five more minutes of conversation was I able to ascertain that Luke taught graduate level seminars in philosophy and mysticism in the Division for Educational Alternatives at a local teaching center. As I continued to sketch, I noted something even more peculiar. Luke's shadow did not have the same density as mine. I shifted my position to mimic the other man's angle to the earth. Even so, Luke's reflection on the ground was visibly lighter; the edges less defined. I considered pointing out the difference but hesitated. An answer might be more confounding than the observation.

After Luke rose, he brushed his pants clean fastidiously. He put the empty can of soda into his briefcase and removed all the cigarette butts from the ground. He hummed as he removed all his litter. I couldn't help but smile. The man not only took special care with his words, but with his movements as well, as if all his actions had the same value and importance.

Within seconds, no traces of his visit to the park remained. Luke nodded appreciatively. I imitated the gesture automatically; the exchange felt silly and satisfying at the same time. Regaining my guarded composure, I watched the stranger studiously. When he faced me directly, I noticed for the first time his different-colored eyes; the right one, a warm brown; the left one, a cool, intense blue. I felt drawn by the blue one almost immediately.

As I unwittingly concentrated on Luke's left eye, almost a minute passed. I decided to speak but unexpectedly found myself without words. We stood there on the rock, bathed in the sun. I had never stared into someone's eyes for such a concentrated period of time. When I tried to disengage, I couldn't. My vision blurred again, as if I had stared directly into the sun. My mouth became dry.

Luke touched my hand and squeezed it. The act broke our connection. I grinned, inhaled deeply, then touched my fingers to my temples, realizing suddenly that my headache had disappeared.

"I'm glad we have finally met," Luke said.

"What do you mean by 'finally'?" I asked.

Dipping his head as if confirming the legitimacy of the question, Luke answered, "Everything happens for a reason."

"Oh. Uh, huh." The man's insane. A lunatic. I wanted him to be deranged so I could dismiss him. I could not entertain seriously what I didn't understand . . . not here, not now, not encased in the body of this peculiar human being. If I ever found a soothsayer, he would look like a soothsayer, not like some gothic cleric in a polo shirt adhering to the no littering ordinances in the park.

Luke put his hand in the air as a parting gesture. Despite

the size and shape of his body, he climbed down the rocks with a marked agility. With his feet apart and his toes pitched outward, he waddled slightly, like a short Chinese panda bear, as he disappeared across the field.

I looked down at my designer slacks and Bass shoes. I tried to ground myself. I didn't need the knot in my stomach to announce the resurging tension. Another migraine had already begun to exert its viselike pressure in my head. In this moment I could accept what was familiar—the pain and the discomfort—more easily than the enigma, and ultimately, the power of the little man who would alter the direction of my life.

2

"Hummm," Larry Cranshaw, the marketing director of IMC, crooned as he paced the length of his office, viewing the poster designs, photographic layouts and illustrations that I had lined up against the side wall. Finally he paused in front of one colorful rendering and leaned over it precariously. The sunken flesh beneath his eyes tightened as he squinted. Holding that position, he fumbled through his pockets, locating a pair of stylish bifocals. Once the glasses had been balanced on the upper ridge of his hawk-like nose, he backed away from the design, then continued his meandering trek across the plush carpet. Not once did Cranshaw verbalize any preferences. In fact, he avoided direct eye contact with me and with the members of my staff gathered in the room.

Colleen sat bolt upright in a chair, her eyes fixed on some indeterminate point on the wall. Her jet-black hair, knit tightly into a long French braid, curled over her shoulder and hung like an exotic necklace. Only the muscles in her jaw, which flexed beneath her high cheekbones, betrayed any signs of impatience. Eddie, a politically radical art director on my staff, danced a cigarette expertly through his fingers, then flipped it into his mouth with the class of an accomplished magician. He flashed a mischievous grin at Lena, one of the illustrators who had worked on this project. Dominick, always the studio chieftain, squeezed Eddie lightly on the shoulder. The smile disappeared instantly from the younger man's face.

"Hummm," Larry Cranshaw murmured once again. Another three or four minutes expired, punctuated with several additional vocal but nonspecific utterances. Finally he turned to me, nodded, then continued his promenade back and forth across the room. The aimless quality of his pacing became more and more obvious. Nevertheless, I found myself tracking his figure with the same persistence with which I imagined a lion might track an intruder in an effort to protect her cubs. We had labored on these designs and illustrations for more than three weeks. They were our babies.

A polite tapping on the door drew everyone's attention.

"Yes, yes, come in," Cranshaw bellowed, obviously welcoming the intrusion.

"Sorry to interrupt you, Mr. Cranshaw, but I need your signature." He signed the paper with a flourish.

"Ellen, what do you think of these designs?"

Her face changed immediately. She leaned back on her hips and cast her head to one side, then rolled the edge of a pen seductively across her bottom lip. A familiar "hummm" erupted from her throat. "Well," she sighed, "I just love the two on the right, Mr. Cranshaw. They're kind of . . . sexy. And the red, well, you know, red."

"Oh," Cranshaw acknowledged. "Yes, red. Hummm. Well, thanks, Ellen, you've been a real help."

He then positioned himself in front of the two posters of Ellen's choice. "I'm partial to the two red ones on the right."

The buzzer on the desk rang once again, bringing the audio on the two desk speakers alive. "It's Artie," the secretary announced in stereo.

"Send him in," her boss replied.

A tall, lanky young man entered the room. An adolescent case of acne still ravaged his face. After introductions, Artie, a trainee in the advertising department, was asked to comment on the display of illustrative ideas.

"Hey," he said, "they're really neat. A whole lot better than the film."

Cranshaw looked at him sternly. Minus two points for Artie.

"Sorry, Mr. Cranshaw." The young man pointed decisively to the piece on the far left. "That's it for me."

"Hmm," Cranshaw mumbled as he peered at Artie's choice.

As the meeting crawled toward its inevitable conclusion, Larry rocked leisurely in his executive leather lounger, discreetly picking his left nostril. "How about taking the bottom of the piece on the left," he suggested, "and combining it with the second illustration on the right? Hmm. Maybe you can lift the star heads from the center poster and include them near the top." He rubbed his hands together like a crazed chef. Two from column A and one from column B.

My attempt to discourage him from mindlessly killing off each poster concept, one by one, caused Cranshaw to assert his rightful and almighty position as the client. The continued drone of his voice dulled my senses. Colleen came to the rescue and took scrupulous notes on his further comments.

Suddenly, I had a fantasy that almost completely disoriented me. In slow motion I rose out of the chair and lunged over the huge desk toward Larry Cranshaw. He stopped talking as his eyes bulged at my approaching figure. Too startled to resist, he sat there impotently as I grabbed the front of his suit, lifted him neatly out of his tufted chair and slammed him through the floor-to-ceiling plate-glass window behind him. The huge pane fractured into thousands of pieces. Once his body hit the open air, he began to scream. I waved, watching with detached fascination as he fell forty-two stories to the pavement below. People scattered in all directions as his body hit the ground.

Splat!

"Can you have it for us by the end of the week?" Cranshaw asked, drawing my attention back into the room.

"Sure we can," I answered automatically, although, admittedly, I hadn't the slightest idea what he was talking about.

As he continued to itemize his needs, I found myself repeating the fantasy over and over again.

"Wonderful. Now that we're all in agreement, let's get to it." Cranshaw slipped his moist, limp hand into mine and gave me a plastic smile. Instant nausea. At that moment the audible pulse in my head became painful . . . another migraine, the second for the day.

Dominick, defeated by the hodgepodge results of the meeting, saluted informally as he headed for the doorway while Eddie and Lena distracted Cranshaw by shaking his limp sweaty hand. Colleen, next in line, stepped right up to the man like a fearless street fighter. Instead of looking at him, she peered through him as if he were transparent. Then she smiled, politely and elegantly, before saying her good-bye.

"Fine job," Cranshaw complimented me as I turned to leave. In some bizarre fashion he had covered himself on every base and, thus, his fear about committing himself during the meeting had now abated.

I knew I had to say something, anything—if not for him, at least for myself. "I want you to know I don't agree with mixing concepts. This is not a salad, Larry, it's a marketing campaign."

"I know," he said, patting my shoulder paternally. "You're a purist, Peter. That's probably why you're so good. But this is the real world, you know."

What the hell does that mean? I couldn't find a polite way to answer him; so instead I nodded the best I could. My anger frightened me. Colleen grabbed my arm and directed me out of the room. The pain in my head had traveled down the back of my neck. I thought about the strange little man I had met a few days earlier in Central Park. Lunacy or lucidity?

As we walked through the outer corridor toward the elevators, Colleen said, "Cranshaw doesn't know what he's doing. Lucky him. Where I grew up, he would have been eaten alive."

"I don't think so," I protested. "In Spanish Harlem, with his personality, he would have probably been a successful pimp or loan shark."

"Is that the way it always goes?" Eddie, still a novice at client meetings, asked.

"Too often," I replied.

"That's not true," Colleen countered.

"True enough for me," I whispered as I pressed the elevator button.

To offset my assertion, she cited examples of more satisfying presentations. "Do you hear me, Peter?"

I had already withdrawn from the conversation. I peered at her through the veil of my own thoughts. One more meeting today, I calculated, and it's over!

"Do you hear me, Peter?"

I nodded blankly at her, focusing on the incredible familiarity of her words. Just that morning I had asked the very same question to someone else. Do you hear me, Raffson? James Raffson, my very own psychoanalyst, had dipped his head slightly as I rattled on in my sunrise session before going to work. In the midst of a sentence, I noticed his chest heaving. I stopped speaking, my tongue frozen on a word. The whistle of air currents whipping through my psychiatrist's partially stuffed nose assaulted my ears. God, the man fell asleep in the middle of my commentary! One hundred and fifty dollars an hour and still he couldn't keep awake. Panic. Could I be that boring . . . or trite? After six years of therapy, what a message! I leaned forward and eased out of the chair quietly. After circling behind the physician, I bent over his slumbering form and put my lips next to his ear.

"Do you hear me, Raffson?" I barked.

James Raffson jumped almost a foot into the air, knocking the pipe out of his hand and spilling his tea all over his desk. When his body dropped back into the chair, he looked up at my smiling eyes. An embarrassed grin rippled across his face.

"Caught you!" I whispered. Somehow I understood. We had circled the same problems for years. How many ways can you describe a migraine headache? How many times can you explore the confusion each time you buy a suit in Bloomingdale's with the stunned awareness that you feel no joy when spending money? How many times can you review yelling at the lady you love as therapy for your own pain? The questions kept coming up like wooden ducks on a circular pulley in a shooting gallery. How could I blame Raffson? He didn't have his own answers, so how could I expect him to lead me to mine?

During lunch we put the final touches on the Lutrec presentation. Dominick and Colleen tacked the sketches and photo comprehensives to the cork wall in my office. Using Pentels and a battery operated airbrushing unit, I made last-minute adjustments on the components for a two-hundred-foot exterior mural to adorn Lutrec's newly constructed suburban headquarters.

"Where's the three-dimensional model?" I asked Henry.

"We're still extending the relief sections."

The medication that I took upon returning to the office had relieved some of the tension in my neck, but my head still pounded. Most of the pain centered now in my forehead. My eyeballs ached. "Henry, do you realize what time it is?"

"It'll be done. Sorry, Peter. Sam screwed up again."

Sam. Poor Sam. He had drowned his brain cells in liquor. When Henry left my office, I kicked the door shut. Two seconds later Maire entered with a neat pile of papers in her arms.

"Later, okay? Tomorrow. Wednesday. Next month. Next

year." I turned her around gently and guided her to the
door. "This doesn't mean I don't love you. I just have to
concentrate on the Lutrec boards." She shook her head
like a patronizing mother as I eased her through the doorway.

Sitting on my stool once again, I twirled the edge of a
fine brush between my lips, dipped it into the acrylics and
lost myself in perfecting the edges of a face in one of the
illustrations. By layering pastel washes of amber over the
irises, I brought the eyes to life. I squinted at the face as I
finished, aware once again of the aching in my own eyes.

Thirty minutes later, seven of us piled into two cabs for
the short trip across town. Dominick read off the checklist
to Henry. Colleen rode in the other cab with Nigel, our
fabricator, who balanced the detailed model of the mural
on his lap. I kept reviewing each point in my head. We
needed to convince them of the efficacy of humanizing
their corporate image.

Once inside Lutrec's offices, we were greeted by the president, Ken Ricotta, then ushered into the private waiting
alcove adjacent to the board room.

"We're going to support you and your staff one hundred
percent on this, Peter," Ricotta assured me unnecessarily.
He flashed a quick smile as he left. Not again, I thought to
myself. I couldn't bear another Cranshaw meeting. Suddenly my vision began to fuzz slightly in the center. Little
vibrating electrical lines cut my sight, obscuring totally
everything directly in front of me. Oh, Christ! This was
the fourth time in a year that this had occurred. Both the
ophthalmologist and the neurologist found nothing after
extensive tests. Panic. A lather of sweat bubbled to the surface, making my shirt stick to my chest. "Get hold of yourself. C'mon." I couldn't withdraw and sleep it off as I had
done on previous occasions. Nothing left now except dim
peripheral vision.

"Dom," I said, "during the presentation, I'd like you to
feed the boards to me from the right side. And don't turn

your back to them. Make sure you face them all the time. Okay?"

Although I couldn't see his face, the void after my request increased my panic.

"Um, sure, Pete," he replied finally.

"Henry, you'll be on my left."

I had to avoid talking to Colleen; somehow she would know.

Just then the door opened at the end of the alcove. We all stood up. I concentrated on fixing Dominick's and Henry's shoes firmly in my mind.

"Peter." The voice came from my right. Ricotta. It had to be Ricotta. I grabbed for Dominick's arm, stopping him from entering the board room as I faced the direction of the sound. Despite the fact that I could not see directly in front of me, I noticed, peripherally, a pair of shoes pointed toward me. "Yes," I answered to the mass of jagged lines in front of me.

"The Evans group will be seated in the back of the room. Try to make them feel part of this. They've become quite a force on the corporate level."

"Ken, it will be done."

Dominick began to move again. I followed studiously behind with Henry to my left. Several times I had to suppress an impulse to turn and run or just collapse into a little ball and roll up inside of myself. Hands were thrust at me. I said many hellos, infusing as much warmth into my voice as possible. Then the room became quiet. You're on, you fool. I searched the ground for Dominick's shoes. Oh, God, Henry was there on my left, facing me. Where's Dominick? His legs appeared. He found a position at a forty-five-degree angle to the right. I mimicked the same diagonal.

"We've been working with Lutrec for four years now," I began. My voice quivered slightly. I concentrated on remembering details of the boards I had just finessed in my

office. Usually I searched the faces in front of me to deter-
mine their initial receptivity to our work. For once I had no
such distractions. The only thing grounding me in this
meeting was the continuous pain in my head. From time to
time during the opening monologue, I gestured toward
what I imagined would be the rear area of the room. The
Evans group. Don't forget the Evans group.

When Dominick handed me the first board, I froze. How
could I talk about what I couldn't see? Then, suddenly, I
remembered the checklist we had reviewed in the cab.
"This rendering," I continued, "provides an overview of the
multimedia approach we have taken in designing the
mural." Colleen interjected our plan to mesh ceramic tile
patterns with polished aluminum reliefs and a stained glass
background. Dominick fielded the technical questions.
When Nigel unveiled the working model, I heard some
murmurs of approval from the rear of the room. I wondered whether it was from the Evans group.

Toward the end of the presentation, Dominick handed
me a layout on an angle. When I turned it and held it in
front of me, I sensed a certain hush in the room. Several
people laughed.

"It's upside down," Henry whispered.

The muscles in my neck and shoulder snapped taut. I
turned the illustration slowly and smiled self-consciously.
More laughter. The meeting concluded with Ken Ricotta's
emphatic support.

As we left the board room, I followed Dominick's shoes.
The pulsating in my head intensified. "Great," someone
said on my left. I nodded. "I agree with your ideas, Peter,
we should take another look at how we can move people."
Several people shook my hand as our entourage moved
into what I supposed was the lobby.

"I've never seen you so slick," Ken said to me in a hushed
voice as he tapped my shoulder. Blind, Ken, not slick.

In the elevator everyone bubbled about the success of

the presentation. "And, Peter, holding the board upside down . . . at Lutrec's," joked Dominick as he laughed. "Brilliant, really brilliant."

It all sounded like nervous chatter to me. Did they know? Suddenly someone touched my arm. "Hey, you're awfully quiet," Colleen whispered to me. Quiet or transparent? I wondered. At that moment being exposed would have been much worse than being blind. I didn't want to be like Sam, pathetic even to those who cared.

"Listen, um," I announced, "I have another meeting. Ah, so, why don't all of you head back to the office and I'll catch up later."

After exiting the elevator, I stood next to the wall and waved good-bye. The footsteps retreated. I waited for at least three minutes until I could be assured they had all cleared the lobby. Then, like a blind man without his cane, I slid my hand along the wall as I headed toward the area with the newsstand. I remembered that the telephone booths were opposite the magazine racks. My knee slammed into something hard and metallic. The muddled image of a lobby ashtray solidified in my peripheral vision. Detouring around it, I walked another twenty feet. The wall ended. I tried to picture the phone booths in my mind. Four units. Each recessed into the wall. But were they directly or diagonally across from the newsstand? Why hadn't I been more observant? My breath became shallow. I had to cross the lobby. I let go of the wall and began walking, brushing against another person within the first four feet. We both made our apologies to each other, then I continued, aware that I might have been knocked off course. I counted each step, reasoning that I had to take at least fifteen to be parallel to the newspaper stand. On my thirteenth step I crashed into the paper rack, knocking it over. Frantically, I tried to pick it up and, somehow, find the papers.

Someone grabbed my arm. A voice behind me but not

connected to the person beside me shouted, "If you can't hold it, buddy, you shouldn't drink."

The strong hand holding my arm guided me away from the hissing voice. The shoes belonged to a woman. "I'm okay, uh, thanks." The force of the grip didn't loosen. "Well, could you help me to a phone booth, please?" We changed directions for a few feet, then stopped. I put out my hands and touched the glass enclosure of the booth. "That's it. Great! Thank you. I'll be fine now."

"Will you?" the voice answered.

Oh God, it was Colleen.

I put my hands instinctively over my eyes, too embarrassed to speak. Finally, I pushed out the words. "You never left the lobby, did you?"

"Nope. I never left."

A pause. "I should have stopped you when you bumped into the ashtray . . . but I wasn't sure. You can't see, can you?"

"A little. I'll be okay. Do you think anyone else . . . "

"Realized?" she said, finishing my question. "No. I don't think anyone knew. You were good, almost perfect, except when you talked to me in the elevator and kept looking at my forehead instead of my eyes."

"Go back to the office. I'll be okay."

"I'm not going to leave."

"Please let me do it my way."

"Maybe that's the problem; it's always got to be your way."

Silence. I couldn't answer her.

"I can take you to a doctor or a hospital," she said.

"I just had tests done last month for the same thing. They found nothing wrong." I slipped into the phone booth. "Please, Colleen, go back to the office." She didn't answer. I shifted my head, searching for her legs in my peripheral vision. "Colleen?"

"I'm still here," she said softly.

I jerked my head to the right. "Please, I just have to keep the little dignity I have left intact. Okay?"

"Okay," she conceded. I listened to her footsteps until they merged with the others in the lobby. I closed the door to the booth and ran my hand across the metal instrument until I located the dial. The fatigue began to overwhelm me. Suppose Jamie is not home? My fingers quivered, making it even more of a struggle to secure the number. Finally, the line connected. Four rings. A fifth. A sixth. Then a voice. Jamie.

"Hello."

I opened my mouth, trying to speak.

"Hello. Is anyone there?"

"Jamie," I said in a barely audible voice. My hand squeezed the receiver. Jamie, oh God, Jamie, I wish you were here.

"Peter? Is that you? Peter?"

"Yes," I said. I couldn't get it out. I knew my voice would break even before I spoke.

"Is anything wrong?"

"No. Well, not really. I—I can't see again."

"Where are you? I'll come get you." The urgency in her voice scared me. "Peter, please talk to me."

"I feel so out of control."

"Peter, it's okay. Tell me where you are and I'll pick you up."

"The Burlington Building. Sixth Avenue and Fifty-fifth Street."

"Don't move from the phone booth. I'll find you." The line went dead. I sat there in my own sweat with my head still pounding. I tried to relax for the first time. The little lines that had destroyed my vision became less intense. I leaned back against the wall, listening to the dial tone blaring from the instrument held in my hand. Depressing the lever with my index finger, I continued to hang on to the receiver so I would not be evicted from the booth. The ticking of my watch became audible for the first time. Pieces of conversations penetrated the glass door. The beep from the cash register at the newsstand sounded every six or seven seconds. Leather heels clicked against the tile floor. Time froze in a cacophony of random, disconnected sounds. Had it been ten minutes? A half hour? An hour?

Suddenly the door to the booth opened.

"Peter, it's me." Jamie touched my hand.

I had to turn away to mask the tears that flooded my eyes. I no longer felt frightened or even sad . . . just empty. I forced a smile. "Hi. Going my way?"

"Yup," Jamie said, guiding me out of the booth, through the lobby and out into the street. "One step down. Okay. Now another. And another." A horn blared. My body tensed. The screech of a policeman's whistle stopped me dead in my tracks. Jamie tugged lightly on my arm. "We're almost there. Keep walking." The door to the car clicked open in advance of our arrival.

"Can you feel your way in?" Jamie asked.

"Yes," I answered. Once inside, I dropped my head against the headrest.

Jamie slammed the door shut. "Thanks," she shouted to someone in the street as she entered the other side of the car.

"Who was that?" I asked.

"Just someone," Jamie answered finally. "You know, to help me double park and all."

"You'd never make a very good liar," I replied. "Was it Colleen?" A pause. "Then it was Colleen."

"She called right after you did. Then I guess she decided to wait until I came."

"The pills," I said to myself aloud. "I almost forgot." I whipped open the glove compartment and searched for the extra vial I had stashed there in reserve. Sure enough, I found them behind a tool bag. I downed two pills and hated myself for needing them.

Neither of us spoke for the next half hour. I closed my eyes, wanting to sleep, but I couldn't let go.

"Jamie, instead of going right home, how about driving to Mohanset Lake."

"Sure, whatever you want."

As the pain in my head subsided, the distortion in my vision began to clear. Nevertheless, when we reached the lake, I still had difficulty seeing. Jamie guided me down a small hill to a grassy knoll that we used to visit when we first moved out of the city.

"Stand here, I'll get the beach blanket." Jamie returned in less than a minute. "Okay, it's ready," she said, pulling me down beside her. I leaned back and rested my head in her lap.

"I'm sorry," I said.

"There's nothing to be sorry about, Peter. I just wish I could help you like you helped me."

"What did I do for you?" I asked, closing my eyes again, almost dizzy from exhaustion.

"You loved me."

Everything faded.

An hour must have passed before I awoke. I rolled to my side, aware that my vision had cleared completely. Jamie stood about thirty feet away, one hand holding the branch of a tree. With considerable expertise, she stretched her foot upward, almost bringing it parallel with her head. It was one of those "How does she do it?" positions that can only be assumed by the most lithe bodies. Jamie had exercised her body carefully, first, as an adjunct to physical therapy as an adolescent, finally, as a statement against the doctors who cautioned her to the contrary. She had fought hard, on a daily basis, to maintain her physical strength and agility. After lifting each leg ten times, she did a back twist touching her head to the ground. Her sandy blond hair spread like a fan on the grass. She noticed me and smiled. I waved, not wanting to interrupt.

Pulling herself upright, she darted toward the blanket. "How do you feel?"

"I'm fine. You didn't finish, did you?"

"It doesn't matter."

"It does. Go ahead, finish."

"Okay, Peter, if you want me to." Jamie walked about twenty paces. Reaching level ground, she flexed her legs like a dancer, finding the exact position of perfect balance. Her lips began to open and close with studied regularity; her eyelids fluttered, then closed. A smile spread across her face. Jamie had slid into a hypnotic womb deep inside.

"I love you," I whispered apologetically, knowing that my words would not penetrate her single-minded concentration.

In one continuous flow, she performed several side-stretching exercises and rolled her body from one position to the next as she had practiced in an advanced Yoga class. Once crippled, she had defied her disability and found a way to respect herself and order her life. I envied her rituals. She had battled a real, definable physical adversary while I merely fenced with invisible phantoms. Her wants had been clear, our marriage the apex of all her fantasies. Why wasn't that enough for me?

When she had completed the sequence, Jamie returned and slipped her hand into mine. "It passed, right?"

I nodded.

Jamie pressed her fingers against mine and exhaled noisily. "I always love it here. Especially now without any people."

"Me too."

A black crow flapped its wings noisily as it catapulted itself from a rock on the lake shore and ascended at a steep sixty-degree angle. At about one hundred feet, the bird spread its wings and glided in a leisurely circle above us. Jamie's clear blue eyes tracked the creature. Her slightly puckered lips fanned into a delighted smile.

"Don't you just wish you could do that?" she asked.

"Yeah . . . from the forty-second floor of the Burlington Building," I mumbled. Jamie grimaced. Her eyes became moist. "For Christ's sake, Jamie, don't cry for me." I stood up, fighting the rigidity in my own body. "Hey, I'm sorry."

"Me too," she murmured.

"Why do you always apologize when *I'm* wrong," I whispered. She didn't answer. Several minutes passed without either one of us talking. Jamie shifted her body several times, then began flexing her foot.

"Here," I said as I knelt beside her and took her leg in my hands. "That ankle's stiff again?"

Jamie nodded. "It rained this morning, remember?"

Applying most of the pressure with my thumbs, I worked my fingers down toward the Achilles tendon. I wished I could reduce my world to simple, physical components. Tendons. Muscles. Vertebrae. Whatever.

"When did it start with your eyes this time?" Jamie asked.

"You don't want to hear it. It's boring. Even Raffson finds it boring. He fell asleep during my session this morning." I leaned back on the blanket. "After all the therapy, all the weekend seminars, all the graduate courses . . . what's the difference any more? Maybe I'd be better off if it were a brain tumor; then some smart surgeon could cut it out and I'd be fine . . . maybe."

A brisk wind whistled through the trees and bent the grass almost horizontal to the ground. Jamie shivered. "C'mon," I said, "you're cold. Let's go home."

"No, I'm okay. If you want . . . "

"Please don't play martyr," I interrupted.

"But it really doesn't matter to me."

The innocence of her answer unnerved me. "Okay," I whispered, "let's just go anyway." We walked across the field together.

"I'll race you," she challenged.

"What about your ankle?"

"That's probably what it needs . . . a good workout. What do you say?"

"You're on."

In that split second, Jamie lunged forward and raced across the field. "Hey!" I protested. When she didn't stop, I chased after her. I could hear her laughter as she jumped a small stream and headed up the slope. Pushing my legs to move faster, I began to narrow the gap between us. She whipped her head around for a second, realized that I was approaching and angled her route toward a more level plateau. Once on the cut grass beside the parking lot, I gained on her quickly. Sweeping my hand out as far in front of me as possible, I tried to grab her, but she twisted sharply to the left. "Never," she teased. Now I dropped the blanket and charged toward her. Angling to the right, she eluded my grasp a second time.

"I'm going to bring you down, smart ass," I continued. Suddenly, she began to favor her left leg. I broke my run immediately. Her hips! "Stop, Jamie." She looked over her shoulder and slowed her pace. As she walked back, a limp became noticeable.

"C'mon," I said. "I'll give you a piggyback ride to the car." As I carried her, my arms tucked around her legs, I wanted to thank the universe for having her in my life. For a rare moment, I felt grounded.

As I steered the car out of the parking lot, my migraine returned. Ignore it, I told myself. "Talk to me, Jame."

"Sure. Let's see. Oh, I got my cello back today from Rensaleer. The sound's so much better. You'll love it. And still no hot water in the apartment. Craig said they would try to have it fixed before you got home."

"If only he meant it," I interjected, the throbbing in my head becoming more distracting.

"He tries, Peter."

"You really believe that, don't you?"

"I guess." She shrugged her shoulders.

My eyes ached again. Automatically I began to squint.

"Are you getting another headache?"

"Yes," I said flatly.

Silence.

"Why don't you pull over and let me drive?" Jamie said.

"I'm fine."

"But you have a headache."

"Will you stop treating me like an invalid?" I shouted. "I can drive, damn it. I've always done everything with these headaches, haven't I?" She didn't respond. "Well, haven't I?"

Jamie slinked back in the seat and stared blankly out the window. "I'm just trying to help," she replied.

I'm losing it. I knew my endurance was fading. My body and its pain had become my enemy. No place to hide any more. I dropped Jamie at the apartment and drove through the neighborhood for almost an hour. I made one stop, at a local jeweler's, and went home.

"Better?" Jamie asked as I kissed her.

"Yes," I lied. Pulling her away from the kitchen counter, I turned her body gently until she faced me. She peered at me quizzically. "I—um—well . . . here." I pulled a small box from my pocket and handed it to her. Jamie stared at it for several seconds. "Go ahead, look inside." She lifted the lid, revealing a stylish gold watch. "Thought you could use an alternative to your Timex." She didn't respond. "Listen, if you don't like it, we could exchange it." Still no response. "Hey, are you going to talk to me?"

"You didn't have to do this, Peter."

"I know," I said weakly.

"Why don't you take it back, okay?"

I grabbed the watch from her and sent it sailing across the room. The impact with the wall smashed the delicate instrument into countless pieces. My mouth dropped open. Why? Why had I thrown it? And then I remembered the pencil I had tossed in anger in the park. What had he said?

Ah, I remembered. "There are many ways to plant a flower." Certainly this wasn't one of them.

Jamie grabbed my arm as I turned to leave.

"Please don't," she said.

Her eyes glistened. I reached out to touch her face. My fingers intercepted a tear running down her cheek. "You deserve better," I mumbled.

"You don't understand, Peter. I know you. I know what's under that pain. There is nothing better for me—ever."

I wanted to believe her. When I put my arms around her, I could feel her hands trembling. Please, hands, stop trembling, I begged a silent God. I knew I could not keep doing this to Jamie; I had to change, somehow, or leave. That silly, ridiculous man in the park came to mind again. The calm I had experienced in his presence returned to me for an instant. I knew I had to find him.

3

Only the neat rows of wooden chairs at the front of the
large expanse suggested a classroom. The floor-to-ceiling
windows and brown industrial carpeting softened the academic environment. I leaned my chair against the back wall;
another university, another graduate course, but the same
me. The muddled conversations that blanketed the room
ended abruptly as the teacher's rotund body bounced gently through the doorway. An easy smile adorned the man's
face as he entered the room, a can of soda in one hand, a
lit cigarette in the other.

Researching Luke's teaching schedule at the university
began with some confusion as to his actual identity. A
fellowship student at the registrar's office realized that my
description matched the characteristics of Professor Chris-
tian Lukas, who, apparently, had been nicknamed Luke as
a child.

Everyone knew the infamous Professor Lukas, either by
direct experience or by reputation. And everyone knew the
appropriateness of his name, which had been more than a
mere abbreviation of his last name. Luke had been the
kind of child who rescued all living things: dogs, cats,
ducks, even worms. He would repair the wings of fallen
birds, doctor an injured squirrel back to health or hand
feed a family of kittens abandoned by their mother. Thus,
his family called him little Luke, after the healer-physician
of ancient Rome known as Lucanus and, ultimately, as St.
Luke. Many said little Luke would have been a gifted veteri-

narian or doctor, but all that was purely academic now, the fellowship student gossiped. Although he, himself, had never taken any of Professor Lukas's classes, "unique," "spacey," and "cosmic" were among the adjectives he used freely to describe this unlikely character who had attracted a loyal following among the student body.

I spent an entire evening debating my inclination to audit one of his courses. Maybe the disappearance of my migraine had been a coincidence, I argued, rethinking every detail of my meeting with him in the park. The man had guessed, at best, about my headache. A guess. A simple guess! It was probably apparent in my body language. Nevertheless, the more I tried to diminish the impact he had had on me, the more I felt compelled to attend the class, any class . . . just one.

Waving his arms like a music conductor leading a slow-motion symphony, Luke asked the members of the class to sit on the floor, encouraging us to gather together in a close circle. He joined the group playfully, then extinguished what was left of his smoldering cigarette butt and set his soda can down beside him. For the next five minutes, Luke sat silently in the half-lotus position, one leg neatly folded over the other, alternately meditating and sharing wide-eyed smiles with each member of the class.

Some students appeared visibly uncomfortable with Luke's bizarre initiation. Others closed their eyes. Certainly, in the battery of courses I had taken over the past eight years, I had met many unorthodox, if not downright senile, instructors. Yet, I, too, found the knee-to-knee intimacy on the floor unnerving. When Luke beamed at me, I felt relieved and smiled. Ah! He remembered me. But then his glance turned toward the next student, giving me no special sign of recognition. I wanted to wave my arms. "Hey, it's me. From the park. Don't you remember? It's me, Peter." I rehearsed alternate lines in my mind, finally cursing my own silence and my obvious need for recognition.

A shared mood of acceptance and permissiveness prevailed in the room. Despite my own caution, I nodded at several other students: a marked contrast to the guarded demeanor I had maintained before Luke's arrival. The second headache of the day subsided as I relaxed and stopped focusing on myself: a time to pause, to feel all the physical sensations fluttering through my body.

Amidst the quiet, Luke's inert hulk cut the form of a Buddhist priest seated before the altar in an Eastern monastery. Just before the class started, I had heard someone refer to him as "the happy monk." Luke was still wearing a polo shirt. He still smiled sweetly through his unkempt beard. But now a pair of eyeglasses accented his huge, uncommon owl eyes. I found myself studying them.

The soft, mellow brown iris of his right eye contrasted dramatically with the piercing, blue hypnotic gaze of the left one, which appeared to follow and hold in its grip all those who crossed its path. Had he been tall, Luke would have been an Orson Welles riding a white cloud into the Land of Oz. Being of less than medium height, his impressive mass hovered close to the ground, giving him an expanded aura of humility.

"Once you are here, it no longer matters why you came," Luke began in a hushed voice. "On the surface, the curriculum will deal with philosophy and the mystics, but learning is the process of unraveling." Luke's voice was unusually gentle, devoid of the impatience or boredom that typified many professors. He slugged down a noisy gulp of soda. "I can teach you nothing," he continued. "The world searches for saviors, when in fact we can only find guides. You won't find truth in this room. For that, you must look inside."

I found myself listening carefully to every word. It was as if Luke had taken command of the very molecules in the room. I tried to hold back, to maintain a reasonable position of cynicism. But, like an unguarded infant, I had been lured already into Luke's commentary.

In a potpourri presentation he mixed Eastern and Western philosophy, weaving a beautiful fabric out of varying
systems of thought. Afterward, as he related Greek philosophy to the teaching of Christ, an odd change in perspective
occurred. As Luke told stories of Jesus, he began to use the
first-person form of narrative.

"As I stood on the surface of the water, maybe only one
hundred yards from the shore, he didn't recognize me,"
Luke whispered to the class. "So I called Peter again. 'Yes,
it's me. And you can do it too, Peter. Come.'" Luke paused
and stared directly at me as if the directive had been given
for my benefit. Several seconds passed before he altered his
concentration and resumed speaking. "And, for a minute,
Peter actually stood on the water. Ah . . . but suddenly, he
looked down and realized in disbelief what he was doing.
Naturally, he sank right under." Luke chuckled. "Poor
Peter." Once again he looked at me. Heads turned. Everyone gazed in my direction. I wanted to protest, but I didn't.
Instead, I shifted my body position several times and
avoided direct eye contact with my classmates as well as
with Luke.

When the man disengaged finally and resumed his rhap-
sody about walking on the water while detailing the facial
expressions of John, James and the others, I found myself
drawn into what ceased to be just a story and took on the
compelling texture of an eyewitness account.

In the midst of the recitation, Luke paused again. He
rested his folded hands on his protruding abdomen and
closed his eyes. "A saint is one who knows he cannot be
made unhappy," he said. "He chooses carefully . . . just as
Christ chose the cross." His eyelids popped open. "Just as
all of you chose to be here. You see, in some fashion, we're
all saints. The problem is most of us are afraid to claim
what is already ours." He nodded his head emphatically, a
gesture that confirmed his thoughts.

Luke rose from his seated position, lifted the long window pole from its hook on the wall and opened the top portions of several glass sections. Then he turned, stood motionless and stared at us with smiling eyes. As he resumed his narrative with intense concentration, he balanced himself against the pole still held in his hand. Like a chubby gymnast, Luke began to revolve ever so slowly around it. Several people laughed. A young woman in a red tunic began to giggle uncontrollably. Luke stopped. Obviously he had been so absorbed in the story that he had not been aware of his body movement. He laughed, too, then returned the window pole to its rightful place. Seating himself among us, he opened a second can of soda, ignited another cigarette and talked to us as if we had been part of an intimate family. His commentary swept me beyond the classroom walls once again.

"In the hot desert, just east of old Jerusalem, Lazarus rose from the dead. Everyone could see him standing at the entrance to the burial cave. His sister broke from the crowd and raced down the hillside shouting his name. When she touched him, the trembling in his hands and face disappeared. He lifted his head slowly, laughing and crying at the same time." Luke rubbed the tip of his nose thoughtfully. "And yet, not a single tear moistened his eyes." The diminutive professor leaned forward. "Not a single tear," he repeated in a whisper, as if to share a secret.

"A fantasy?" Luke challenged in a more boisterous voice. He put his hand out toward us much as a blind man might do in soliciting a donation. "Well, what do you think? A fantasy? A dream? Or, indeed, a kind of journey most of us know nothing about?" No one answered. Luke then continued the lecture, fencing masterfully with a multitude of concepts about life and death in rapid-fire sequence: Kant, Buddha, Aristotle, Sartre, St. Thomas, Freud—an anarchist's mix created with ease and expertise. As colored objects and playful sounds dazzle the young child, all

philosophies awed Luke as special and wondrous . . .
though, he confided, they were often grossly inaccurate.

I couldn't put my finger on exactly what did it, but I was
hooked and relieved at the same time. My own pain and
tension had taken an intolerable toll in recent years. My
relationship with Jamie had begun to crumble. My business
had slipped into an obvious decline. Nothing had worked:
no therapy, no soul-searching, no vacation from the hot
spots. Wherever I went, I always brought with me the one
thing I couldn't conquer: myself. In this classroom, in this
man's presence, suddenly that didn't seem so bad. Finally I
had found someone who not only could outtalk and out-
think me, but who, I believed, knew that elusive "something" that I had searched for since my undergraduate
days. I hated the thought of a master or guru. Certainly this
hairy, overweight, chain-smoking sage addicted to carbon-
ated soda defied such categorization. His simplicity and
humility, almost to the point of embarrassment, held a different promise, one that opposed my current lifestyle. Perhaps that incongruity lured me more than any other single
factor.

A perspective on life wove its way through the lecture. I
wanted to hold the very quick of life with the same soft and
loving embrace that Luke exhibited. I would have given
anything to see like that man. And what was the risk? I had
begun to lose everything I valued anyway.

As the students cleared the room, I moved hesitantly
toward the front blackboard, then stopped dead in my
tracks. I remembered a former idol, a psychology professor,
who claimed to hold the key to personal liberation while
secretly wasting himself with gallons of bourbon. Was Luke
authentic? The "happy monk" nodded at me as if giving
me permission to leave. Instead, I edged closer.

As one student left, he called, "Hey, Luke, thanks, . . .
great class." Another radiated her delight as she hugged
her teacher. A third held on to his arm possessively. Sud-

denly, I realized the teacher had turned to face me.

"Are you still planting flowers with pencils?" Luke asked.

"So you did remember," I replied, smiling. He nodded his head ever so slightly. "Well," I continued, "do you have some time to talk?"

"Sure, Peter." Luke beamed as if he had anticipated the request. Pausing for a second, he slipped his meaty fingers into the loops of his pants and pulled them upward on his portly frame. I fantasized that if Luke suddenly decided to brush his teeth in the middle of the classroom, it too would seem like a natural, appropriate move. Luke distinguished himself not so much in what he did as in how he did it.

Sitting in the chair beside me, he lit a cigarette with the tip of an expiring butt. Then he unfastened his leather briefcase, which had been waiting by the front desk, and withdrew yet another can of cream soda. Taking a sip, he eyed me closely. His gaze became hypnotic.

"I feel peculiar," I admitted.

Luke tipped his head in acknowledgment. He gazed off at some indeterminate point in space, lingered there for several seconds, then faced me again. "Can I help you?" he asked.

The same question that he had asked in the park! I looked away when I realized my eyes had begun to tear. I had never before experienced such a genuine flow of warmth from another man. "I don't know where to begin," I said, avoiding Luke's eyes.

"Why does it matter where you begin? You've already begun. This is just a step; we take many steps along the path."

"I don't want to give you a sob story. How can I? On the surface, I have everything I ever wanted. The woman I married is special, sensitive and caring. I have my own business, a commercial graphic arts studio, until recently a flourishing one. But it's a fake. I'm a fake. I go to Bloomingdale's and buy five suits I don't need in order to soothe my discontent. But instead, I only feel empty, hollow." I wiped a thin layer of perspiration from my forehead. My pulse pounded in my temples. "I keep looking for an answer, but I don't even know the question." I stopped, self-conscious about my intensity. "I know I'm rambling."

"I'm only aware of how beautiful it is for you to share this with me," Luke commented.

Reassured, I continued. "You know, when I was a kid, there was always somebody who wanted to be a doctor, a musician, a banker. Well, I was completely lost in that crowd. Me—I was still trying to figure what it was all about when they were already hustling. When I told my father I was thinking of majoring in philosophy, he said to me, 'Hey, did you ever see any want ads in *The New York Times* for philosophers?'" We both laughed. "I guess I've been believing I have to live with all this—the confusion, the anger, my damn headaches. But right now, I feel different. I really think you know something—I'm not even sure what I mean when I say that but, Luke, I . . . I want to learn from you."

"Okay," he said softly. "If you want, you can take some of the other courses I teach here at the university."

"No, Luke, that's not exactly what I meant. I've heard you have private classes in your home where you teach more about expanding our consciousness. Can I join those classes?"

"Yes, if you want to."

"Thank you. Really, thank you." Was this me, really me? I had been groomed to be cocky. My business had thrived on it. I never imagined finding safety by revealing what really went on inside of me. And yet this chair had become home plate; this stranger, a coach rather than an adversary. I wanted to bring everything I thought to the surface, to say everything, to hold nothing back.

"Is there something else?" Luke questioned.

"Yes, absolutely yes." Go for it, Peter. "I know this might

sound strange, but, well, could I buy you breakfast and dinner whenever you're free? Maybe, during those times, I can
ask you my questions. I'll be your best student." I held my
breath. Had I played the fool?

Luke bobbed his head up and down. "Give me your
hands," he said softly. I hesitated. Maybe the man was crazy
after all.

"Are you afraid?" he asked.

"No," I replied, thrusting my arms out and presenting my
palms. Despite his request, he never once looked at my
hands. He kept staring into my eyes, as if he had concentrated on the silent spaces between my words and sen-
tences. In that apparent vacuum Luke found his answer.

"Okay, Peter, if I can help you find what there is for you
to know, I will. When you get what you want, I will be getting what I want."

I sighed in relief, having anticipated a negative response.

Luke handed me a small yellow business card. Unlike its
conventional counterparts, this form did not contain the
usual information. The four letters of Luke's name had
been hand-printed carefully and artistically in the center,
just above a handwritten telephone number. Title, position,
address, even alternate numbers, had been conspicuously
omitted.

As we rose from our chairs simultaneously, Luke
searched my face with his uncanny eyes.

Sensing my own transparency, I retreated a half-step,
which did not go unnoticed. My diaphragm knotted
beneath my rib cage. For the first time in my life I had
moved toward something I wanted instead of moving away
from what I feared or disliked.

Luke tapped my shoulder affectionately. With a single
nod, he ended our meeting.

Three weeks later, Luke left the university to devote all
his energy to teach and tutor people privately and in small

classes. Yet some people insinuated that Luke's removal from the staff had resulted from an investigation conducted behind closed doors.

Many faculty members and parents had questioned Luke's influence over his students. Two sets of parents had registered complaints with the president's office and the dean's office. They accused Luke of luring their children to his home and either hypnotizing or drugging them. Both of the students involved, who remained loyal to Luke, dropped out of school to protest the charges. They subsequently left their homes, refusing to reveal their destinations.

Numerous and conflicting rumors circulated throughout the university at the time. Supposedly, during one meeting with the administration, Luke answered most of the questions with questions of his own. And his statements, consistent with his style of conversing, were more like openended riddles than concrete replies. The school had never endorsed Luke's individuality enthusiastically. Now his soft and accepting manner infuriated administration officials. To end the controversy, the president asked for Luke's resignation.

Another version depicted Luke denying the charges emphatically but admitting that he had a unique and pervasive power. When asked to define this power, he laughed. The request dangled awkwardly in the room. Luke then turned his penetrating eyes toward the president, who became frightened and bounded from the room to escape his gaze. Another board member dismissed the meeting and ultimately refused to reconvene it. He maintained his distance by using registered mail to notify Luke formally of the termination of his services.

A third account met with the most enthusiastic reception from the student body, but not because of its credibility. In this version, the investigating committee asked Luke to sit in a high-backed chair in the center of the room. He refused by shaking his head. The investigators sat around a large mahogany conference table, grumbling and snorting their disapproval of this break from academic protocol. Hissing tongues ejaculated charges in an unending barrage. Luke waved his arms above his head in a circular motion . . . a prehistoric warrior neutralizing hostile territory. He never uttered a word. The only pronounced activity in which he indulged was the sipping of soda from a can.

When they had finished firing their remarks at him, they demanded an explanation. After standing for several seconds in silence, amused and perplexed, Luke grunted. The sound that came rushing from his vocal cords held no malice or aggression . . . like the sound of an elephant clearing his throat. He leaped up onto a chair in the center of the room. For a moment he paused, thoroughly pleased with his nimbleness. Dipping his head as he bent his body forward slowly from the waist, he acknowledged his bewildered audience with a humble bow. Without further ceremony, he unbuckled his belt and dropped his pants and underwear to his knees, then proceeded to urinate on the carpet. Not a full blast, just a carefully controlled, partial voiding of his bladder. This height of institutional transgression halted immediately when two guards interceded, lifting Luke bodily off the chair and throwing him out of the building. People still point sometimes to the curious yellow stain on the rug in the president's office as evidence.

The facts about Luke's departure disappeared in a whirlpool of conflicting narratives. In the end there were never any official claims or charges. Nevertheless, the fingers remained pointed. Only the man's private students appeared uninfluenced by the accusations.

Luke, himself, dismissed the subject, saying, "These stories say nothing about me, but they do tell us much about the beliefs and fears of those who repeat them. To the closed mind, the truth could appear to be a lie, or a lie might have the appearance of truth."

4

I clutched at Luke like a starved man lunging for food. My commitment to attend some home classes and talk informally with him during recess periods escalated quickly into a compulsion to make daily contact with him. In effect, I tried to question Luke at every possible turn. I revised my work schedule and, for months, became his shadow.

Each weekday I raced into Manhattan like a crazed disciple, jumping red lights and speeding on grassy meridians in an effort to accompany Luke to breakfast. Sometimes, we arranged to have dinners together as well.

To my surprise, Luke asked as many questions as he answered. He insisted that every problem brought with it the gift of a solution. I found the notion hard to digest. What about my migraines, which had brought me, literally, to my knees for years? How many prescriptions had I filled? How many medical examinations had I endured to no avail? Almost once a day I had had to retreat to a couch or bedroom, often leaving a project in shambles in order to escape the agony.

Rather than have me indict my own migraines, Luke encouraged me to accept my body and its signs. "Could you imagine," he said to me once, "having a cancerous brain tumor and loving it like your very best friend?" I laughed. The notion was patently absurd.

One afternoon, as we sat together on an isolated bench in Washington Square Park, Luke noticed me pushing my fingertips against my forehead.

"Is it one of those headaches again?" Luke asked.

"Yes," I answered. "But I'll be all right."

"Of course you will," he agreed. "But first you might want to clear the migraine. You can't hear music if there's noise in your ears."

I smiled despite the pain. The vise that had gripped my head since early morning spasmed the muscles at the back of my neck and jackhammered a sharp sting repeatedly between my temples.

"Close your eyes," Luke said. I followed his instructions. "Good. Don't try to minimize your pain. Do the reverse. Concentrate on it. Your body is giving you a message. Allow yourself to feel it fully. Try to think of the pain as a friend and, like a friend, you have to learn to trust it."

The words seemed all wrong. I dug my fingers deep into my thighs. Hold on. Don't resist. The commands I muttered to myself were ludicrous. I reconsidered the bottle of orange capsules in my jacket and their promise of relief within twenty minutes.

Luke placed his hands solidly on my shoulders. The strength of that contact bolstered my confidence. For the first time I did not fight the throbbing assault. I thought my skull would explode, but, instead, the aching exceeded the boundaries of my head, releasing me finally from the pain as if my consciousness and my body had undergone a slight separation. I opened my bloodshot eyes, unmasked and disoriented.

"What do you see?" Luke asked.

"You. The park." The words tumbled from my mouth. I couldn't quite focus my attention on the question.

"Stay with it. What else do you see?"

I shook my head. "What do you mean?"

"Close your eyes again," Luke whispered.

As my eyelids fell, I heard the distant thunder of metal hitting metal. And then I saw my friend, Helene, amid the twisted steel. Pretty Helene, contorted and crushed.

"Please," I mumbled, "I can't do this."

"You can, Peter," he insisted. "Tell me what you see."

Memories, real and imagined, flooded my mind. "It's Helene, my sister." Her mouth was stained with blood, her eyes fixed and vacant. The muscles in my face began to twitch.

"Follow her, Peter." Luke's hypnotic voice subdued the panic, but I couldn't hold back the tears; hating death, hating her death. "Go with her as you went with the pain," Luke prodded.

"I can't," I protested, forcing my eyes open.

"I'll go with you if you'd like," Luke offered.

"I don't understand," I insisted as my headache began to overwhelm me again.

"You will. Just close your eyes. This time welcome the pain." Luke paused for half a minute, then asked me another question. "What do you see now?"

To my surprise, I saw myself standing beside an iron gate. Two coffins descended slowly into the frozen ground. Thick flakes of snow blanketed the other grave sites. I had returned to the cemetery often, party to what had always been a solitary ritual. But this time I noticed another mourner beside me, a man whose rounded silhouette reminded me of Luke. That presence comforted me. I had met death twice in the last three years. My mother first, then my dear Helene. I promised them I would always remember. Sometimes, I coveted the anguish of that lonely ritual as the only way to recall their presence.

Despite my attachment to Helene, the entwined memory of my mother often dominated my thoughts. Alone in the soup of old images, I visualized her rummaging through the refrigerator on the last night. The final climb up the stairs. The last eleven o'clock news. I heard the last breath my mother inhaled while watching *The Late Show*. I described each minute detail to Luke. My mother's pasty-white face haunted me.

"I never told her I loved her," I whispered.

"Do you want to tell her now?" Luke asked.

"But she's dead."

"If you think about her, if you see her beneath sealed eyelids, then she's not dead for you. Nothing really ever dies."

With my eyes held firmly shut, I peered into the face in front of me. "I love you . . ." I couldn't finish the sentence. I withheld the last word.

"Are you finished?"

"No," I admitted. I stared in my mother's face. I re-created my parents' bedroom around her deceased form. However, this time I sensed Luke in the room with me. Impossible. A distortion of memory. "You're still here, Luke, aren't you?"

"Yes," he confirmed, moving closer to me on the bench. "When it's no longer necessary to be here, I will be gone."

I didn't understand. Instinctively, I braced myself by bending forward and wrapping my arms around my legs. My internal focus drifted back to the bedroom. I heard a younger, less inhibited voice within me say, "I love you . . . Mommy." At that instant, the wrinkles disappeared from my mother's face, leaving in their wake a soft, peaceful smile. The omission had been rectified. I had said good-bye. "Mom," I murmured again.

"It's okay. You can let her go now, if you want to."

Now Helene's face poked its way rudely to the forefront of my consciousness. Her divorce and her twenty-fifth birthday had all occurred within a month of her death. We had been friends since childhood. The imprint of her freshly cut hair and extravagant new clothes stayed with me as a sad commentary of her last effort to hide her burgeoning depression.

One Sunday morning, Helene hit the accelerator to pass another car and sped head-on into an oncoming trailer truck. I refused to go to the scene of the accident, where

police spent three hours separating her body from the
jagged metal and morning groceries. Her laughter and
comic routines had ended. Irrevocably. Without warning.
Helene . . . how I missed Helene. I always remembered the
accident: the screech of tires that I never heard, the twisted
metal that I never saw. Now, with Luke at my side, both on
the bench and in my daydream, I conjured up a completely
different image. I described her laughing green eyes as she
stood waist-high in a swimming pool of ice cream, her
major earthly addiction. Her joy brought a smile and tears.
The outrage I had bottled up for over three years began to
drain.

"When it's no longer necessary to be here, I will be
gone." The words Luke had spoken ten minutes ago
echoed in my head. Would this man disappear like some
cloudy apparition? Had he already left? I froze. The shouts
and laughter of children from a distant playground drew
my attention momentarily. The wind whistled in my ears.
I became afraid to open my eyes and lose the deep quiet
within.

"Do you want to go now?" Luke asked softly.

Relieved, I looked at my strange, enigmatic friend. Without hesitation, I hugged him in a display of affection I had
never shown toward another man.

As we left the park together, a little boy, chasing after a
ball, crashed into Luke's legs, then tumbled to the ground.
The child's face began to crinkle, a prelude to crying. Tears
flooded his eyes as a wailing sound gurgled from his throat.
In a quick, agile movement, Luke knelt down and lifted the
little boy back onto his feet.

"It's okay to cry," Luke said soothingly, his face creased in
a simple smile. "But you don't have to. You didn't hurt me
and I watched very carefully when you fell and I don't
think you hurt yourself either." The boy relaxed his face,
stopped crying and looked at Luke with an amazed expression. "There—see," he added appreciatively, wiping the

tears from the child's cheeks. "Now both you and I know the same thing."

Luke retrieved the ball from under a nearby park bench and placed it in the little boy's hand. The youngster smiled and ran back across the grass toward his friend, turning around continually in order to catch that one last glimpse of Luke.

The incident in the park with my migraine, reinforced by the tenderness with which Luke had treated the little boy, broke the dam for me. In subsequent meetings with him, memories, frustrations, guilt and anger poured out like rushing walls of water. Even the incident with Denny Morton, who had casually assassinated the kitten, bubbled to the surface and, in review, lost its sting. Jessica Simon died one final time and Malcolm Green was forgiven finally. The more I talked and questioned my unhappiness directly, the more comfortable my world became. By facing my demons with Luke's help, I eradicated much of the pain and cleared my vision. Eventually the migraines disappeared. Even my conceptual talents as an art director seemed enhanced. I no longer encountered creative blocks. Visual ideas gushed easily from a bottomless well.

A multitude of beliefs about myself and my past had altered during this bizarre and wonderful apprenticeship. Luke argued repeatedly that "happiness heals," but the transformation appeared almost magical.

Nevertheless, my relationships with people improved dramatically. Without the wall of anger in front of me, I found I could express affection more freely, especially with Jamie. Although a mammoth amount of my time had been consumed by Luke's classes and my design studio, the remaining moments, although limited, allowed me to touch my wife with a softness and caring that had previously eluded me. In business I relinquished my daily requirement of perfection for myself and my clients; yet, at times, I worried about becoming passive.

"You see, Peter, you'll always climb the ladder," Luke
said. "There's no way around that. It's just that when you're
happy, you won't notice the act of climbing. You'll look
back and it will seem as if the rungs on the ladder simply
grew beneath you."

That first year with Luke passed quickly. Sometimes, it
seemed like a day; sometimes, a whole lifetime. The more I
studied and confronted myself, the more I believed I owed
Luke a debt that I could never repay. That imbalance, on
occasion, made me uneasy. I noticed, also, that in the two
periods when I had not seen him for a week or two, some
of the old phantoms and frustrations bubbled up, almost as
if Luke's presence directly influenced and, perhaps, even
controlled my comfort and clarity.

5

My business prospered again, allowing Jamie and me to purchase our first house: small, Victorian, with gingerbread woodwork lacing its feminine peaks and its curved, wraparound porches. Jamie not only had taken charge of finding the right house, but had invested much of her time and energy in restoring the interior. Oak fireplace mantels and mahogany banisters were stripped of layers of paint and refinished. She challenged eighty years of rust and decay, rejuvenating a wood-burning cooking and heating stove in the kitchen. We wallpapered the bathrooms in antique patterns she had located in specialty shops in the city.

But no room in this house could compete with the nursery for her interest. Each week she would make something special for the room: a mobile of fabric trinkets found in thrift shops to hang above the crib, a simplistic rendering of a father, a mother and a child scratched into a piece of slate to decorate a wall, an oversized teddy bear fashioned from leftover fabric to sit on the bureau. The memories of the cold, sterile wards in which she had spent her childhood loomed in the background, increasing her dedication to provide a safe and caring world for the children she might ultimately have.

In the evening, when I went to Luke's, she would practice her cello, sometimes for two or three hours at a stretch. Jamie joined two string ensembles. She buried herself in Bach, Haydn and the other early classicists, whose compositions grounded her with their repetitive order and predictability. Once she became pregnant, she played her instrument in what was to be her child's room. "Music feeds the soul for both born and unborn people," she declared, ". . . and this baby and nursery are going to be filled with loving vibrations, even if I have to do it all by myself."

The last part of her comment lingered with me for days. "All by myself." Perhaps we needed to spend more time together. Initially, Jamie had been supportive of my association with Luke, but lately her silence on the issue had become marked. In March, Luke left for a month-long trip to Europe. With the meetings and classes suspended and my work situation less demanding, I focused more of my attention on Jamie. Each night during this period, I tried to do something festive with her: see a Broadway show or a ballet or take a buggy ride through the park.

One evening, after we had stacked a pile of logs in the bedroom fireplace and ignited them, I turned to my wife as she crawled across the bed, her enlarged abdomen hindering her movements.

"Okay, fat lady," I joked, "I have a small, modest surprise for you."

Jamie propped herself against two pillows and eyed me mischievously. She twirled the front part of her shoulder-length hair into a sloppy tassel and fashioned a thick mustache across her face. "Well," she countered, "I have a surprise for you."

"Who goes first?" I asked.

"Ladies first." She pulled her nightgown tightly over her stomach and said with mock ceremony, "Oh, little friend, dream child of Peter and Jamie, arise and make yourself known." I laughed. Jamie put her index finger to her lips. "Shhh!" She stared at her enlarged abdomen. I approached slowly, following her lead by focusing intently on her belly. Then, suddenly, the cloth moved.

"You're kidding," I bellowed as I sat beside her. Jamie

pointed to the opposite side of her stomach, guiding my
attention. Another movement from within broke the curve
of her abdomen. "Wow!" I said, "Some magic trick."
Jamie's eyes filled with tears. "Our baby's alive, Peter,
really alive." After sliding into the bed beside her, I placed my hands
carefully on the rounded surface of her pregnant belly.
"I'm ready," I whispered to the unborn person inside.
Jamie giggled; her stomach bounced up and down.
"Hey, Jame, c'mon, cut it out. You're disturbing our
child." She nodded playfully and held her breath. We both
stared at her belly again; this time no movement. I
shrugged my shoulders. "Nothing's happening."
"Be patient," she countered in a quiet voice.
"When did this start?"
"This morning. The first kick happened right in the middle of Dvořák's concerto in B minor."
"In B minor," I echoed. We both laughed. "Wait. Stop
moving. I think I feel something. Yes. Yes. The baby's moving. Absolutely. That was really strong." I put my face
against her stomach. Something rounded and firm shoved
against my cheek. "There she is again," I observed.
"How do you know she's a she? Maybe she's a he."
"Well, we can't call the baby an 'it.' It's not an 'it'; I
mean, it's a person." We laughed again, then plotted the
baby's movement for the next twenty minutes.
"Jame, I know I haven't been around as much as I
should."
She smiled at me and played with my hair. "I'm not com-
plaining."
"If you did, I guess I wouldn't feel so guilty about it.
Between classes and sessions with Luke, I guess I've been
pretty scarce. Look around. Except for the bathrooms, you
did this house single-handedly. I know how much it means
to you, but I had to spend the time getting my head together . . . so I could live with myself and really appreciate you."

"I know," Jamie said almost sadly. "Maybe it's me, Peter. Maybe I don't have enough to give you."

"Don't say that. Don't ever think that." I turned her face toward me. "I love you and you are all that I need. It's going to be different; you'll see." Jamie looked away. "Okay, what is it?"

"What's going to happen when Luke comes back?"

"I'm not going to stop participating now, but I'll ease off soon, I promise. Besides, I have a wonderful idea. You ready?" She nodded. "Luke is starting a new course; it'll focus on improving intuition and psychic awareness. I have always felt someone really important has been missing from the group. So did Luke. So you're invited. Officially. How about joining the Tuesday night class?"

Jamie shook her head. "No. I can't do that."

"Why?"

"You know why. I'm terrible in groups. Besides, I'm not a member of Luke's exclusive club."

"There is no exclusive club. Jame, you'll love it."

"I won't. You've seen me with Luke. I get tongue-tied in front of him. Those weird eyes of his. And the way he stares at me."

"He looks at everyone the same way. I'll hold your hand during the whole time in class," I offered with a big grin.

"I know, you want to make a joke out of it."

"Sorry," I said softly. "I really want you to come. It's about time. Jame, we'll be together more. I know you want that."

Jamie closed her eyes. "Peter, I am so thankful for what he's done for you."

"For us," I added.

"Okay," she said, opening her eyes, "for us. But I'm just not comfortable in that kind of situation. I'm no good at group games. I just wouldn't know what to do."

"But you would. You'll see. How about coming to one meeting? If you don't want to go after that, fine."

"Could I think about it?"

"Sure." I counted to ten aloud. "Okay, what's your answer?"

"I don't have one."

"Jamie, are you scared?"

"Sort of, I guess."

"About what?"

"About losing you."

My mouth dropped open. "I don't understand."

Jamie sat up. "Okay, I'll go."

"Wait a minute. You didn't explain what you just said."

"There's nothing to explain, Peter. I'll go. That's what you want, isn't it? So, please, don't push me."

"Okay," I said. The fire roared in the silence between us. I don't think I ever quite realized what an impact my time with Luke had made on Jamie. I forced a smile. "Still want my surprise?"

She nodded her head.

"Give me a second." I left the room and returned with a package in my hand.

Jamie untied the ribbon and then, as if opening the crown jewels, she lifted the tape gingerly and freed the wrapping paper without ripping it. When she looked at the tiny photograph contained in the small three-by-five wooden frame, she gasped. "Peter, Peter, where did you find this?"

"In one of the boxes when we moved. I thought you might like it framed."

"Oh, yes, thank you." Her eyes glazed as she admired the tiny yellowing photograph taken in one of those coin-operated booths. Jamie ran her fingers across the glass as if trying to touch the dark brown skin and grand smile of the bulbous woman staring out at her. She rolled off the mattress, placed the picture frame on top of the television set and returned to the bed. Not once did she take her eyes off the portrait.

"What do you think, Peter?"

"I think Mary-O looks great on top of the TV."

Jamie shook her head. She reclaimed the portrait and positioned it on the nightstand beside her. "There, that's better. I want her closer to me." Her eyes squinted as she continued to peer at the photograph. Her body began to rock in a just perceptible front-to-back motion. "I can still hear her, just like she's in the room with us. The lullaby she used to sing to me; it's so clear, even now."

"I know," I said, but she didn't hear me. A soft humming filled the room, a humming that allowed Jamie to keep the only beautiful thing in her childhood alive. I used to be jealous of Mary-O. Maybe that was why I had to frame her picture and bring her into our bedroom. Somehow, I needed to test myself. Now I knew. I no longer felt competitive with the bigger-than-life black lady from Jamie's past.

"Maybe Luke could help you find her," I volunteered.

She turned toward me. "How? What do you mean?"

"The new course, remember? Extending our awareness, maybe even increasing our psychic ability." Jamie stared at me blankly. "You're still going, aren't you?" She nodded affirmatively, but her whole body stiffened. Scared to come and scared not to come. "Jame, trust me," I said. "Trust Luke."

"I'll try."

Jamie looked back at the old photograph. Mary-O had asked her to trust her, too, and then disappeared.

6

Using my knuckles, I knocked softly on the large wooden door and waited. Jamie stared at the ornate brass latch, her eyelids quivering nervously. Her torso arched backward to counterbalance the weight of the baby, who in the eighth month jutted out in a pointed mound in front of her. I stepped behind her swollen figure, put my hands below the bottom of her belly and lifted upward.

"Ah," she sighed, leaning against me and smiling. "That's what I need—my own private crane."

The buzzer released the door latch, inviting our entry.

"Ready?" I whispered.

"Ready as ever," she answered somberly.

"You'll have a good time," I assured her as I turned the curved handle and opened the door.

We had arrived late; thus, as we entered, we encountered the group sitting in silence, the traditional opening of Luke's gatherings. Gregorian chants recorded in a monastery in southern France slipped off the tongues of robed monks and echoed into the room through stereo speakers mounted near the ceiling.

Stepping over bodies, we found a place near the couch, seating ourselves on a massive Oriental rug, which covered most of the wood-planked floor of Luke's living room. The bare, pale yellow walls of the loft embraced the space. I kept a firm grip on Jamie's hand, squeezing it often. I could hardly believe she had come. Somehow, I imagined she shared the same notion as she busily catalogued everything and everyone in the room.

Some class members lounged on the floor near us. Others seated themselves in chairs and on the couch. A mixed montage of people . . . from businessperson to psychologist, from social worker to artist, from teacher to gambler. There were eighteen people in the group. Within four months there would be only twelve.

Jamie had been right. With the exception of her and one other person, these were the handpicked members of Luke's inner circle. Although I would never have defined us as an exclusive club, we did share almost two years of common experience. Many of us had enjoyed great personal growth during our association with Luke.

Rudy, who had lived with Luke for many years, broke the silence by asking those present to regroup in a circle on the floor. His soft, cherubic features exuded an uncanny sweetness. Jamie sighed in relief. I knew she would find comfort in the gentle manner of this expatriate of the computer business. His distended stomach swept out from under a turtleneck sweater and bounced haphazardly over the ledge of his tightened pants as he supplied cushions to those who wanted them. He squatted beside me, touching my forearm affectionately. I returned the gesture, aware of Jamie watching me. I shifted my body, moving closer to her until our legs touched. Her face relaxed into a momentary smile.

Luke, completing the circle, nodded to Rudy, who rose on cue and switched off the stereo. Different patterns of breathing became the most prominent sounds in the room. Tucking his loosened polo shirt neatly into his pants, Luke began his visual procession, regarding each person closely, greeting them with his silence and intense talking eyes.

He began with Hera, whose limp, plump form lay face down, flat out on the rug. Exhausted from having run in high gear all day as a preschool recreation and dance coordinator, she had fallen asleep immediately after her arrival.

She had successfully disguised her identity as a resident of suburbia by dressing like a tarot-card reader from the East Village. For several minutes, Luke stared at her back. Suddenly, with a quick jerking motion, she awoke as if someone had poked her.

"Hi!" she sang with an embarrassed giggle. "I, uh . . ." Hera shook her head playfully, aborting an excuse that would have ended in an apology. She extended her hand toward Luke, but by then his eyes had turned toward the other members of the class.

When he came to Jamie, he smiled. His eyes brightened noticeably. The blue one seemed to swell and move slightly forward in its socket. Some students had claimed that, if a person were unafraid, with Luke's sanction they could look into that eye and see a triangular torch burning deep inside. I always wondered why people needed to create myths around their teachers, as if the lessons and clarity they imparted to others were not enough. Although Jamie and I both scoffed at such an assertion, I knew what she must have been thinking as she stared into his crystal-blue iris. For several seconds, she remained straight-faced, frozen; then she grinned as a way to camouflage her uneasiness. I put my arm around her, remembering how unnerving this ritual had been for me the first time, though now I found comfort in these wordless greetings. Many people I knew could make their words lie, but their eyes tended to reflect the truth.

As Luke continued to stare at Jamie, she nodded politely, yet forcefully, trying to break his focus. Although she had met him several times socially, I don't think she had ever seen him so intense. The muscles in her body tensed. She glanced at me, then retreated behind closed eyelids until she knew Luke had turned from her.

At that moment Max Sorenson entered the room, late as usual, his large, playful walrus mustache hiding his mouth. The lamplight danced on his huge forehead and shiny bald crown. He squatted between Luke and Rudy, nodded to all his classmates in one sweeping motion, then smirked jubilantly at Jamie and me.

"You made it," he mouthed to my wife. Before she could answer, Max eyed Luke, who had apparently been waiting for him to finish. "Sorry," he whispered. This large, demonstrative person, who had come initially to Luke's previous classes as my guest, had not only been a dear friend but also had served as Jamie's psychotherapist for two years. The two of them had developed a special camaraderie. Sometimes I wondered whether Max had needed Jamie as a patient more than she had needed him as her doctor.

Luke yawned, then stretched playfully. Everyone focused their attention on him as he popped open a can of cream soda. "All learning begins with trust." He leaned his head back and gulped some soda. "So maybe what we have to do is learn to trust each other." He smiled at us like a kid with a new chemistry set and introduced a "trust" exercise. He asked Max, considerably taller and heavier than most of his peers, to lie down on the rug. The class encircled him, each of us kneeling beside his prone figure. Instructing us to use only the index finger on each hand, Luke asked us to lift Max into the air.

"How can we possibly do that?" asked Claire, a public relations executive whose rural Louisiana origins still molded her speech.

"Perhaps we could try before we judge it," countered Luke in a soft and reassuring tone. "Remember, try to see Max floating easily upward."

Each person slid two fingers under his body. We began to apply pressure in unison. To everyone's amazement, Max lifted effortlessly off the floor. As we pushed him higher, we rose to our feet. Finally, with our arms fully extended, we held him near the ceiling, high above our heads.

"Fantastic," Max blurted from aloft.

After several minutes, we returned him safely to the ground.

"Okay, who's next?" Luke grinned broadly.

"Oh, I love it. I just love it," squealed Hera, the second to be held aloft.

I had the very same sensation, surprised at the sense of security and warmth I experienced when supported by only the fingers of those gathered beneath me. Jamie took her turn, though she clutched her belly, never quite letting go throughout the exercise.

Jessica, the only other new member of the group besides Jamie, took her position on the floor reluctantly.

"I warn you," she whispered into her husband's ear, "if this degenerates into one of those huggy-touchy scenes, I'm leaving!" Woodrow looked away from his wife, embarrassed because many of us had heard her comment.

After we reassembled back into a loose circle, Luke removed the cigarette that had been dangling from his lips and addressed us again.

"Without speaking, I'd like each of you to turn in place so that you have your backs to each other and you are facing the outer walls. Once everyone is comfortable, we'll turn the lights off."

As people shifted position, Jamie, her legs bent beneath her, arched her torso forward, taking great pains not to put any pressure on her distended abdomen. Then, despite her pregnancy, she reversed the movement gracefully, like a ballet dancer, aligning her body once again over her knees. She knew her joints would stiffen if she remained in any one position too long.

Noting her maneuver, Luke tipped his head and peered at Jamie through his eyebrows, then saluted her by smiling and pointing his folded hands in her direction. Poised in that position, he closed his eyes.

Jamie put her lips to my ear. "What was that all about?" she asked.

"Give him time," I whispered.

"I would like each of you," Luke directed, opening his eyes again, "to be more sensitive to yourselves, your bodies, your own space. Be aware, as you wish, of the others in the room. We can use our voices but not words. Whatever communication takes place, it will not involve eye contact or verbalization." He paused. "Does anyone have any questions?"

"I don't see why we have to turn out the lights; that seems a bit adolescent to me." Jessica, a school psychologist, who like Jamie had come to class to accommodate her spouse, spit her words like bullets. Her crisp verbal assault startled everyone.

Woodrow glared at his wife. "Oh, come off it, Jess!" he barked.

Her face turned crimson.

"Maybe if I explain what we might achieve with the lights out," Luke said softly, "you'll feel better about the exercise." He lit another cigarette, guzzled from a new soda can that Rudy had supplied, then dipped his head sharply. He put his hands together again, palm to palm, and touched his fingers to his lips as if about to pray. "Vision and language are probably the two most active means we use for staying in touch with our environment and with each other. In the dark, we will minimize these functions and heighten others . . . whichever they may be. It's a role-shedding exercise that I believe you'll all enjoy," Luke concluded.

The harshness melted from Jessica's face, erasing lines from around her eyes and softening the rigidity of her jaw. "Thank you, Luke," she murmured, entranced by the sweetness of his voice and the fatherliness of his demeanor. He smiled at her with delight, accepting her so easily and completely that his manner alone disarmed her anger and fear. Even Jamie, who shifted positions continually to redistribute the weight of her abdomen, appeared calmed by his explanation and tone of voice.

"So," Luke added, "does anyone else have any questions?" The room fell to silence. "Good, let's begin." Rudy turned off the lights.

About five minutes passed in silence. Reggie and Dan, who sat to my left, jostled each other in the darkness. They shared an obvious allegiance to Luke. Both had been students together and had dropped out of the university during the controversy over their teacher. Weeks after leaving their own homes, they reappeared as Luke's house guests. Reggie catered to Luke with such dedication that some suggested he acted more like a disciple than a student.

In contrast, Dan returned to school while still in residency at the loft, ultimately earning his doctorate in psychology. Now he took the initiative in the class unwittingly.

He had a well-developed talent for flatulence, a residue of years spent playing hopscotch with colitis. Often his intestines outtalked his mouth. Perhaps in an effort to camouflage such sounds, Dan began to rub his hands together noisily. Within seconds almost everyone in the room followed his lead. I joined in the activity as well. Flesh slid against flesh—a sandpaper symphony.

After several minutes the hand-rubbing stopped abruptly. I laughed in surprise at the uniform cessation; so did several other people. Another period of silence followed, longer this time.

Jamie raised her arms to stretch her back, feeling the strain of sitting on the floor. Then, remembering Luke's suggestion, she explored the space around her hesitantly. Pushing her hands upward, then out to the sides, she touched what she believed was my arm. She ran her fingers along the skin, coming across an unfamiliar scar on the inside of the wrist. Jamie jerked her hand away frantically and cuddled her arms in front of her chest.

Someone rose to his feet, rudely breaking the silence in the room. Moving legs made the floor creak under the rug. The erect figure paused, exhaling a long hollow sigh. With dragging feet, it paced the center of the circle. Ears strained to listen. Muscles contracted. Then a blanket of silence.

I searched the darkness behind my head, locating precisely the position of the person standing and yet the fixing of that position in my mind had nothing to do with sight, sound, or touch. In some fashion I "sensed" or intuited the person's presence.

Suddenly, springing over a student, who gasped, the figure moved swiftly away from the circle. It seemed to vanish, but in the next moment it came into the center of the circle again. Jamie grabbed my arm tightly. She didn't know these people as I did. I considered aborting the game and going for the light switch, but at that very moment the standing figure brushed by my shoulder, hurtled through the murk like an apparition, and was gone, having penetrated deep into the darkened house.

A door opened slowly in the hallway. A switch clicked. A flash of light whipped through the room, then the door slammed, draping everyone in total darkness again. Suddenly the heavy rain of urine hitting the water in the toilet bombarded the room.

Laughter filled the chamber. Jamie released my arm. The toilet flushed. Rudy opened the door, grinned triumphantly at us, then turned off the light and returned to the darkened room.

Several other participants, now considerably more relaxed in the dark, began to laugh in concert. Another grunted. The atmosphere turned carnival. The children hidden behind these adult faces began to emerge. This interplay persisted for several minutes until, one by one, each person fell silent. Finally, a few muffled grunts and then a hush. Heavy breathing. Scattered laughter. Bodies changing positions. Several sighs, a cough, more coughing . . . and silence.

Max entered the arena by humming one continuous

note. His intent was lyrical and sincere, his tone rounded and full-bodied like a voice in a Christmas choir. I joined by harmonizing as best I could. Several others participated. Within minutes, the room filled with a soft chorus of humming voices.

The volume increased slowly. And increased. Then, as if some giant vacuum were sucking the sound out of each person, the crescendo built more rapidly. I found my mouth drawn open as I chanted louder and louder. Max's voice strained with intensity.

Jamie had difficulty participating. What appeared spontaneous with the other group members required a definite, self-conscious effort on her part. The anonymity of darkness protected her privacy as she experimented, first with a whispered chant, then a full-bodied singing voice. Yet in spite of the involvement, she held back.

Nevertheless, in general, the embrace of the chorus intensified. We could have been soldiers bonded together by the rally of a patriotic marching song. The sound increased. Someone's first pure shriek ignited the others like a match thrown into a pool of gasoline. The loft filled with a wild cacophony of shrills. Unrestrained. Intense. Furious. A guttural and sensual release, primal in nature. No one could stop now. I wanted to reach for Jamie but couldn't.

A common thrust enveloped everyone in the room. The sound became almost intolerable. As it continued, my limbs grew lighter and lighter. Beads of sweat lacquered my face. I rocked back and forth. And then I had the most peculiar sensation of being drawn outside of myself, momentarily freed from my body, taken aloft by the energy that flooded the room. I experienced an incredible movement, like a glider soaring upward on an ascending air current. The shouting became the rush of passing wind. Dizziness overwhelmed me as I realized that I was not drawing any breaths. I panicked, grabbed my chest, and forced

myself to inhale consciously. Extending my arms, I touched
Jamie on one side of me and Dan on the other in an effort
to ground myself. Each of them grabbed my hand instinctively.

As the voices grew more exhausted, they began to rise
and fall in pitch on their own energy. At last they sputtered
like an engine running out of gas. After driving ourselves
to near exhaustion, we stopped abruptly . . . as if prepro-
grammed. Some laughed as Luke switched on the light. A
party atmosphere prevailed. I threw my arms up like a gymnast and exhaled loudly. Jamie, squinting to avoid the
glare, pulled her legs together and curled them beneath
her body. She wiped a thin layer of perspiration from her
forehead.

"Remaining nonverbal, why don't we all just turn to the
center of the room and face one another," Luke suggested.
We shifted positions noisily.

As eyes met, faces smiled. I looked at Jamie, but she
stared at the floor. She now shared something with these
people, something elusive yet intimate. Give her time, I
told myself. She needs time. I rubbed her sizable belly gently and whispered, "I'm really glad the two of you are here
tonight." She pressed my hand tightly on her abdomen.

That's our baby, she wanted to say but didn't. That's what
is important, she thought, not any trust exercises or games.
Misinterpreting her grip on my hand, I smiled broadly.
Finally, I thought, she, too, had experienced the magic of
one of Luke's classes.

The mood changed rapidly. Smiles faded. Jessica shifted
her body sideways, her eyes riveted to the floor. Hera began
to comb her hair with her fingers. The old masks slipped
into place. And yet something had changed.

Warm breath humidified the air. Hands began to twitch
nervously. Fingers picked at the corners of chairs as feet
tapped out versions of the Morse code. Suddenly Claire,
nicknamed Lady Claire for her distinctive Louisiana accent,

gasped as she looked at me. Her cheeks grew ashen and her lips lost their color. Her entire body seemed encased in a heavy shadow. I looked at every part of my body nervously, checking for any wounds or blood. What am I doing? I thought suddenly. Ah, another part of the games. I began to smile, but the seriousness of Claire's expression cut my reaction, sobering my mood immediately.

"Claire, what is it?" Luke asked calmly. "What's wrong?"

Unwilling to alter her focus, she continued to stare at me and babbled almost mechanically. "I see two—there are two eyes hangin' over Peter's left shoulder. They're as plain as day. Just hangin' there and—and lookin' right at me."

I jerked my head to the left but didn't see anything.

"Claire, why does that frighten you?" Luke asked, his voice still relaxed and soothing. Why didn't he challenge her? It was silly; obviously, there were no "eyes" over my shoulder.

When Claire turned away and concentrated on Luke, her panic subsided. Slowly she eyed me again and sputtered, "Death . . . it comes to you from over your left shoulder."

If I could have hushed Claire, dissolved her observations, I would have. To counter her commentary, I found myself half smiling in a facial expression that seemed oddly familiar. When I glanced at Luke, I realized that I had unwittingly duplicated one of his poses. Jamie stared at me, then peered back at our teacher. I knew that she had detected the similarity. I forced a more complete smile, not wanting this incident or my face to alienate her from the class or destroy whatever small rapport had developed. C'mon, Jamie, smile back at me. Suddenly, there was a strange distance between us.

Claire spoke again. This time, as I listened, I observed her face growing lighter and darker. Each time she gaped at what she identified as "floating eyes," her face became shadowed, as if the lights in the room had been dimmed. I scrutinized each lamp. The lighting had remained con-

stant. Maybe the exhaustion from shouting during the previous exercise had fatigued me to such an extent that my
vision had been affected. I wanted to stop the illusion, but
somehow I couldn't withdraw my concentration from
Claire. The voices around me faded. Even my concern for
Jamie became secondary. Only Claire existed in a vivid fashion.

She continued to gawk at me. Now, when she looked at
Luke, she complained that her vision had been blurred by
a yellow mist that enveloped everything.

"I have the same impression," Hera offered. "Sort of a
yellow haze all around you, Luke."

"I think everybody's really trying hard to make something happen," Jessica volunteered with less antagonism
than her previous comments.

"What do you mean by 'make it happen'?" Luke asked.

"Like squinting your eyes as Claire seems to be doing,"
Max interjected thoughtfully. "If I squint for any period of
time, my vision blurs. Everything looks fuzzy and kind of
yellow from the walls. And, well, that's not the normal way I
see something."

"Is there only one way to see things?" Luke asked.
"Maybe, just maybe, squinting is a way to help your eyes see
what they normally would look through or past." He
turned to Claire. "Everything that comes to us, whether we
are sleeping or awake, whether we label it real or not,
whether we squint or keep everything in equal focus . . .
those things that come to us and through us do so for a
reason. If you knew that and trusted that what you see
could not hurt you, but only be useful to you, would you
still be afraid? And would you want to dismiss it?"

"No," she answered in a barely audible voice. She did not
want to be afraid or deny what could be useful to her. The
distress began to dissipate. Luke dealt with everything in
the same way. Rather than challenge or go against people's
experiences, he moved with them, trying to guide them

through what he always identified as the lesson. I guess even illusions or hallucinations would have lessons.

Sandy, another student, reported seeing the two eyes as well. Her comment jarred me. How could she substantiate someone else's fantasy? Self-conscious about being spotlighted a second time and remembering Jamie, I scowled, then grinned at my wife apologetically. Her face reflected her deep concern and growing confusion. I wanted to tell her that all this had nothing to do with me. Nothing had changed. And yet I felt that Luke had drawn me in even further than I had anticipated. I shifted my attention and watched him as he sat Buddha-style, in utter tranquillity, on a soft leather chair. I envied the man's uncanny ability to be in apparent control of himself and any situation presented to him.

"The weirdest thing," Sandy volunteered, "is that I could swear now, if I could see a bit clearer—well, don't laugh, but it would be your face, Luke, over Peter's shoulder."

"Are you frightened?" Luke questioned without any reaction evident in his face. Again he did not question the validity of her perception.

"No, not now. I'm okay," she said.

Jamie, apparently unable to contain herself any longer, bent down on her knees in front of me. Everyone stared at her. She turned to confront Claire and Sandy, unwilling to let their statements go unchallenged. But when she looked into their faces, the sincerity of their expressions stopped her. Jamie blushed. She turned herself around and placed her hands on my left shoulder but then withdrew them suddenly.

"What's the matter?" I asked.

She didn't answer but just withdrew to her original space and kept peering at her hands.

Max knew how difficult it had been for her to challenge the class and, indirectly, challenge Luke. He tried to draw her attention, to communicate his support, but she never looked up at him.

Sandy looked over my left shoulder again and announced that the eyes had disappeared. Claire also noted the change and grinned weakly. Her face lightened once more, or at least that was my observation.

"Peter," Luke said, staring at the floor, "seeing Claire's face getting lighter and darker is not a skill. It's not a statement of your power either. It has always been there to see."

My God, I thought to myself, is he reading my mind? I couldn't look at him. The shock of exposure and vulnerability left my thoughts momentarily in disarray; yet I still trusted Luke implicitly.

A sleepy-eyed participant consulted her watch and rose hurriedly. Her announcement of the time signaled the end of the class. People began to leave. Max stood up when I did. We both helped Jamie to her feet. She hugged me with a definite urgency. I smiled at her, then grinned at Max. Everyone appeared concurrently exhausted and invigorated.

Luke climbed out of his chair, hugged me and Max and then, with special emphasis, embraced Jamie. If she had relaxed, I knew she would have been flattered by the attention. I could have kissed Luke for his graciousness toward her.

To Jamie, everyone and everything appeared so interconnected: a spiderweb with Luke at the center. When she said her good-bye to Rudy, he bowed politely, the epitome of decorum. At least she could trust him, she told herself. Extending his arm, he opened the door for her. Suddenly, as she noticed the tiny scar on his wrist, her diaphragm knotted beneath her rib cage.

We passed through the lobby and out the front door in silence. A thick mist hung over the street. The brooding factory buildings, only recently converted to apartment dwellings, cast dark shadows on the sidewalks. At night the empty caverns of SoHo were neither quaint nor reassuring.

"Well?" Max remarked as he and Jamie stepped into the street. Mischievous and twinkle-eyed, he lifted his eyebrows, repeating the question with his rubbery face. "Well?"

"Am I to assume you're talking to me?" kidded Jamie, responding in kind to Max's frivolity.

"Uh, huh," mumbled Max, doing a clown routine. "You surprised me tonight, little lady. I didn't see the eyes either, but I wasn't willing to challenge someone else's apparition. I admired what you did."

"Truthfully, I don't know what came over me," she replied. An awkward smile fluttered across her face.

"Jame, why'd you pull away after you touched my shoulder?" I asked. She slipped her hands into her pockets with obvious haste. "Hey, what's that all about?"

Max came to her rescue. "You and I, ol' buddy, are pros with Luke's classes," he said to me. "What Jamie needs is a good night's rest, not an inquisition."

I nodded my agreement. "I'm really sorry, Jame, I don't mean to push you."

Max threw his arms carefully around Jamie. "Good night, pregnant lady."

Jamie stroked his back affectionately. "We sure do love you, Max."

"The same," he replied succinctly, disengaging from her while tapping her belly lightly. Then he shared a husky Russian-bear hug with me. We waved our last good-byes and proceeded to our cars.

Unlocking the door to the front seat, I felt invaded by an uncomfortable sensation. I had enjoyed the evening, as I had always enjoyed and been stimulated by my evenings with Luke . . . but tonight the gears had shifted and I wasn't sure if I or anyone else was ready, least of all Jamie. Had I made a mistake inviting her? She slid in beside me, leaning back against the headrest, and closed her eyes.

I rubbed her arm as I waited for the car to warm up.

Jamie began one of her breathing exercises. As she relaxed, her clenched hands separated in her lap. My mouth dropped open when I saw small red blotches on the tips of her fingers, almost as if her skin had made contact with something very hot. I remembered the look of surprise on Jamie's face as she pulled her hands away from my shoulder very abruptly . . . like a person who had been burned. That's silly! Impossible! And, yet I hadn't noticed the redness earlier in the evening. I thought of questioning her, to find out if she had hurt her hands cooking during the day, but I wanted to keep my promise not to push. She would tell me when she was ready. I backed off but felt even more uneasy.

As I steered the car out of the parking space, I looked at the exterior of the building. Luke stood at a window in his loft, gazing down into the street. His right arm stretched upward in some kind of gesture that I did not understand. A distinct yellow glow, almost golden, outlined the man's body, reminding me of that hazy, sundrenched image of Luke during our first encounter in the park.

I glanced back to Max's car. He, too, leaned his head out, eyeing the glowing figure in the window. An odd expression rippled across Max's face. His forehead creased as he turned to meet my eyes. Our gazes lingered on one another for several seconds, then parted.

Both cars proceeded down the street, the slick pavement hissing under the rubber tires. Luke's haloed figure remained frozen at the window.

7

Although he drove carefully and slightly faster than he considered prudent, Max winced when the car hit a bump.

"I'm sorry," he said, tapping Jamie's arm affectionately. "Are you all right?"

She nodded affirmatively, then pressed her back against the seat and moaned as the muscles in her abdomen tightened. She tried to concentrate on developing a rhythm of shallow breathing in order to neutralize the pain of the contraction but couldn't. Jamie had held off for almost two hours, waiting for me despite the insistence of her doctor that she go to the hospital. Even now she could hardly believe that she was making this journey without me. We had worked months together practicing Lamaze. "Peter," she murmured, half in desperation, half in protest.

"I'll find him," Max assured her.

When the contraction subsided, she turned to the large, gentle man seated beside her. Thank God for Max, she thought. "If it's a boy, we'll name him after you."

Max had to look away in order to avoid exposing his glazed eyes. Why hadn't it been Jamie instead of Mona? he wondered. Nineteen years before, he had taken his first drive through the night with another woman in labor, but that time it had been his wife and his child. During the ride Mona cursed him for her pain. She pushed him away when he tried to touch her. Even in the hospital she lashed out at him for being treated rather curtly by the resident and nurses. "If you had a little more balls, you'd make them toe

the line," she jeered. He knew he had never fulfilled her
desire for a strong macho-type man who would fight symbolic duels on her behalf. She had always interpreted his
gentleness as weakness. Portions of her loud, ribald cri-
tiques still echoed in his ears, though he and she had been
divorced fifteen years ago. He looked at Jamie, who smiled
softly at him. Why hadn't it been her? He watched her long
tapered fingers rub her extended abdomen delicately. She
hummed a lullaby that he had once heard her play on the
cello. Then her face cringed as she puckered her lips and
puffed quickly, trying to soften the pain of an approaching
contraction.

They entered the hospital through the emergency
entrance. Max held Jamie's hand as a nurse guided her
through a long corridor in a wheelchair.

"We have to prepare her, so I'm afraid, for now, Mr. Halsted, you can't go beyond this point."

"Oh, um, I'm not Mr. Halsted."

The nurse eyed him curiously. "I see. Well, Mr. Halsted
or no Mr. Halsted, we'll take her from here."

"Max, . . ."

"I know," he said. "Jamie, I'll find him."

He watched the elevator doors close behind her, then
searched for a telephone. Rudy gave him the same answer
that he had given Jamie; he would try to find me. I had
arrived earlier in the evening and then left with Luke for
dinner without mentioning any specific destination.

There was nothing more Max could do, and, yet, he
didn't leave the hospital. He wandered back to the lobby
and sat on a chair near the main entrance. Despite the
futility of his gesture, he had to stay for Jamie. Max wondered whether he knew her better than anyone else. She
had been his therapy patient for two years. He knew what
she had overcome in order to stabilize her life. He had
loved her then, Max supposed, but his professional ethics
had blurred that recognition.

In fact it had been my impetus that resulted in a relationship expanded beyond the traditional boundaries.

I had contacted Max at Jamie's recommendation, soliciting his service as a consulting psychologist for my business. I wanted to have all my illustrative and art concepts thoroughly analyzed for their effectiveness in triggering underlying psychological impulses before we made presentations to our clients. These consultations added a convincing authority to my studio's work. In the process Max and I became good friends.

Had it been anyone else, Max told himself, he would have refused such an alliance despite the fact that he, too, had found such an idea intriguing. He knew now that his interest in Jamie had influenced his affirmative response. It allowed him to reenter her life as a friend after his role as therapist ceased. And, ironically, tonight he played substitute husband.

An hour passed. Max stared through the glass doors. He imagined Jamie in a small cubicle, all alone, enduring the contractions without any support. The idea seemed intolerable to him. He tried Luke's loft again. No success. Max paced the corridor. He wanted Jamie to know she was not alone; he convinced a nurse to give her the message that he had been waiting in the lobby, cheering for her. A second hour passed. Perhaps Mona had been right, he thought. Should he have forced his way past the nurse and remained with Jamie? When the receptionist motioned to him, he pointed at his own chest quizzically. Yes, she nodded.

"Mr. Sorenson?"

"That's me," he replied.

"There's a call for you. Over here, on line three."

"Hello," he said.

"Max, it's Rudy. We got him. He's on his way."

"Finally," he sighed.

Max checked on Jamie's condition; she was still in labor.

He asked the floor nurse to inform her that her husband would be there soon, then collapsed back into his seat. He would leave when I arrived, no longer needed. Max wondered whether he would always be the orphan: an outsider, a human being always on the edge of relationships. His one chance at a family had disintegrated when Mona left him with their two daughters and moved to California. His role as therapist enabled him to be involved with the lives of others, but the nature of those connections was always tangential and temporary.

No one understood except Jamie. They shared a special bond. More than anyone else, she knew the loneliness of being a child alone in an institution and of the importance of a family. Max's father had been a Lutheran minister in Austria before the onset of World War II. Hitler's expanding German confederation, which included sympathizers within the province in which Max's father lived, put the cleric's missionary work in direct conflict with governmental policy. His marriage to a Gypsy further infuriated the authorities. The resulting crackdown on his ministerial activities forced them to flee to the United States. Max was born a year later, but before his second birthday his parents were killed in an automobile accident. The war destroyed any possibility of reuniting the child with relatives in Austria. As a result a child welfare agency placed him in an orphanage. He remained there until he turned nine, then lived in successive foster homes until he was sixteen. The need to belong still plagued him. Most of his patients tried to escape their families whereas he tried to find one. But Jamie had had the same goal.

The elevator didn't move fast enough for me. I leaned the huge package, which I had kept in the trunk of the car for almost three weeks, against the railing and watched the number of each floor as we passed. How could I have fouled up on the one night that really mattered? I always left instructions, either with Maire at the office or with Rudy, as to my whereabouts. And yet, on the one night that I forgot, our baby decided to be born. I couldn't even remember what Luke and I had discussed over dinner, though, at the time, I treated our conversation as duly significant. Despite the several classes in which Jamie had participated, I knew she did not understand or share my need to be with Luke. And why should she? He did not help her to cure herself of crippling migraines or teach her acceptance in the face of anger. Those had been my gains. In fact the strange nature of the exercises in this latest series of group sessions left Jamie, often, uneasy in the man's presence.

Finally, the eleventh floor! I burst into the lobby, balancing my bundle to one side. I saw Max immediately.

"Where is she? Jesus, Max, I didn't blow it, did I?"

"The first one usually takes the longest," he assured me.

We jogged down the corridor toward the obstetrics wing. At the reception desk, an attendant called ahead. I could pass, but Max had to stay behind.

"How do I say thanks?" I whispered to my friend, embracing him firmly.

He returned the hug, then pushed me toward the double doors. "Get out of here," he said. His voice wavered.

I grabbed his shoulder one more time, squeezed it, then ran. A nurse directed me to another elevator. At the next floor I bolted from the automated cubicle and jogged toward the nurses' station.

"I'm Peter Halsted. My wife—she's here, she's about to have a baby."

"Yes, Mr. Halsted." She dialed a number on the phone and announced my arrival. The nurse nodded several times, then smiled. "Congratulations, Mr. Halsted. You have a daughter. Six pounds, two ounces."

"Oh, it can't be," I blurted. She needed me for the delivery. "Are you sure? Are you absolutely sure she gave birth?"

The woman stared at me. "Yes, of course I'm sure. Your wife gave birth about forty minutes ago. She's probably still in recovery now. You won't be able to see her until she's out. So have a seat and I'll let you know."

They kept me waiting for an endless hour. How could I ever make it up to Jamie? I felt like a manic-depressive: hating myself, regretting my absence, then, suddenly, high as a kite, elated by images of a little girl, our little girl, weighing all of six pounds, two ounces.

Finally, the pediatrician took me to a glass-enclosed section containing at least ten infants. A nurse, wearing a mask and gloves, held up a tiny newborn child that they identified as my daughter. I stared at the baby, amazed. I laughed aloud when she flexed her little fingers in front of her face. I wanted to hug her; most of all, I wanted to hug my wife.

I had to wait another thirty minutes until I could see Jamie. She lay sleeping in her bed when I entered the room. I placed the enormous package carefully on the night table and squelched my first impulse to kiss her. Let her sleep, I counseled myself. I sat in a chair beside her bed, loving and admiring her. Contented to watch her, I remained by her side for almost forty minutes until she stirred. As she opened her eyes, I took her hand gently and kissed it.

"How's the sweet mama?"

"Oh, Peter," she whispered. "She's so beautiful and she's ours."

"I saw her," I said. "She looks like you."

"Us. She looks like us."

And then Jamie began to cry. I didn't have to ask her about her tears. "I'm sorry, Jame. I wanted to be here just as much as you wanted me to be here. Believe me."

Jamie tried to control her sobbing. We both knew that I had been with Luke instead of with her. The doctor had explained to me that in my absence she could not go through natural childbirth. Therefore he convinced her to take a spinal. Although she watched the delivery through a mirror, she didn't feel any pain. I knew she had wanted to feel everything, to birth her child to life in the most conscious way.

I reached across the bed to touch her. She turned away from me and stared at the wall.

"I didn't know, Jamie, I swear. I came as soon as I found out you were here."

"You promised it would be different," she whispered.

"And it is! What happened was just a mistake. C'mon, turn around, please." She didn't respond. "I have something to show you."

Jamie turned her head as I unveiled a dollhouse replica of our Victorian home. She couldn't stop the smile that exploded on her face.

"I've been working on it for months at the studio," I continued. "Colleen, Dominick, Ann—well, I think just about everyone helped. It's been in the trunk of my car, just waiting for today." I smiled. "It's perfect to the last detail. And look here," I said, pointing to the three little figures placed on the front porch. "There's me, you, and the baby. And up here—see." A little plaque over the miniature front door said: JAMIE'S FIRST FAMILY.

She wrapped her arms around me and squeezed as tight as she could. "Oh, God, yes, my first real family." Her arms trembled slightly. Suddenly she pulled away and peered into my face. Her fingers tracked the outline of my lips. "When the baby looks at you, Peter, I want her to see your smile . . . not Luke's."

I couldn't respond to her comment. I only knew that I was afraid to smile.

8

Jamie and Rachel, as we named her, arrived home on a quiet Sunday morning. I had hung a huge welcome banner on the front porch and lined the steps to the second floor with roses.

"You're so crazy," Jamie said to me, "but I love it."

In the weeks that followed, we focused much of our attention and energy on our daughter. Her presence in our lives made the bond between Jamie and me even stronger. And yet neither of us ever talked about the delivery again, as if we had silently agreed to bury the incident. Conversations about Luke were also conspicuously absent.

Jamie and I had never even discussed the red blotches on her fingertips after that class, although Max talked to me about a conversation he had had with her on the very same subject. She had not burned herself cooking that day. Instead she attributed the tiny blisters to the unexpected intense heat she encountered as she touched my shoulder. Max dismissed the incident as something he would diagnose clinically as an hysterical symptom, not unlike a welt that will bubble up on the skin of someone hypnotized if the person believes he has been touched by something very hot. "If it had been anything more than that," he concluded, flapping his bushy eyebrows, "anything, you know, not of this world, then you would have also felt such intense heat." His analysis made perfect sense. Certainly her state of mind during the first class was anything but calm and centered. And yet why heat? No one had suggested she'd feel heat before she approached me. As I think back now, I should have discussed the subject with her. Perhaps we could have avoided what inevitably followed.

It was exactly twenty-two days after her return from the hospital that Jamie had the first dream. I didn't realize then that from that moment forward our lives would never be the same.

I had arrived home late from an evening group session with Luke. I missed having Jamie with me but hesitated to push her to return. Nevertheless, as soon as I saw her, I blurted out the question. "Jame, when are you coming back to class?"

She peered at me for a few seconds, then said, "Next week. Okay?"

"Okay!" I bellowed enthusiastically.

As Jamie prepared for bed, she thought she felt a warm breeze near the bed. She guided me to the spot, but it had apparently dissipated.

"I'm not crazy, Peter, I felt something."

"I believe you."

For several minutes, we explored the atmosphere of the room. I even stood on a chair and placed my hands near the ceiling. No draft. No warm breeze. Giving up, I left the room, locked all the doors in the house, then returned to the bedroom.

As we lay in bed, Jamie curled her body next to me. "Doesn't anything in the class ever scare you?"

"No, not really. Why should it? What we're learning will help us not hurt us."

I ran my hands down the small of her back and caressed her soft, warm flesh. Jamie's fingers danced on the interior of my thighs. Ever since that communal shouting experience in Luke's initial class, she admitted to feeling freer sexually. Hands touched. Legs entwined. The doctor had recommended abstaining for a month. We knew we had just begun to cheat; only three weeks had elapsed since Rachel's birth.

Our mouths found each other. We rolled over and over, moving like the summer tides. Back and forth, our energy surged until she opened herself to me . . . letting go. My body moved slowly upward against her until I entered. Jamie released a soft hum. The rhythm changed as we pushed up against one another. Our bodies heaved together. Our breathing matched the fire of our thrusts. I cupped my hands gently around her breasts as I searched her mouth with my tongue, bringing her closer. Then, as I felt her pushing off the bed, speeding hypnotically toward her climax, I opened the doorway to my own orgasm. Simultaneously we surged over the edge, tossing and groaning, culminating in our own moisture. Our energy came like waves, rushing and peaking, rushing and peaking, until the passion was spent. Together, we floated downward, the muscles in our bodies coming to rest. We fell back, sinking deeply into the mattress, still locked in each other's arms.

Sleep engulfed us like a dense ocean fog. For Jamie, a door unlocked as crisp mountain air scented with jasmine enveloped her. A brisk wind skipped across green fields, encircling stony ridges and granite peaks that loomed like tall skyscrapers against a distant sky. Flowers and leaves sighed sensuously in the breeze. The sun floated just over the horizon, a giant apricot suspended gracefully above the landscape.

Walking sprightly, her stride firm and strong, Jamie approached a plateau. In an Indian-style pouch, she carried Rachel comfortably across her chest. The baby's eyes opened, carefully watching her mother's face against patterns of clouds. Jamie's hiking grew more casual. She stopped to pick wild berries as she ascended the windward face of the mountain. Her hair swept forward into her face. She paused, resting on a giant, rounded boulder.

The green valleys began to turn purple and blue. The night mist rose from the ground, gathering in the canyons as dusk approached. Yellow and red rivers streaked the sky.

Jamie hummed to her daughter as she stroked her face. "Ah ma lady, ah ma lady." Rested and at peace, she began to climb again toward the peak. The wind increased significantly. The temperature dropped. She buttoned her denim jacket and secured the bright green Scottish plaid blanket around Rachel. Mist enveloped the base of the mountain completely. A thick, impenetrable cloud rolled up the hillside. Jamie hesitated. She stood absolutely still and studied the area as if looking and listening for some distant calling. Twice she spun around in place. Then, in an easy, deliberate movement, she took off the carrier and laid the baby on top of the blanket on the ground.

Suddenly the dense cloud enshrouded the entire mountain. Jamie tried desperately to clear the mist from around her head. It limited her vision to several inches. She bent down to pick up her daughter. Rachel and the baby sling were gone. Her body went limp as she searched frantically for the cloth cradle, the blanket, anything. She opened her mouth to scream, but no sound came forth. Dropping to her hands and knees, she probed blindly with her fingers.

With a *whoosh* she experienced herself drawn out of her body and propelled airborne to an uncharted location above the mountain. The wind whipped the clouds and sent them racing across the horizon. Jamie peered down through their thick patterns to see herself standing on the mountain. Portions of the fog cleared to give her an unobstructed view. She watched herself run, frantic and alone, through the fields amid towering stone monuments.

"Rachel! Rachel!" The sound of her voice reverberated against the rugged terrain and returned unanswered. Perched on the opposite side of the peak, her daughter sat motionless, bewildered though not distressed. Apparently she could not hear her mother's cries.

As Jamie surveyed the scene, her awareness took in a large, black and white spotted horse standing on a crest near the summit. Still viewing the activity from a position outside of her body, she felt compelled to focus on the animal. At that moment, as if activated by her gaze, the horse began to rock its head from side to side in slow motion. Its muscles rippled along its majestic form. It began to prance and parade in wide, irregular circles. Jamie glared at the animal as it turned its head skyward to confront her.

She felt a wild, silent scream thunder inside as she perceived the horse's watch-eye, a pure blue iris floating in a sea of white contrasting dramatically with the other brown one. They stared at each other. Then the horse disengaged, looked past her gaze and began to lunge down the jagged slope.

Her viewpoint shifted as she felt her consciousness slam back into her body. Now, as she gaped up the mountainside, the charging horse moved directly toward her child. Mesmerized by the fury and majesty of its body in flight, Jamie stood paralyzed, her feet cemented to the ground.

The sound of hoofbeats crashed against the limestone surface that exploded under the rampaging impact. A white, foamy lather glistened on the chest of the animal. The wind velocity increased. The horse hurtled over a second ledge; only one long field separated it from tiny Rachel, who tumbled off her blanket and came to rest in the path of this approaching fury. Jamie's eyes bulged as the distance narrowed between the animal and her baby. Still transfixed in horror, she could see the sweat dripping off the horse's body. He kept coming and coming, closing the gap. His hooves echoed thunder through the mountainside. His weight and power threatened to crush the baby as he sped to within yards of Rachel's little form.

Seconds before the impact, Jamie awoke. Her body lifted off the bed in a powerful thrust. Her arms flew into the air as she fell onto the floor.

"Christ," I murmured, awakened by the sound of Jamie's body slapping the hardwood floor. I jumped out of bed and bent to embrace her. She stared blankly into space, her torso quivering in silence. Gathering her up from the floor, I stroked her forehead. Jamie turned slowly and squeezed out a limp smile.

"I'm okay," she sighed. Her hand touched my arm.

"A dream?" I asked.

"Almost too real to be a dream." Suddenly she gaped at me for a second then jumped to her feet. "Rachel! I have to check Rachel!" Jamie bolted from the room. Once upstairs she stood over the crib for several minutes and stared at our sleeping daughter. Eventually she forced herself to leave.

"You want to tell me about it?" I asked when she returned to the bedroom.

"I don't want to go through it again now. Maybe in the morning, okay?"

I tucked my arms around her. We both lay awake for a long time.

Jamie thought only about Rachel, her wonderful, lovely baby. She tried to blot the horse from her mind, but its strange eyes and foaming mouth continued to haunt her.

9

Shining soft auburn hair framed her face. Freckles dotted the skin around her electric amber eyes. When she clapped her hands over Rachel's tiny form, her large plump body vibrated in concert.

Terry's fingers galloped playfully up and down my daughter's stomach, making her cackle and coo with delight. After sprinkling white powder, she rubbed the baby's satin skin in small circular motions, completing what would become a nightly ritual. Terry had entered our lives three years before when Max, her mother's friend and occasional lover, recommended her to me for a free-lance art assignment. No one could have anticipated then her move from the studio into our home. And yet, as she set the stage for her first night of baby-sitting as part of a live-in trade that enabled her to attend graduate school full time, I knew Jamie's assessment of her maternal instinct had been correct. Terry tickled and hugged the baby with a natural ease. Rachel's joy was obvious. She waved her hands and dropped the rattle that had been trapped between her index finger and thumb.

"Just too big for that little hand, huh?" Terry said softly. "Well, okay, here's your blanket." Rachel hugged the material awkwardly, then smiled brightly. "That's it. Just hold that pose." Terry grabbed the large pad from the counter, removed a thin charcoal stick from the box beside it and drew only a few lines; yet these thin, single strokes created a chin, an infant's puckered lips, an eyelash, the inside curve of an ear—in combination, the delicate hint of a newborn smile. I admired her drawing as I stood by the doorway to the living room. Terry stopped and looked behind her.

"I didn't know you were there," she said.

"You two were having so much fun, I didn't want to disturb you."

"Tell Jamie not to worry. I know it must be hard—her first full evening of separation from Rachel, but we'll be okay."

"I know that," I answered. I knelt down beside my daughter and stroked the bridge of her nose with my finger. She giggled. "I love you, little lady," I said softly, then kissed her before leaving to pick up her mother from an early-evening rehearsal for a local string ensemble. As I rose, I glanced at the sketch again. "The drawing . . . it's beautiful."

Terry smiled proudly. She held up her hands like a surgeon, turned them over for my inspection, and said, "What do you think, maestro, are they the hands of an artist?"

I laughed. "Ah, good memory."

"For certain things. You were pretty crazy in those days, Peter."

I nodded my head and remembered in surprising detail the occasion of our first meeting.

We had been in the midst of photographing background references for a ceramic wall piece. On that particular morning the model failed to appear as scheduled. Rather than lose precious time, I insisted on replacing him myself. With due fanfare, I had Dominick and Maire help me dress in old Prussian armor. A tall, statuesque dapple-gray horse waited in the cleared area in front of the studio where the photographs would be taken. Megan, a woman with dark eyes, a black turban and outrageous patent leather platform shoes, loaded two electric Hasselblads with film. When I climbed into the flimsy antique saddle, she laughed. So did Colleen, who looked up from her drawing board in amazement.

I drew the reins in tight and backed the horse against the seamless paper covering one entire wall. Despite the obvious harassment, I was determined to succeed in the role.

"Let's go, Megan; I'm ready." I pranced the horse in small circles, striking different poses as we moved. The rapid-fire whine of the motor drive on the camera filled the studio. At that moment, Maire ushered a young woman into the area. I angled the horse in their direction and did an aborted gallop toward them. Both women dashed to the side walls.

"That was good," Megan shouted. "Looked great in the camera."

Maire recovered quickly, but the stranger, introduced as Terry, did not. She kept her back pressed against the wall, holding her portfolio in front of her like a shield.

"You're Max's friend," I said to her.

"Sort of," she answered.

"We got stuck for a model this morning. Give me half an hour and we'll talk. I promise." She nodded shyly. "Good," I concluded, turning the horse and trotting back to the seamless backdrop. For the next thirty minutes, I assumed a variety of poses, finally becoming bored with the process. I directed the horse to a position near the front entrance of the studio and whispered in its ear. Then I shouted and galloped toward the easels and drafting tables.

Terry had been the first to yell. Others, who had been hunched studiously over their work, were rudely awakened from their concentrated efforts. Instinctively they darted in different directions as I guided the animal into a jump over the reception desk. Tucking its legs gracefully beneath its huge girth, the horse cleared the obstacle easily and landed steadily on its special rubber hooves. A roar of laughter filled the chamber. Several people gasped. I slipped from the saddle. Handing the reins to the photographer, I motioned to Terry. She approached me very cautiously.

"I don't normally dress this way," I said, removing my

helmet and breast plate. "Welcome." I shook her hand.

"Hi!" she blurted self-consciously.

"Max says you're a good designer."

"Maybe . . . well, Mr. Halsted . . ."

"Peter."

"Well, Peter, I'm only in my third year at Pratt."

"I know," I said.

"Do you want to see my portfolio?"

"Nope," I quipped, eyeing her intensely. "Put out your hands." Terry complied obediently. "Now look at them. Are they the hands of an artist or not?"

She stared down at her own hands. For a moment they seemed disconnected from her body. She observed them in a way she had never done before, taking note of her long fingers and the sculptured network of bones and muscles on the backs of both hands. They were strong and agile in appearance.

"Well?" I asked, putting my hands on top of my head and pressing down in an effort to stall an approaching migraine.

"I never thought about it before, but, yes," she answered, her face relaxing into a smile, "they sure could be the hands of an artist."

"Good, then you're on. See Dominick, he'll get you started." The migraine assaulted me with such ferocity that I couldn't continue to talk. I jumped up the stairs, three at a time, without ever introducing her to the production manager or waiting for her agreement to my proposal.

The memory faded as I watched Terry lift Rachel into her arms, still smiling over the compliment I had given her about her sketch.

"You know, I never explained why I left so rudely that first time we talked. A migraine had hit and I needed to take care of it."

"That's what I figured. Maire explained your 'strange' behavior to me right at the beginning. For a while there, you were either shouting at us or holding your head."

"And now?"

"No comparison. You know when I knew you'd changed?" I shook my head. "Well, it was late one night. You had returned from one of Luke's classes. Larry and I had been bickering over who spilled the India ink all over the floor. Do you remember what you said?" I shrugged my shoulders. "You told us that you knew we really didn't want to argue and that you would clean up the mess yourself. You were so . . . soft."

The chimes of the hall clock signaled the hour. "Wow, it's eight already. I have to run," I said, kissing her lightly on the cheek. "We'll be home before twelve."

Holding the baby over her shoulder later that evening, Terry cleared the dishwasher despite Jamie's insistence that she need not do anything else beyond, at times, helping with Rachel. But Terry wanted to give more. Her friendship with Jamie, which had begun after a few chance meetings at the studio, led to the current barter arrangements that included room and board. She had moved in with my enthusiastic support and fallen in love with the baby immediately.

Rachel began to whimper at about 9:30. Responding to the cue from this month-old child, Terry ascended the stairs and went directly to the nursery. After placing the baby on her stomach in the crib, she massaged her back. Rachel curled her legs under her body and drifted into a deep sleep within seconds.

Terry went back downstairs into the master bedroom on the first floor, where she turned on the television. Using the remote, she switched through the stations three times with little interest, finally settling for an old Ingrid Bergman film.

An hour passed. The music swelled as Bergman ran down the hallway of an eighteenth-century mansion. Terry floated away, her eyes glued to the television set. The drone of the TV drowned out most noises, but then some rustling in the house distracted her. She checked the clock. Too early, she mused, but nevertheless she slid off the bed and marched into the hallway. "Jamie? Is that you?" Silence. She moved through the living room and entered the kitchen. Nobody there. "Peter? Jamie?" No answer.

Before returning to the bedroom, she scrambled up the stairs to check the baby. Rachel was sleeping peacefully. An almost inaudible hum rose from the crib. It sounded like the purring of a kitten when being stroked.

Terry returned to her movie. The action had shifted to the interior of an airplane. She frowned, having missed a critical segment that left a gap in the story line. Again she sensed activity in the house. She called, "Jamie? Peter?" Still no answer. Her body went rigid. Someone was standing at the door to the room. She knew it. For several seconds she could not turn her head, afraid to look. She inhaled deeply. "Move," she begged herself. "Move!" With a snap of her head, she faced the door. No one was there. Currents of air churned in the room.

A cold chill washed through her body. Terry saw a yellow-ish mist enter the room. It moved in a low zigzag pattern: a luminous body of energy, almost three feet wide by four feet in height. Each turn brought it closer to the bed. Its path appeared calculated.

First she threw her hands out in front of her as a gesture of self-protection. Then she crept off the bed slowly, backing away from the yellow light. Very gently the force penetrated more deeply into the room. Terry slithered around the perimeter, keeping as much distance between herself and the light as possible. The luminous body came to rest above the bed, hovering over the mattress.

She tiptoed toward the door, planning each step. As she crossed the path of the intruder, a warm, distinct breeze engulfed her. Flashes of childhood summers on the coast of Maine. For an instant all fear subsided, leaving her surprisingly tranquil. But as she neared the exit, her panic returned. She flung herself through the door, slamming it behind her. Terry darted upstairs into Rachel's room, threw the blanket over the child, swooped her up into her arms and sprinted downstairs into the kitchen. She stopped with her back against the wall. Her mind raced. Her chest heaved up and down. The bedroom door remained closed. The television was still playing mindlessly. Shifting the sleeping baby into one arm, she dialed Jamie's friend, Cleo.

"Cleo, it's Terry. Help me, please. I'm alone with Rachel. There's something here . . . in the house."

"Take the baby and run," Cleo barked. "I'll call the police."

"Wait . . . it's not like that."

"What the hell does that mean?"

"It's a presence . . . or something."

Cleo again ordered her to leave the house immediately and wait in the car. Terry hung up the phone and left through the side door. Her little Saab became home base. She felt safer once she locked the doors. Breathing more easily, she started the motor, turned on the radio and rocked Rachel in her arms as she stared expectantly at the house.

Within minutes, an old, battered Dodge convertible came swerving around the corner. Sliding to a halt just behind Terry's car, Cleo jumped out into the street, poised like a guerrilla fighter closing in for the kill.

"Are you okay?" she asked as she slid into the seat beside Terry. Shaking her head affirmatively, Terry detailed her experience. Cleo pushed the blanket from Rachel's face and checked her "little princess." The strength and determination of the older woman's face reassured Terry.

Although tall and lanky like a model, Cleo's presence was intense and at times distinctly masculine. Her hair was cropped close around the ears and the back of her head.

Jamie and Cleo contrasted in style and statement. Yet their diverse personalities complemented each other and strengthened their friendship. As a birthday gift, Jamie once had had an astrologer plot and read Cleo's chart, which resulted in an incredibly accurate picture of her friend, a double Aries, the most determined and dominating of all fire signs in astrology. Cleo dismissed the reading as superstitious nonsense.

"C'mon," Cleo commanded, interrupting the last portion of Terry's commentary.

"C'mon where?" Terry asked.

"Let's go to it. I can assure you that no woman has ever been molested by any yellow mist."

The women entered the house cautiously. Terry, still clutching Rachel, refused to go any farther than the kitchen. The antics of her own mother with tarot cards, astrology charts and tea leaves seemed mild compared with what she confronted now.

Cleo chuckled and patted Terry's shoulder with parental indulgence. Leaving her and the baby by the kitchen table, she entered the hallway and turned toward the bedroom. She slowed her approach. Her last step, which brought her within inches of the closed door, was taken in slow motion. The yapping of the television set penetrated the walls. Cleo hesitated, rubbing her square chin thoughtfully. Then, cocking her head like a charging boar, she threw the door open, fully prepared to confront Terry's intruder.

She leaped at the bed, her fists frozen in the air as part of the psychological posture of assault. To her amazement, she did not perceive anything unusual. No luminous body. No weaving light. Relieved but disappointed, she pursued her investigation further by running her hands across the top of the bed. She stood in different parts of the room, ready to experience a breeze that never materialized. Yet, she had to admit that the air seemed distinctly warmer in this part of the house. Giving herself one more opportunity to confront Terry's phenomenon, she tramped around the entire bedroom. She spread her arms wide as if to encompass the great void. Then, with daring and bravado, she lay down on the bed. Still nothing. Her hand slapped the neighboring bureau. She left the room feeling cheated.

Terry waited expectantly as Cleo reentered the kitchen.

"Nothing. No yellow light. Warm, but no breezes," chimed Cleo with conviction.

"You do believe me?" questioned Terry.

"Two months ago, I'd have chalked it up to your imagination, saying you've been listening to too many stories about Peter's archangel, Luke. So, a reflection of light from the hallway or maybe the TV and you think you're seeing a suspicious yellow mist." She rubbed her chin again. "Funny thing is, I do believe you."

As she completed her last comment, Cleo walked decisively to Terry and removed Rachel from her arms. "I think we can take her back to bed now." Cleo headed for the stairs. Rachel's eyes opened. "Hi ya, little princess," she said, smiling awkwardly. "Cleo is just going to take you right upstairs and put you back into your cozy crib. Close your eyes, that's it, close your eyes, little princess."

Alone, but feeling more confident, Terry marched down the hallway. The bedroom door stood ajar. The television still blared. With determination she walked straight into the room, exhaling a deep sigh when she found nothing. After turning the television set off, she returned to the kitchen.

"Now," Cleo said, "if you would kindly put up some java, I'll keep you company until the wandering gypsies return. In fact, I'm sure we can hunt down something interesting to eat . . . hopefully before something else happens and we all become victims of Peter's little escapade."

"What's that supposed to mean?"

"Come now, Terry. To you, he's Mr. Wonderful. It's all over your face most of the time. I'm the only one left to lend a little sanity to the situation."

"I don't think I want to listen to this."

"Of course not; no one wants to see their balloon burst."

The two women settled into an uncomfortable silence. An hour passed before the front door rattled.

Jamie and I, having seen Cleo's car parked out front, moved rapidly into the house.

"Over here, in the kitchen," Cleo greeted us. "Well, now, did you guys have an eventful evening?"

Terry appeared pale and drawn.

"Is everything okay?" I questioned.

"Rachel?" Jamie queried nervously.

"Relax, everything's perfectly okay. How could it not be? I'm here. Seriously, everything is fine . . . for now. But we did have an adventure, to say the least. Go, Terry, you're on." Cleo had completed her master-of-ceremonies routine.

Jamie refused to listen until she checked the baby herself. When she rejoined us in the kitchen, Terry told her story about the yellow light and the breeze.

Jamie eyed her intently, thinking about the current of air that she herself had once detected in the room.

"Well, I guess I can leave this in your qualified hands," Cleo said to me sardonically. "You students of the beyond can figure this one out. You do know my opinion on this whole affair." Cleo faced her friend directly. "Jamie, I know this might sound repetitious, but I can't say it too often. This isn't a game. This whole business with Luke and that group of weirdos sounds a little too creepy for me. And maybe it's not only creepy; maybe it's dangerous."

Jamie tried to ignore Cleo's statement. "Thanks for being here, Cleo," she said as she hugged her.

"Any time. We can all be thankful someone was here *this time,*" Cleo added, emphasizing the last two words of her statement.

"My thanks too," I offered.

"You're welcome. And don't worry, I wouldn't leave without planting a big one on you," she said, kissing me lightly with a theatrical flare. Patting Terry on the head, she opened the door. "Tra-la-la."

I smiled, shook my head and said, "She's a pip, that one." Terry laughed.

"Now wait a minute," Jamie snapped, trying to suppress the smile that had already blossomed on her face. "She really was right here when it counted."

Terry sobered immediately. "I'm sorry."

Jamie confronted me. "I know Cleo's a bit much at times, but she went out of her way . . . and she means well. Can't you be more forgiving?"

"You're right, Jame. I guess it was all those innuendos about us and Luke. You don't have to defend her—really. She does what she does. It's okay."

"Then it's finished?" Jamie asked, touching my hand.

"Finished," I agreed.

Terry nodded. She, too, wanted to believe the entire sequence of events was finished.

10

Rush hour had just begun. At the corner of Fifth Avenue along a section of Fifty-ninth Street that bordered Central Park, five old horse-drawn carriages assembled in a neat row beside the curb. The horses stood on motionless feet, worn by the daily burden. Their manure created uneven mounds on the blacktop; their tails swatted darting flies.

By late afternoon, the tourist trade had ebbed. These relics of another century waited patiently for their evening clientele. A young coachman, inexperienced and obviously uncomfortable in his top hat and long tails, watched Jude, one of the more seasoned drivers, mix hay and grain for the horses. The old man, bent and weathered by the sun and rain, muttered as he filled his canister. The edge of his sleeve dipped into the moist mixture. A brown sauce of saliva and chewed tobacco crusted on his lips. He looked up momentarily and stared at his horse amid the cluster of parked coaches. The huge black and white spotted animal danced restlessly in place, constantly flexing the muscles in his legs and pushing against the leather straps that confined him. Jude spat on the ground and turned back to his chore. He never noticed the large man, dressed in jeans and a sweatshirt, ambling toward the carriages.

Max did a slow city shuffle past the caravan of antique vehicles by the curb. He carried a small bag of groceries under one arm and a gift for Rachel under the other. Although the role of godfather was a bit vague nowadays, he delighted in having the honor. The hand-sewn baby quilt, complete with gingham and calico patches, allowed him to demonstrate the seriousness of his own commitment. Did he have the same rights as a grandfather? he wondered. Or, perhaps, an uncle? And did this make him Jamie's god-husband? Max laughed aloud. Shifting the grocery bag to the arm holding the quilt, he pulled out an apple. Just then, the antics of a mime impersonating a mannequin in a store window across the street drew his attention. He shook his head and grinned, then returned his focus to the fruit in his hand. As he opened his mouth to consume his first bite, a bag lady, moving all her worldly possessions in an old rusted shopping cart, crossed his path. Max watched her for a moment, then offered his apple to her. The woman snatched it from his hand and smiled shyly as she polished the skin of the fruit on her tattered jacket.

"And a good day to you, ma'am," he said respectfully. The lady ignored him and kept walking.

Max Sorenson loved New York City. His ardor was boundless and without embarrassment. Anything west of the park signified his part of town. He claimed that all creative people in the city lived on the Upper West Side. Seldom did he stray from his chosen Eden, but, as this day ebbed, he made an exception, not wanting to return to his empty apartment until necessary. The horse-drawn carriages that he surveyed held a special significance for him: he had ridden in one only once ... but that was when he was married.

Wisps of shoulder-length hair jumped casually in the breeze and outlined his bald crown as he crossed the cobblestones and neared the curb. He tugged on the ends of his thick mustache as he admired one particular horse. The muscular and massive black and white animal commanded all his concentration immediately. Max couldn't help but notice its peculiar eyes. The right one was a typical brown, but the left appeared humanoid with an intense blue iris on a field of white. He edged closer, barely containing his amazement. The strange eye mesmerized him; he couldn't turn away. When he reached out to touch the side of the horse's neck, the animal bucked and reared, throwing its front hooves wildly and grunting an angry, violent protest. Max, his arms gripped around his packages, fell backward, narrowly escaping injury as the animal's powerful legs lunged in his direction. The noise of hooves chipping the curb sent the other horses into a frenzy. Several drivers charged their coaches.

"Are you crazy?" Jude screamed at Max. "Get away from that animal if you want to stay alive." The coachman cursed the intrusion under his breath.

Max scrambled to his feet while the horse snorted and banged his foot on the black macadam. Although a touch dizzy, he extended his hand to the old man, who turned away abruptly. Undaunted, he continued, "I know a man who has eyes just like that horse."

Jude glanced back at Max, ready to fire a barrage of obscenities, but the softness and sincerity in the other man's face voided his anger. "Only a horse can have a watch-eye," he countered in a raspy voice.

"What's a watch-eye?" Max asked, still having difficulty with his balance.

"A stiff pain in the butt if you ask me," the coachman grumbled. "Some say that a horse with a man's blue eye is evil. Others spin a different yarn. They'd say if you owned a horse with a watch-eye, you'd hear the voice of God. Well, I've owned him for years now and I ain't never heard nothin'."

Once Jude finished stirring the mixture in the pail, he left Max without any parting comment and moved slowly toward his coach with a hobbled gait. He's part of the city's mosaic, Max told himself, glancing one more time at the very humanlike eye of the horse. His equilibrium returned, but, somehow, the fall left him shaky. At that moment two nuns stopped beside the same animal. Max raised his hand, opened his mouth to warn them, but paused midstream and watched with curiosity as the two sisters stroked the horse. For a brief moment the animal appeared sedated; the ever-flexing muscles in his loins relaxed. One nun turned and smiled directly at the aged coachman, who remained straight-faced, his leathery skin dried and fixed.

Celine tiptoed quietly across the hall. Her huge, chunky form, hidden beneath a floor-length Grecian robe, jiggled with each carefully placed step. She held one hand over her mouth so that she would not burst out laughing. As she extended her arm to surprise Max by tapping him on the back, she tripped, crashing into him and knocking the keys from his hand. He fell against the door of his apartment but avoided falling by steadying himself against the portal frame. They gaped at each other. Celine began to laugh, at first sheepishly but then more forcefully as she gazed at his startled expression. Her giggles quickly became contagious, and they both broke into hysterics. It took them more than a minute to recover.

"Maxy, I've been thinking about you all day." She pinched her lips together, assessing his form curiously. "Did anything happen?" Without waiting for an answer, she added, "You know, you look awfully pale."

He touched her hand and squeezed it lightly. "That's my cosmopolitan pallor."

"What about answering my question?"

"Well, let's see," he said, scratching his shiny crown. "Did anything happen?" He paused, pushing the tip of his nose down against his mustache. "Sprinted a bit in Central Park and . . . oh, yes, a horse tried to flatten my distinctive middle-aged body this afternoon." He laughed and assumed the pose of a bullfighter.

"Not funny," Celine snapped protectively. "Come. Come with me." She led him into her apartment across the hall.

"Here, sit down. Some spirits will restore the shine to your cheeks." She mixed a concoction of bourbon, tequila, chamomile, sarsaparilla, and lemon.

"You're kidding," he protested.

"I told you I was an alchemist in my last life. Here, drink it," she counseled, delivering it to his lips. "Let's go, drink up." He sipped a little from the glass and grimaced. "You're a big, overgrown baby. Did you know that?"

"Here," he said, handing her the glass, "feed what's left to the rats tonight."

"Don't say I didn't give you a chance," she countered, removing the drink and placing it discreetly on a small table. "In 1306, when I was a Jesuit, I saw a man just like you. He was breathing, like you are, but his skin was chalk white—like yours. He had been mauled by an animal and part of his lifeforce had seeped out of him. A very danger-ous state."

"Oh, I see," Max said, trying to conceal his smile.

"Go ahead. Make fun. I'll love you just the same." With that announcement she took her shoes off and literally jumped into the chair on top of Max.

"What the . . ."

"Shush," she said. "I'm rebirthing you with my own body. That's what I saw Brother Daniel do with the man who had been mauled, and it worked."

"Celine, I wasn't mauled, but if you persist in sitting on me, I'm going to expire."

"In this particular case, Maxy, my few extra pounds," she said, giggling at her own underestimate, "will aid the process." She kissed his forehead while she remained on his lap.

The weight of her body made it difficult for him to breathe, but he didn't say anything. He patted her back, acknowledging her caring despite the discomfort of her rather radical remedy.

"There . . . there," she said, noting his face, which had

become flushed. Leaping off him, she bounced into the bathroom and returned with a small hand mirror. "Now look. See—your color is much better."

He stared at his own face. His cheeks glowed as if powdered with rouge. He didn't have the heart to tell her that anyone would look like that if they had been suffocating beneath her more-than-ample form.

"Thanks for the . . . rebirthing," Max volunteered as he rose from the seat and kissed her, more intimately than a friend but less passionately than a lover. For fourteen years they had lived across the hall from each other. When one was lonely, the other would play companion. On occasion they bedded down together. Sometimes Max played surrogate father to Celine's daughter, Terry.

"Before you go, I want to show you something." She guided him into a small room decorated by a painted landscape that continued across all four walls. Compasses, a protractor, ruler, and graph paper filled the opened shelves. Printed disks, divided like pies into twelve slices, hung from a wire. A planetary ephemeris charting celestial formations for people born between the years 1900 and 2000 lay opened on the desk. Several piles of books on the planets had been stacked haphazardly beneath one window. Celine gave in-depth astrological readings to her clients and made tapes for those who contacted her by mail. But only for her most intimate customers and friends did she reveal her interest and trust in tarot cards and tea-leaf readings. In the metaphysical circles she traveled in, she had developed quite a respectable following.

"What do you see?" she asked Max when she pointed to the two cups on the table.

"Hummm," he grunted, bending over to smell the contents. "I'd say... jasmine."

"Well, of course, silly. But I didn't mean that. Look again."

He humored her a second time. "I would say by the looks

of those leaves, you have already had your tea." Max smiled gayly as Celine pushed him down into the chair.

"Listen, you clown, that's first-quality jasmine. In my sixth life . . . "

"Now hold on. I'd love to hear about your sixth life—I've heard about so many others—but I have a patient who should be arriving at my office just now."

She held him in his seat. Her seriousness surprised him. "In my sixth life, when I did readings for the Court of St. James, we used jasmine, of only the best quality, to glean things about the future. I didn't mean to do a reading this morning, but I had just finished sewing your shirt and, well, I brewed the tea and then let the leaves fall for you. You're not angry, are you? I mean, I should have asked your permission first."

"You know, you're a jewel." He kissed her playfully. "If they ever got you downtown for psychoanalysis, they'd never understand." Max couldn't admit to her that he didn't understand either. He accepted Celine, oddities included, but he could not seriously entertain her beliefs despite his own involvement with a man such as Luke.

"I'll show you something," she said, spreading the leaves on the surface of the table. Her eyes scanned them like intricate roadmaps. "Here and here. Something is moving close, but I'm not sure you're ready." She glanced at him. "No, not by the looks of you." Celine stared at the leaves again. "Here, get a load of this. These curves and that indentation—a hoof. That means . . . why, of course, a horse."

"Nothing like the power of suggestion to get you started," Max chuckled.

"But it's here, truly. A hoof."

Max looked at the leaves. "I feel like I'm taking a Rorshach. It looks more like a butterfly to me."

She pushed Max back into the chair. "You don't know how to read them. It's not a guessing game like the tests you give your clients. Reading leaves is much more precise. Here, on the lower leaf, the overlap of the little veins on a north-to-south axis signifies the hoof or horse as a symbol of the split between two opposing forces in your life." Celine shrugged her shoulders. "I know it might sound foolish, but maybe you should get to know that horse."

Max laughed. "Do I look like the outdoor type?"

"Something is coming, Max," she repeated. Her intensity cut his humor. "It's just a symbol . . . but, I, uh, feel something concrete. Make friends with that horse, Max, before . . . " She turned away.

"Hey, you can't stop now," he insisted. "Before what?"

"Before something happens."

"Like what?"

"I'm sorry," she answered meekly. "I don't know. But look, every leaf in the cup has a crack across the main vein." She shook her head. "That's not a good sign."

Max rose from the chair, twisting the ends of his mustache thoughtfully. "I've never known you to be spooky," he whispered. He trusted her intuition, although he believed she did her parlor games—the stars, tea leaves, and the like—as an excuse to allow her to vocalize what she knew. He could dismiss her charades as silly but not her instincts. Max tiptoed to the door, then turned suddenly and shouted "boo." Celine gasped, then shook her head again. "See," he said with a mischievous smirk, "now we're even."

11

The old Victorian home, set among manicured lawns, gave Jamie a sense of stability and security. A reasonable ideal, she assured herself as she exited her house with Rachel in one arm and a cello in the other. With her knee she pushed the antique rocking chair beneath the canopy of the porch. Her eyes scanned the line of gladiolas she had planted in the spring. Jamie enjoyed the predictability of nature; she liked to watch the world flower, confident that it always would. It's a matter of positioning, she told herself, just as she had positioned the gladiolas halfway between the birch trees and the house, exposing them to the right mixture of sun and rain. She believed that if she did her part, nature would do the rest, at least the part of nature she had befriended. Droughts, blizzards, floods and other catastrophes had been conveniently excluded. Jamie believed she had earned the right to exclude them, if not for herself, then for the child in her arms who had made her own survival worthwhile. She squeezed Rachel, blew a kiss to her hundred-year-old house and entered her car. In twelve minutes she knew she would be at a county park.

A flock of geese flew in formation only twenty feet above the field. Jamie watched them until they disappeared behind the trees; then she removed the baby from a large cradlelike wicker basket and nuzzled her on the small slope near a stream. Rachel's giggling escalated her mother's assault. She tickled her child's stomach and munched on her nose, losing herself in the wrinkled little face and smiling lips. The baby poked her fingers into her mother's mouth and cooed. "Oh, I love you," Jamie hummed to her daughter. "I love you, I love you, I love you." She smothered Rachel with kisses. The sun bathed them in warm yellow hues, the soft breeze rippled the grass gently around them. As she rocked her child in her arms, she coordinated instinctively that motion with a yoga neck exercise. Round and round in wide, easy turns. Her head swiveled on her shoulders. The vertebrae released their energy. Six clicks echoed in her head.

She placed Rachel back into the basket. Standing erect with her hands raised over her head, she twisted from side to side, stretching to the limits of her ability. Arching backward, she touched the ground with her fingers. After finishing a set series of movements, Jamie began her last breathing exercises.

Resting near the basket after completing her studied repertoire, she scanned the park. Her eyes fixed on a couple with a crippled child. In an elaborate procedure, they lifted the little boy, his legs weighted with braces, out of the wheelchair and onto a swing. His body perched awkwardly on the small wooden seat. Yet he laughed during the entire process. The father strapped him securely into the swing. The mother jostled and joked with her son. Very gently they pushed him aloft. Shouts of reassurance. Huge, rosy smiles. A noisy celebration.

Unexpected tears streamed down Jamie's face for the little boy, not for his leg braces or wheelchair, but for the warmth and joy showered on him that had been absent in her own childhood. She, too, had once been crippled, a victim of rheumatoid arthritis. By the age of three, she had already felt the constraints and disabling effects of the illness. By the time she was five, her joints had swelled and stiffened. The radius of movement in her arms and legs decreased sharply, the pain constant and at times overwhelming. At night, from beneath her covers, she listened to her father blame his wife for their predicament and refuse to have another child, fearing it might have the same disease as Jamie . . . a disease he described as a curse. When she was six, her parents divorced.

In those last days before they separated legally, both her mother and father concluded that they would be unable to care for Jamie, who by this time had become completely immobile. They informed their daughter that they would take her to a special place that would cater to her needs, a "nice" place with other children. They painted playland images.

The long afternoon ride to the state hospital became the most difficult journey in her life. She pleaded with her mother to keep her at home, promising not to be a nuisance. Her mother insisted that this solution suited everyone's best interest.

The clothes her mother wore on that particular day left an indelible imprint on Jamie. It floated back to her in vivid detail, red roses on a white field. They had strapped her to the car seat to prevent her from falling. Jamie remembered lifting her left arm slowly through her own nausea and grabbing onto her mother's skirt. During the last minutes of the ride she clutched the garment so tightly that her fingers became numb. Jamie clung to the connection, refusing to relinquish her last hope. Even at the institution she maintained her grip on the clothing. Her mother pulled her arm, imploring her to release the skirt. The requests turned to angry reprimands. Tortured and pulled in opposite directions, they both cried—hollow sounds, dry and brittle. Finally, two hospital attendants pried her hands loose.

As they lifted her carefully out of the car, Jamie held her breath in disbelief. Her mother turned away . . . she never left the car, never entered the large gray building. As they wheeled Jamie toward the entrance, she cried out only once. A last plea. Unanswered. The distant ring of her own voice reverberated in the stark brick courtyard.

For five long years, she was confined behind those walls,
just one of several hundred children who had been separated from the mainstream. Many of them floated in a
secretive, nonverbal world of their own; so Jamie found
herself even more isolated. Alone among the lonely.

The first weeks were the worst. She cried herself to sleep
every night. The doctors and attendants tolerated her
adjustment with professional indifference. Her will to live
dissipated quickly, followed by a dramatic loss of weight.

The spark of life might have completely escaped her
were it not for an orderly named Mary-O. A heavy and
jovial woman from the island of Jamaica, she gravitated to
Jamie immediately. The child's silence and submerged
intensity sparked her interest.

Each evening, after completing her chores, Mary-O sat
with this little girl. She massaged her unused legs and
talked to her incessantly. Her teeth twinkled in the light.
When she laughed, the single silver earring she wore
bobbed up and down. Jamie began to live for Mary-O's visits. The kindly old woman sang calypso songs and told her
voodoo stories. Sometimes, at night, Mary peeked in on
Jamie before going home, kissing her lightly on the forehead.

Jamie's grandparents decided to remove her from the
hospital just before her eleventh birthday. Standing on
crutches in the hallway as they processed her papers, she
stared at the silver-haired strangers with sad faces. She bit
her lips, rocking back and forth on the wood supports.
Suddenly, her face brightened as Mary-O came lumbering
toward her.

"Wouldn't have missed you for the world, honey."

Jamie dropped her head. Mary-O bellowed, her eyes filling with tears. "You write to me now, don't you forget your
old Mary-O."

As Jamie began to sob, Mary held her to her own heavy,

warm body. "Don't cry now, ma lady—you're going to be just fine. Ah ma lady, ah ma lady," she crooned, rocking gently.

Within two weeks of becoming her benefactors, her grandparents sponsored a trip to Iowa, where Jamie was to be treated by a well-known arthritis specialist. There, under careful supervision, she underwent a series of operations. Her hip sockets and portions of her knee joints were replaced with Teflon counterparts. The surgery gave her the freedom to walk. With huge dosages of steroids and a regimented intake of cortisone, her condition improved steadily.

Her general mobility increased markedly. But the medication racked her system, imbalancing many autonomic functions. She took pills to control the side effects of other pills. Her courage to persist came from Mary-O's short, supportive letters.

"Mary-O's so proud of her lady. So proud."

Jamie hummed, "ah ma lady, ah ma lady," over and over like a mantra as she entered the door of school for the first time.

Her playmates teased her about her swollen face and limbs, a standard side effect of cortisone. They nicknamed her "fat face." The doctors used diuretics to control the swelling. This further interfered with her body chemistry, draining her system of vitamins and other nutrients. Responding to her lethargy and depression, her physician added antidepressants to her daily diet of drugs.

At twelve, Jamie was reunited with her mother. Having remarried, she now believed she could care for her daughter, who returned hesitantly to the woman who had placed her in a state institution six years before.

By sixteen, Jamie walked without a limp, but the side effects of the medication marred her days. The pills grounded her, dragging her down like anchors. One afternoon, instead of ingesting several of the eighteen capsules she took daily, Jamie threw them into the toilet. Too frightened to confront her mother, she placed a long-distance call to her Uncle Richard, a chiropractor, seeking his support.

"Jamie," Richard said succinctly, "if you don't want to take the drugs, then don't take them."

She began to cry. His answer, so direct, respected her wants—the antithesis of the edicts of her doctors.

Richard, who possessed a wealth of knowledge about homeopathic and herbal medicine, suggested various natural remedies, including a daily regimen of yoga exercises and an involvement with a musical instrument, which would provide the needed calisthenics for her hands.

"But who will tell Mom?" Jamie asked. "I can't, Richard. I can't." Her voice became barely audible. "Could you do it?" she pleaded. "She's your sister. She'll listen to you. Oh, please, will you do it?"

Despite the hysteria of her mother and the dire predictions of the physicians, Jamie, with strong support from her uncle, remained aloof from the medication and refused to ingest another pill. Her health actually improved without the medication. Yoga and the cello became her religions. Her moods softened. Her energy doubled.

"Dear Mary-O," she wrote. "It's like a miracle. I'm well, I'm truly well." The letter came back with "addressee unknown" stamped haphazardly across the name.

Mary-O's boisterous laugh still filled her ears, even now in the park. She smiled a silent thank you. Jamie promised it would be different for her own child.

As she watched the father continue to push the little boy on the swing, she stared at his harness of chrome and steel. "If he were mine, I'd always keep him by my side," she whispered to the wind. Jamie embraced her own daughter; her hands trembled as she squeezed her tightly to her breast.

Minutes later her focus changed as something indistinct drew her attention elsewhere. A strange energy flowed through her body. Everything blurred, except for a small bridge built over one of the ponds; it beckoned to her. At first Jamie resisted the pull. Stubbornly she remained seated although she wanted to rise. Finally, she allowed her body its movement. Carrying Rachel on her hip, she walked across the field and climbed the planked boards of the old bridge.

Standing on the structure overlooking the water, she noticed her inability to concentrate on anything other than the immediate foreground. People and sounds merged into one hazy tapestry. Her eyes searched the pond and neighboring rocks nervously, her vision drawn immediately by the glint of a small metal object. Securing her grip around Rachel, she crossed over the bridge to investigate. As she bent down, she discovered a gold ring. It was the very one she had lost a year before in the same park. The inscription from her Uncle Richard still showed.

Jamie filled with excitement, but her exuberance soon clouded. She felt powerful and yet, oddly enough, out of control. She lingered on the bridge, fondling the ring. Several minutes later Terry appeared.

"I'm sorry I'm late," she exclaimed, kissing both Jamie and Rachel.

"That's okay. I still have more than enough time for my rehearsal before I meet Peter." As they strolled back to the wicker cradle, Jamie recounted the events leading to her discovery of the ring. Her words reignited her initial enthusiasm.

"So what do you think, Terry?"

"I don't," she answered. "It's over my head."

Jamie smiled. "Well, anyway, I'm . . . grateful. Maybe that's all that matters."

The two women embraced and Jamie departed for the trek into the city with Luke's class as her ultimate destination. As she crossed the lawns, Terry called to her.

"Jame, be careful."

Jamie waved her assurance. Twenty minutes later, en route to the city, she recalled Terry's comment. "Be careful . . . about what?" she murmured to herself.

12

Spring Street, the hub of SoHo. Art galleries, sculpture studios and health food restaurants blended into the brick and stone landscape of refurbished factory edifices. Freshly painted buildings hid behind networks of sagging fire escapes. A young woman, her hair dyed orange and her long legs grounded in combat boots, strutted across the street. An old man, his arms filled with books, trudged along the sidewalk, barely noting the neon lady who had whizzed by him. Elegantly dressed tourists tramped into a store selling ambrosia teas and coffee.

Everyone knew about Toby's Temple, except perhaps Toby, a stuffed parrot poised on a ledge by the entrance of the restaurant named in his honor. Beyond the wooden bins filled with herbs and beans stood a twenty-foot oak counter behind which five chefs dished out a variety of vegetarian and Mideastern delights. Toby's benefactor, a dark-skinned, gaunt man dressed in a white robe, greeted each patron individually.

This eatery had become an informal meeting place for those who arrived early for Luke's class. Seated at a front table with two others from the group, I drifted in and out of the conversation as I awaited Jamie's arrival.

"I think Luke might be going too far this time. I mean, after all, sure he's gifted . . . but sometimes he acts downright strange," suggested J. Collisandro Fawcett, a thirty-two-year-old former lawyer, former Canadian citizen, former Reikian therapist, former heterosexual. In addition to his cerebral gymnastics, Collis, as he liked to be called, had a startling way of positioning and manipulating his tall, lean body, intertwining his arms and legs like a human pretzel. His angular features and sharply chiseled nose gave him the appearance of a hawk.

"Well, aren't either of you gentlemen going to voice an opinion?"

"Collis, what do you really want?" I asked.

"To analyze the man, what else?"

"Maybe, but what I'm hearing is annoyance," said Paul, a mathematics professor.

"That's ass-in-ine," Collis hissed. "Just dump it back in my lap. You sound like Luke, only he does it better."

Paul smiled parentally, indulging Collis's tantrum.

"You know, you're curious to me," Collis said, shifting his attention to me. "You don't talk too much in class, yet your presence is very strong. What goes on under that strong silent routine of yours?"

I put down my spoon and stared directly into J. Collisandro Fawcett's eyes.

Unknowingly I mimicked Luke's gaze, a fact that Paul shared with me later. "And if Luke is a bit strange," I said, "why would you be uncomfortable about that?"

"Who said anything about being uncomfortable?" Collis shot back.

"Your voice says you're uncomfortable; Collis, don't you ever listen to yourself?" Paul winked at me.

A second later I veered away as I caught a glimpse of Jamie, cello in hand, entering the restaurant. Walking briskly to the table, she greeted everyone warmly by shaking hands. Collis mellowed when her fingers touched his. "Oh, c'mon, Jamie, you can do better than that." He laughed, using his sudden burst of joviality as an excuse to hug her. She submitted to his embrace awkwardly.

Standing by the chairs, we chatted for several minutes before Jamie and I excused ourselves and took a separate table in one of the tatami booths. We removed our shoes, then seated ourselves on pillows around a low table.

"How'd the rehearsal go?" I asked.

"Good, really good. We started practicing a Debussy piece. A little daring for me, but I kind of liked it—I think." A full smile burst onto her face when she held up her hand and wiggled the finger with the gold ring on it.

"Wow, you found it? Probably spent the last couple of years in a coat pocket."

She told me the story quickly.

"See, then it is working," I said softly.

"What's working?"

"The classes, the exercises . . . what we're learning at Luke's," I answered.

"Oh, Peter, my finding the ring was just a coincidence."

"But what about the intuition to get up and walk to the bridge . . . and the sense that everything was blurred except the foreground?"

Jamie took my hands. "I can't explain that, except, maybe, those things sometimes happen."

"That's just it; they do happen. If we just dismiss them, then there's nothing to learn from those experiences. Are you dismissing what happened to you?"

"Of course not. Here," she said, lifting her hand and flexing the finger with the ring, "how can I dismiss what's in plain sight. It's just that you want to tie everything in with Luke."

"I just want you to be open. Okay?"

She stared at the ring a long time before answering. "Okay," she mumbled finally.

Gusts of wind slammed against our faces as we left the restaurant. Air currents whistled through narrow alleys like a shrill chorus of nervous witches. Old posters, clinging limply to the walls of an unoccupied building, flapped in the stiff breeze.

As we crossed the street, I looked up and noted several familiar figures pass by the windows of the lower floor in Luke's duplex. Looking to the top floor, I almost stopped short, intrigued by what appeared to be two hooded figures. Black robes covered their heads. When they spotted me gaping at them, they backed quickly away from the glass panes.

Once inside the loft, we lost ourselves in the embrace of many hellos. For the first time Jamie relaxed her guard and returned each person's hug with the exception of Rudy's. Her body became instinctively rigid for his greeting. When his eyes saddened like a child who has just been rejected, Jamie reconsidered her response. Maybe the touching in the darkness had been innocent. Maybe Rudy was as he appeared: a soft, gentle soul. Maybe she had been needlessly prudish in her response to the intrusion of his arm. Jamie touched his shoulder and smiled at him. I wanted to cheer her gesture. She had indeed abided by her commitment to stay open to the experiences of the group.

With a bit of fanfare, I made an announcement about Jamie's discovery. I knew that everyone within earshot would connect her "find" to the classes. Several people crowded Jamie, wanting details of her story. Rather than shrinking from their requests, she smiled and detailed the events in the park.

Unobtrusively, I separated from the group gathered around my wife and wandered into the kitchen. I ambled casually into the dining room, then the rear den, searching for the bizarre figures I had seen in the window. Finally I stopped at the circular staircase leading to the second floor and closed my eyes to heighten the receptivity of my ears. I didn't know what to expect and subsequently heard nothing unusual. Suppressing my impulse to continue this little unauthorized investigation, I rejoined Jamie and the other students.

Collis and Paul had followed the others, seating themselves on the floor along the perimeter of the room. Dan, sitting opposite them, smiled with eyes closed. Deedee, another permanent guest in Luke's house, guided Jamie to a place beside her. She stroked Jamie's blouse, admiring the material. Lady Claire checked my shoulder for apparitions, then flopped down on a mound of pillows, obviously relieved. Jessica, Woodrow and several others sat beside her.

Predictably, Hera and Max arrived late, although they came independently of each other. Hera, always a bit flustered, performed an absurd curtsy, almost tripping on her floor-length bolero skirt. Max caught her by the shoulder, returned her to a respectable upright position, then hugged each person in the group.

"Your condition has stabilized, eh?" he whispered to me, checking my pulse with an authoritative air. "No more mysterious eyeballs balanced over your shoulder, I hope."

"You turkey," I laughed. Pulling my wrist away, I withdrew a sketch pad from my hip pocket and drew three quick caricatures of Max. "For you," I declared, ripping the top sheet from the pad and handing it to my friend.

Max laughed at three bald-headed figures, each decorated with a familiar bushy mustache. One had his hands over his mouth, the other over his eyes, the last over his ears. A halo floated over each of them.

"A Rembrandt it's not," he said, holding his chin with his hand and striking the pose of an art historian. "Too symbolic." Max folded the sketch neatly, bowed theatrically, then found a place in the group beside Jamie.

"How's the baby?" he asked.

Jamie's eyes sparkled. "Oh, Max, I learn so much from her. It's amazing."

"What's something you've learned from her?"

"Well, like letting go . . . being a kid again . . . we're really lucky to have her."

Max dipped his head and smiled. "I know."

"Problem is," I interjected from across the room, "she's

starting to look like her godfather."

"Don't listen to him," Jamie insisted, touching Max's face awkwardly.

The intimacy startled him. "Well, um, any tidbits of news to share?" he questioned.

Jamie shrugged her shoulders. "Just the ring, which you know about and, oh, yes, a very bizarre dream."

"Tell me about it."

"Will there be a charge, Doctor?" she kidded.

"Only if it's boring."

Jamie's dream didn't bore Max. When she described the charging horse in detail, he had to hold his face steady in order not to betray his surprise. Max felt that by giving credence to her dream, he might scare her. Only months later did he share with us that the horse in her dream duplicated, in almost every respect, the one that had bucked him in Central Park. He asked her if she had ever seen such an animal, perhaps inserting him unconsciously into her dream. She had thought of that, she said, but insisted she had never seen such a horse. The subject dampened any further conversation.

Ten minutes of class time elapsed with Luke still conspicuously absent. As everyone continued to sit together, points on the circumference of an irregular circle, their talk dwindled into silence. I sat beside Rudy. He lives here, he would know, I reasoned. Unable to dislodge the image of those two hooded people, yet embarrassed to confront my host directly, I spoke in a hushed voice. "Have you been having masquerade parties here lately?"

Rudy smiled. "They have called what we do here by many different names."

Amused and confused by the answer, I could not decide whether Rudy had replied seriously or was purposely inscrutable. Another ten minutes passed without a break in the restless silence. Extravagant Hera, seated in a full-lotus position, filled and emptied her lungs noisily. The peculiar quiet and lack of activity had made Jamie fidgety. She closed her eyes and hummed the Debussy piece she had practiced earlier in the day. Max watched her, straining to hear her barely audible concert. Collis, his left leg miraculously wrapped behind his head, grimaced at Dan who had belched.

Paul addressed Rudy. "Is Luke coming tonight?"

"I don't have the slightest idea. I had assumed so, but that was only an assumption," Rudy responded cheerfully.

"Is he upstairs?" Collis inquired.

"No," Rudy replied matter-of-factly.

The parlay of questions and answers broke the mood. Whispered conversations cropped up throughout the room.

Still another ten minutes passed. Several students, led by Collis, started to put their coats on with obvious displeasure.

Wanting to combat the submerged resentment, I addressed the class. "Luke once told me a very interesting story." All heads turned. "Maybe some of you have heard it too. It deals with, well, I guess you'd call him a distinguished therapist who taught at major universities and lectured all over the world. Despite his busy schedule, he maintained a private practice.

"Because he lived in a remote part of the state, patients had to drive hours and hours to see him for what they believed would be a traditional forty-five minute session. Many loved him and valued his counseling intensely, but others ridiculed him angrily for his unpredictable behavior.

"In one incident, he excused himself in the middle of a session. The patient assumed he had gone to the bathroom, of course. Ten minutes passed, then twenty . . . then the entire forty-five minutes. The doctor never came back." I wavered for a moment, aware that I had taken charge of Luke's class unwittingly, then cleared my throat self-consciously. "Well . . . that patient got really angry and stormed out of the office only to discover a very disturbing sight in the garden. The therapist, on his hands and knees, was weeding busily around his tomato plants." Scattered laughter erupted throughout the room. "When the patient confronted the doctor, the man said, 'I gave you such an excellent twenty minutes; I thought we were through.'"

More laughter sprinkled throughout the room. Max smiled to himself, remembering how often he would have liked to disappear in the midst of therapy sessions with some of his clients, but somehow he wasn't willing to take the risk. I continued. "The real surprise comes when you find out this guy not only was booked solid, but had a waiting list as long as your arm."

"I guess," I added, "it was worth it to them. One man's fifteen minutes could be worth another person's five hours. If anyone here is annoyed with Luke, you might want to think about that." I paused and faced Collis. "Is Luke worth waiting for?"

Hera removed her jacket, nudging Collis, who did the same. Several others returned to their places. Max stared at me approvingly. Deedee engaged Jamie in another conversation, stroking her arm lightly as she talked. Rudy disappeared into the kitchen. Still feeling a touch self-conscious, I stood up, hugged Jamie from behind as I passed, then stood by the window. I leaned my forehead against the pane, staring into the wet street below.

From beneath the canopy at the entrance of the building, three distinct figures emerged. I watched Luke and two nuns walk from the building toward Prince Street. It clicked! The figures at the window! Their black habits glided smoothly over the pavement as if motorized. Luke bounced playfully between his companions as he crossed the street.

What the hell is he doing out there? I murmured inaudibly. My reaction felt like the antithesis of the anecdote I had just related. Respect what the man does, I told myself.

The three figures receded into the distance. I kept telling myself that I trusted Luke, but then, suddenly, I broke from my stance at the window and walked briskly across the room. I couldn't stand it a moment longer; I had to know why he was walking away from the scheduled class with two nuns.

I crossed the room quickly, passing Jamie again. I couldn't help but notice Deedee fondling my wife's hair as they talked. Something about the other woman's manner bothered me, but I couldn't quite define it. I grabbed my coat, tapped Max and said quietly, "C'mon, Max, let's go."

"Are you kidding?" he asked, turning to me in disbelief. "Right after your eloquent defense of Luke?"

"Please, just come."

Noting the round red button at the elevator shining its IN USE, we scooted down four flights of stairs, jumping down two and three steps at a time. On the way down I explained my actions to Max.

By the time we touched pavement, Luke and the nuns were gone. Surmising they had turned the corner on Prince, we jumped into my Volvo and screeched from the curb. The car bolted into the air as it bounced across a pot-hole. A light rain had begun to fall, making the street slick. At the intersection, I ignored the traffic signal, skidding into a left turn. An elderly woman waved her umbrella scoldingly at me.

"You take the right side and I'll watch the left," I said. We found no sign of Luke or his companions.

"Circle around on Sullivan and we can come down Prince from the other direction," Max advised.

As I made the turn, I shook my head. "I feel like an ass, Max. What the hell are we doing? If Luke wants to take a hike with some ladies of the cloth, who are we to inter-fere?"

"Maybe you don't trust him," Max suggested. I answered with my silence, avoiding Max's eyes.

Veering back on Prince, we spotted him several blocks ahead, no longer accompanied by the nuns. As the car angled into the right lane, an oil truck blocked our path. I backed onto the curb, then eased my car alongside the obstacle, finally passing it. Oblivious of the drizzle, Luke promenaded leisurely along the avenue. I slammed on the brakes as traffic snarled again and whipped my vehicle to the curb; then Max and I jumped into the street.

We shouted to Luke. No response. We jogged toward him on the sidewalk, calling his name. I reached him first and tapped him on the shoulder. "Luke," I said, winded, as I came abreast of him.

Luke's head turned away, facing into a colored-light display in a store window. "Luke," I pressed incredulously as Max joined me. Ever so slowly, the man turned. It was not Luke. Instead, an individual of almost the exact same height and weight stood before us; even his beard and carriage bore an uncanny resemblance to Luke's.

Apologizing profusely, I began to explain our mistake. The man just smiled, his face like an infant's, clean and undefined. He touched the collar on my jacket. He pushed his fingers awkwardly through the thick, soft fur, apparently incapable of processing the barrage of language being thrown at him. I stopped talking and gaped at Max. Returning my attention to the stranger, I stroked his shoulder reassuringly.

"It's okay. We made a mistake." I spoke slowly and softly. "You have a nice day, now. Okay?" No response. "We're going, so 'bye now. Okay? Well, 'bye." I smiled, nodded, waved, finally disengaging in order to retreat to the car with Max. I kicked the front tire. "What a jerk I am! That sweet retarded guy was just trying to make it through his day and we had to make his life even more complicated."

As I started my car, I stared at the strange man still standing in the exact spot we had left him. Suddenly, the two nuns that I had seen before came outside and patted him approvingly on the shoulder. Very gently, they turned him and, with their backs to us, guided him down the street.

We returned to the loft, bewildered. We could tell by the texture of the stillness that Luke had arrived in our absence. Everyone sat quietly in a loose circle, their attention focused on the chubby Buddha staring at the floor. Max and I squatted beside Jamie.

Lifting his head, Luke greeted both of us with the penetrating gaze of his luminous left eye. He spoke in a hushed tone. "I am not always who I seem to be."

13

As Luke began the meeting, he asked each member of the class to seal himself or herself off from the intrusion of anything outside of his or her own body. He requested total concentration. Counseling us to focus only on our cerebral cortex, he described precisely its physical appearance and location in the brain. His colorful and concise verbal road map served as our guide.

"Now I want you to find an old memory. Go far back. When you get to the right place, withdraw it as you would withdraw a folder from a file cabinet. Everything will be there for you; all you need to do is reach in and get it. Trust yourselves to have that ability."

Jamie visualized everything Luke had said. Like an enthusiastic tourist, she strolled through the caverns of her mind. Suddenly, the image of a rag doll that she had played with as a child popped into her head. She had cut off its legs, believing the doll would then be more like her. Others in the group had similar experiences or, like Hera, they could not find any available "folders" to scrutinize. Still disturbed by the incident with the man on Prince Street, I began the exercise uncomfortably. Everything appeared muddled to me. No clear roadways in my cerebral cortex such as Luke had described. No neat rows of cells swelling with data from my past waiting to be plucked. When Luke signaled the end of the segment, I could not easily disengage.

Large, dark forms darted in and out of my vision—definite, yet indistinct. They moved over me like elastic amoebas, changing shape and density. I wanted to flee. My chest tightened when I heard a muffled scream filter through the watery veil of those dark figures.

Jamie tapped my shoulder, startling me. "Welcome back. You waited all week for class; I know you don't want to miss it now." I leaned over and kissed her. She's coming around, I thought.

Luke's voice dominated again. He had hoped the exercises we had just completed would heighten our general awareness.

"And don't be concerned if you didn't see anything. Each of us lives on a different schedule. Each of us has a different shield to pierce, different walls to . . ." Luke continued. His voice became garbled for me again, like a record played at slow speed. I fought to maintain my grip on the activity presented, but I slid uncontrollably into a twilight state. Unidentifiable whispers spiderwebbed around me. Suddenly, a sharp object pierced my buttocks, but without the experience of pain. Instinctively my hand jerked from my side and slipped under me to protect the area from further assault. I pushed the phantoms aside, finally surfacing back into the class.

Luke stood with Jamie in the center of the living room. He whispered to her while cupping his hands over her ear. She nodded her assent, smiling like a little girl participating in some harmless adventure.

The interaction between Jamie and the short monkish man continued despite the scrutiny of the others. Obviously Luke liked her. I could not have been more pleased, I told myself. As my wife and Luke talked more, I strained to hear but their voices were hushed purposely. What had I missed? The others waited patiently for Luke to finish and address them again. I inhaled deeply and smiled. I watched Jamie take Luke's hands and laugh. He pulled her gently against his body and whispered again. Affection flowed freely among the students, a natural product of the removal of walls between them. And yet I found myself ambivalent about what I observed. Why did Jamie and Luke touch each other so much? What was simple affection and what was seduction? The unwelcomed questions kept coming and coming. I put a clamp immediately on my growing concern, reminding myself that I had asked Luke to give Jamie extra attention to help her feel more comfortable in class. How could I question his responsiveness to my own request?

I never answered my own questions. The slow-moving forms invaded my consciousness again, crowding out other thoughts.

Luke beckoned to Paul, asking him to come behind Jamie and lift her off the ground. Paul placed his arms gently around her waist; he flexed his sculptured muscles, smiling at an invisible camera, then lifted Jamie's 115 pounds off the floor with ease. Luke put his hands on Paul's shoulder and moved him back a few feet. On cue, Jamie closed her eyes. Her brow creased as she concentrated with unusual intensity.

"Lift her again, Paul." Luke's voice was hushed, expectant.

Paul bent his knees slightly and locked his arms lightly around Jamie's waist again. He straightened his legs and attempted to lift her off the floor. His face contorted with surprise as he strained and reddened slightly.

"Wow . . . she feels at least fifty pounds heavier. What happened?"

"Before I explain it, would anyone else want to try?" Luke inquired. Max and Dan came forward. I, too, stepped into the center of the room—my movement tentative, my eyes vacant. Jamie looked at me curiously.

As Dan repeated the experiment, Max nudged me, "Are you okay?"

"Sure," I replied, gripping Max's forearm for emphasis. "I'm just fine."

Dan's experience duplicated Paul's. Max and I took our turns. Each of us encountered a dramatic change in Jamie's weight.

Energy rippled through the class. Collis, Lady Claire, Woodrow and the others appeared appropriately impressed. "It's a very simple exercise," Luke explained, nursing his can of soda. "This one barely scratches the surface, but it illustrates the power of our energy. In the first part, Jamie centered all her energy in her head. She concentrated upward, experiencing herself as light and buoyant, like a balloon. Then, she centered her energy in her hips and concentrated downward into the floor. I suggested she envision herself solid, heavy, and connected to the earth's core. And so the second time, Paul had difficulty lifting her. Her thoughts altered the effect of her own density and weight."

Luke drew his audience to him with his eyes. "The only limits we experience are those we impose on ourselves."

I marveled at the simplicity of the experiment. It mirrored what I, myself, had devised as a running technique— using the fantasy of filling my body with helium in order to reduce the sensation of weight.

Dividing the class into groups of twos and threes, Luke had everyone repeat the exercise. It worked for them all.

Once again the intrusion of dark forms into my peripheral vision plagued me. I turned my head from side to side repeatedly. Jamie pulled me aside.

"Peter, what's going on?"

"Is it that obvious?"

"It is to me."

"Well, I'm not sure. I keep seeing and hearing something. It feels really familiar, but I can't identify it." Jamie wrapped her arms tightly around my waist.

Luke strolled over to us and smiled. "Whatever it is, Peter, allow it." He nodded his head. "The difference between what we call fact and fantasy is merely a judgment. What I'm suggesting is not to judge."

"I don't understand," Jamie interjected.

He smiled thoughtfully, slipping his thumbs through the loops of his pants and pulling upward. "Ah, but perhaps you do. Do you ever critique what your daughter does? Do you ever think of some of her actions, facial expressions or sounds as silly and others as valid?" Jamie shook her head. "I didn't think so. You're simply open to everything she does. Well, if we can be that way with an infant, why can't we be that way with ourselves? Believe me, it takes a lot less energy, ultimately, to accept and use what we know rather than deny it." He folded his hands in front of his chest and tipped his head.

Rudy came up to us and whispered something to Luke.

"Ah, yes, thank you for reminding me." The short, impish man skipped into the center of the room, then clapped his hands several times. "I think we should go on now. Would everyone lie down on the floor beside each other with each person's feet by the next person's head . . . in a long line starting from the far wall."

Max flashed a big grin. "Ah, ha, more fun and games," he whispered to Jamie and me as we all found our places. Hera locked wrists with Paul. The others took positions in the line. In a natural, easy movement, Luke joined us. He closed his eyes. Twenty-four-year-old Deedee squeezed into the space beside him. Her smile was a perpetual come-on. This renegade from Manhattan, Queens and Brooklyn Heights giggled more often than talked in her attempt to seduce most everyone she met, regardless of sex.

Dan took a position next to Deedee. His eyes rolled like marbles, tracking her thighs. Aware of his interest, Deedee ran her hands up the inside of her legs as she arched her pelvis upward. Dan enjoyed the game. She faced him, then licked her lips.

Luke rose from his position at the end of the line. He promenaded past us like an elf surveying his troops. "Okay, let's everyone lock wrists with the person next to you.

Good. I want each of you to find a point on the ceiling and concentrate on it. Have you all found a point?" Luke waited respectfully for a minute before resuming.

"Okay, now just let yourself look at the point you've chosen. Fill your whole body with it." His voice softened, became deeper and richer. "As you continue to stare at the point, your vision will begin to go in and out of focus. Allow it. Go with your eyes. You're beginning to experience fatigue. Your eyelids feel heavier . . . and heavier. Go with it. Now, very slowly, I want each of you to relax your eyelids and let them close." When we all closed our eyes, Luke turned off the lights.

"We're going to go on a beautiful journey to the other side of the sun. All of us. Together. I want each of you to go with what I say," he said softly, emphasizing each word. "Now, concentrate on your breathing; feel your chest rising and falling, rising and falling. Now, inhale . . . hold, exhale. Each time you empty your lungs, you'll feel yourself sinking, ever so slowly. Floating downward. Sinking deeper into the floor. Inhale; hold it—good. And now exhale gently as you allow yourself to float freely. That's it; just let yourself go," Luke continued, almost whispering in a monotone. As he talked, he moved from person to person, placing his hands on our chests and pressing down each time we exhaled. He wanted us to experience fully the expanding and contracting of our ribs. Everyone breathed in one cadence, inhaling and exhaling in unison. Their general respiration ebbed. Twitching and moving of limbs stopped.

"You've floated through the floor and are drifting into open space. The descent is slow and secure. Against your back, you can begin to feel the heat of the sun, which is below you. We are going to float down to it and around the other side. Inhale, hold . . . exhale. As we get closer to the sun, it will become even warmer. I want you to absorb the warmth, become one with the warmth. In the heat and the light is energy. It's the source. Now you're moving down beside the sun. It's coming up on your left as you continue to float downward. Without opening your eyes, I want each of you to turn your head slightly to the left and look at the sun." Luke paused to survey the turning heads. Several people did not respond. "Very gently, don't be afraid, just turn your heads to the left and allow yourselves to see the sun." Two more heads turned. Neither Lady Claire nor Jessica moved. Claire smiled as Luke's meaty fingers moved her face. Jessica resisted momentarily, then eased her head to the left.

"I know it will be bright at first . . . very, very bright. But as you continue to look at it, you will adjust to its brilliance. If you are not afraid, it will not hurt your eyes." Like a gentle sergeant, Luke kept us locked in a rhythm with each other. "You're moving down under and around the other side of the sun." He watched all the heads moving as we experienced ourselves going around the far side of the sun. "Good. Look carefully at the yellow light. Allow yourself to take it in."

Jamie began by digging her fingers into the rug in an effort to stabilize her body. She moved around the other side of the sun and heard the remote clamor of hoofbeats. Gliding in slow motion, Jamie stared at the brilliant yellow ball with thousands of miniature electric explosions in its molten core. Then from the center of the sun, a face materialized. As she strained to see, the features became more apparent. Luke's watch-eye gazed at her. His expression, simultaneously intimate and impersonal, filled her. A peculiar but pleasant vibration filtered through her body as if she were being massaged from within. For an instant Luke's face turned into a horse's face . . .spotted black and white. Despite the warmth of the sun, a deadly cold washed over her. But as Luke's face returned, so did the warmth. A chorus of hoofbeats resounded in her ears while she moved behind the sun.

Max, Collis, Paul, and Sandy also saw Luke's face in the fiery center of the sun. They floated by it, stunned and awed by their own perception. Only Jamie saw the spotted horse.

Sweat beaded on my forehead in the heat of the summer sun. As I gaped into the almost blinding light, I detected an eye in its center . . . Luke's clear blue watch-eye. As the light grew more intense, it consumed the blue iris.

Then the bottom dropped out for me. Like a missile dropped at high speed from a jet, I catapulted downward. My body tumbled over itself, descending into a bottomless cavern. The sun retreated. Drawing in an endless breath, I tried desperately to stabilize myself. I clenched my fingers around the wrists of the person next to me, to no avail. Down and down I plunged. Out of control. Abandoned. Speeding to nowhere. My body came to rest abruptly on a white rectangular platform. Bars, highly polished vertical beams fashioned out of wood, surrounded me on all four sides. My fingers grabbed them. Despite my mammoth efforts, they did not budge. I peered up at the sun as I crawled into a corner. Exhausted, I fell asleep. The drone of garbled voices awakened me rudely. Large, dark spongy forms blocked out the sun, intermittently casting shadows over the cage. My teeth began to chatter as my hands grew numb.

Large armlike appendages extended from one immense black form. With infinite care it turned me onto my stomach. Other huge gloved hands held me down; someone drove a knifelike wedge into my buttocks. I heard myself scream, but it was from another time. They rolled me over, patted me like a newborn puppy, then abandoned me again. Within seconds another group of phantoms arrived. Their shapes differed slightly; their voices sounded higher in pitch. They also turned me face down on the platform as another knifelike wedge pierced my buttocks. They left me sobbing. I was myself and yet I observed myself.

I shouted to the receding figures. They ignored my calls, chattering to each other in a mumbled alien tongue. But then one figure, with a shrill bark, spoke in a language I

understood. The words *oxygen* and *deprived* stood out. Bending my ear in their direction, I heard *brain damage* and *retar-
dation*. The image of the man in the street flashed before
me, his hands stroking my fur collar. The sun grew larger.
Overloaded sensorily, I hadn't realized that I had begun to
ascend. When I looked over my shoulder, my cage assumed
the more recognizable form of a giant crib. As three phantom figures approached it, images of the nuns in Luke's
window darted before me. Then I realized the murky
amoebas from my dreamlike state had also been nuns.

Pieces of an old puzzle fell from an unlocked compartment in my brain. The strange forms, which I had seen as
vague images from time to time over the years, had shape
and content finally. As I floated up toward the light,
warmed by its heat, I remembered. The memories crystal-
lized. Hospitalization at the age of five with a collapsed
lung and other respiratory complications. The operation. A
surgeon's fears of oxygen deprivation and possible brain
damage. Those images, which had haunted me all my life,
belonged to this experience. The nuns in this Catholic
facility had cared for me. The wedges represented their
needles filled with medication.

Strange laughter intruded. I looked back over my shoulder for one last glimpse of the receding scene. The ladies
in robes looked at me. Now, for the first time, I could see
their faces . . . Deedee and Collis, their cheeks squeezed by
the starched white liners of their habits.

The third nun's bowed head lifted slowly to reveal the
face of the retarded man that Max and I had chased down
Prince Street. I looked into his dull, happy gaze. Extending
his hand through space, the man held out a small red rose,
but he could not bridge the distance. I grabbed for it in a
futile gesture. Suddenly, everything went blank. Something
jarred inside. Had I been sleeping? The sun reappeared
suddenly beneath my closed eyelids.

Continuing the meditation, I visualized myself floating

around the sun until I encountered that luminous blue eye again. My concentration sharpened dramatically. My body felt more buoyant than ever before. I had broken down a wall and freed myself from one nightmare only to encounter another. I continued my ascent, choosing to surface.

As Deedee rounded the far side of the sun, her pupils dilated despite the intense light. The increasing warmth unlocked the pores of her skin. Her nerve endings tingled. Her lips parted. She gazed hypnotically at the yellow-white source. A physical and very personal energy filled her. Her mouth dropped open as she pushed her tongue out like a little girl catching raindrops. Her muscles tightened and released. A rocking motion dominated her body. The driving rhythm of her increased pulse and rapid breathing swept over her. Deedee pushed her pelvic bone toward the sun. The temperature surged inside of her, matching the intensity of heat that blanketed the surface of her body. As she stared at the sun, she threw her head from side to side, gritting her teeth until the energy peaked and boiled over. For a moment her consciousness melted into the sun. Thrusting convulsively, she alternately relaxed her muscles and slammed them locked until every ounce of tension was spent. Limp, yet filled, Deedee's damp figure floated steadily upward.

Luke's melodic voice echoed soothingly. He directed each of us to continue our ascent until we felt ourselves resting on the floor. Starting with the toes and legs, we awakened ourselves slowly.

Almost everyone had opened their eyes when Rudy jumped up and switched on the lights. People stretched and twisted like early-morning risers; grudgingly, we climbed out of the residue of twilight sleep. Dan and Paul sat up first. They exchanged tentative smiles. With a catlike movement Collis sprang to his feet, then paced the perimeter of the room.

Jamie lifted herself slowly from the rug. She bent in the snakelike motion she used to adjust her back. A ripple of clicking noises emanated from the base of her spine. Using both hands precisely, she jerked her head to the left and right. Scanning the bodies on the floor, she fixed on the inert figure of Luke.

Groggily, we formed the traditional circle on the rug. Collis, Dan and Claire began to talk at once. Luke suggested we take turns sharing our experiences with the group. One by one, in the order in which we sat, the members told their stories.

Carefully deleting references to Deedee, Collis and the retarded man, I relayed my experience, appreciative of being liberated from yet another past trauma but haunted by the new images I saw. When Jamie talked about the horse and related it to the one in her dream, her frankness surprised me as did Luke's somber response to her story. Max found the reappearance of that same horse unsettling. He remained uneasy about his awareness that her apparition mirrored the horse he had encountered in the park.

Deedee giggled at Max. "Hey, big boy, just take a look at your bald head. I think you have a sunburn."

Max touched his forehead, running his hands back across his barren head. Feeling the tenderness of his skin, he jumped up and trotted to the bathroom. Several seconds later he returned. "Not to repeat what's obvious, folks, but I think I really did get a sunburn." His eyes darted from Luke to me. I stared at his reddened crown. Had it been the power of suggestion? Or the trick of some sort of hypnosis? Although I remembered reading about such phenomena, I had never believed it. It's going too fast, I told myself, overdosed suddenly by what I perceived in plain view.

"How come we all saw some similar things?" Collis asked.

"Perhaps," Luke answered, "instead of me fielding all the questions, why don't you discuss it among yourselves?" He lit a cigarette and inhaled heavily.

"Collis," Paul began, "maybe that was simply what there was to see."

"Just what's that supposed to mean, Professor?" Collis snapped. "Very metaphysical, Pauly, but I'm not in the mood for conundrums. I want to know what's going on."

"What's a *conundrum?*" Hera asked.

"A riddle, a puzzle," I volunteered.

"I'd like to propose a simple question. Why was Luke's face part of the sun?" Dan asked.

Paul shrugged, repeating his original point. "It just was . . . why does it matter, why?"

"Christ, all of a sudden you think you have all the answers," Collis retorted.

"Maybe it would have been my face," offered Woodrow, "if I had conducted the exercise. Luke's voice, as the guiding voice, was so much part of the trip."

"Perhaps there isn't any one answer for all of us," I suggested. "I mean we all had different experiences . . . very personal. Maybe that is because we each have different lessons to learn."

"I'll say." Deedee chuckled, holding her eyes at half-mast.

"Do you want to share it with us?" Collis snorted. When she pulled away, he leaned over and spoke directly into her ear. "I'll bet you tried to fuck the sun," he sneered.

Deedee glared at him, then brought herself immediately under control. She puckered her lips sensually and threw him a kiss. "At least," she announced out loud, "I don't go around humping the world from its rear end."

Collis sizzled.

An awkward minute expired. Luke looked at everyone, drawing their attention. Lowering his head, he clasped his hands around his large girth. His voice whispered its message. "Instead of searching for the meaning in concepts and words, instead of looking outside for what's already within, be with yourself. You have the answers. You have always had the answers."

The weight of his words suppressed any conversation. I leaned forward to speak but stopped. My mind drew a blank. Jamie folded her arms protectively in front of herself.

Collis, in a total mood change, introduced his next suggestion boldly. "So far, the meaning of every experience here is by inference. I want to do something concrete . . . concrete and spectacular."

"Like what?" scoffed Jessica.

"Like . . . like this." He lifted a flowerpot off of the fireplace mantel and placed it in the center of the rug. "Like move this flowerpot without physically touching it."

"And what will that prove?" Max questioned.

"I don't know . . . maybe nothing. But then again, if we can move the pot, we'd have an indisputable example of extended energy," he replied.

"But that wouldn't really tell us anything about what we can know from within," I countered.

Rather abruptly Luke rose from his chair and bowed his head to the group, signaling the end of the class. Although surprised, everyone prepared to leave with the exception of Collis and Dan. After a brief discussion, they encircled the pot and held their hands over it. With their eyes closed, they concentrated on moving it. Max and Paul shared a grin. Hera and Deedee laughed out loud. Most of the students stayed to watch these two men and to lend support to their intention.

One by one they gave up. Luke stood at the exterior door, hugging everyone as they left. I remained for a few more minutes, watching Collis and Dan until they abandoned their project, leaving the flowerpot alone in the center of the large hall.

"Peter," Jamie called from the outer room.

"I'm coming," I answered. As I turned toward the door after retrieving my jacket from a chair, I jerked my head around for a last glance. The pot appeared to be in a different place . . . three or four feet to the left of its original position. I approached it warily, noting a deep depression in the rug where I had seen it originally. I reviewed Collis and Dan's movements in my mind. Neither had touched the pot.

I turned to leave only to encounter Luke. "Is there anything you want to tell me?" he asked.

"Well, sort of," I answered. "It's about that silly flowerpot. I could have sworn it moved."

"And so?" Luke responded casually.

"Did it?"

"Why ask me?"

I rubbed my forehead and sighed. Jamie took my arm, but I still hesitated. "If I say the pot moved, that's absurd. Yet, I, uh, think it did. What could have moved it?"

Luke's left eye glimmered like a torch. He extended his right hand forward as if to harness a power more potent than his words. For a moment he might have been mistaken for a priest about to bestow a blessing. Maintaining that singular pose, he said to me, "We tend to explain events in terms of causes. And we think of the cause as first and then the response as second. But that's only a fabrication, a mind game. The cause of what we see and do is not in the past, but in the future. It comes from the future. Sometimes we have to wait until tomorrow to know the reason for what happened today. Be patient; we are only just beginning."

He patted me on the shoulder, embraced me, then surprised Jamie, who stood beside me, by handing her a carved, clothed figure about sixteen inches high. "Here, this is for your daughter. It's a Native American kachina doll given to me by my grandfather. The Zunis believed this figure and others like it contain their god-spirits. According to folklore, this is the kachina doll of happiness."

"I can't take this," Jamie said in awe, holding the figure in front of her like a newborn infant. "It was given to you,

Luke. It's very, very beautiful and probably very precious to you."

"All the more reason for you to take it." He guided her hands back toward her body so the doll remained cuddled in her arms. "Please."

Jamie blushed and hugged him. "I don't know what to say."

"Be happy," he replied.

As we moved toward the door, I noticed Collis watching Jamie and me from the darkened hallway. He had something like a fisherman's spool in his hand and a very peculiar grin on his face.

14

The wall of tinted glass, forty-seven stories above the ground, sparkled like Italian crystal as an eerie doomsday sunlight filtered through it. In the distance, the city's steel and cement dinosaurs stretched their necks skyward. Only the twin towers in lower Manhattan managed to ease their top twenty stories above the red-brown chemical mist belched from the rooftops and streets below.

Most of the occupants of the boardroom ignored the view, but I found it more compelling than the strategy meeting to which my staff and I had been invited. The towers I saw from this very room had inspired the illustration we created for the "Save Our City" campaign poster, which had been plastered all over the New York City bus and subway systems in recent weeks. Now, as I surveyed the same vista, a host of new images bombarded me. Luke's recent classes had helped free me from the limitation of contemplating only that which was possible. As I sat there, facing southwest, I envisioned hundred-story fans on the Jersey shore blowing the thick and pasty air pollution out to sea. These moving air currents would activate stainless-steel windmills in Queens to supply the inner city with its electrical energy. I saw enormous white fiberglass vacuum cleaners constructed on either tip of the island. Gigantic suction units would draw the air through massive spring-fed filtering screens to recirculate it on the street level. Gardens and trees would grow from the rooftops of every building in Manhattan.

"Pete," Dave Gillette said, "what do you think?"

The daydreams dissolved as I refocused on the meeting. "With the recent surveys on market receptivity and the demographic profiles you've given us on the target audience, I don't foresee any problems."

Two contrasting groups sat around the oval mahogany table. Dave Gillette, a divisional vice-president, headed the team of executives clustered together on one side of the huge polished slab. Impeccably dressed in fine-tailored suits, they nodded their heads as their superior itemized key points. Speaking with rapid precision, Gillette ejected words from between lips that barely moved. He spat out a series of specific demands, thinly camouflaged as requests.

In counterpoint, my staff and I dressed casually. Open shirts, denim jackets, and jeans adorned our bodies. Relaxed. A studied informality. Our clients expected illustrators, artists and designers to be different, even strange. We obliged quite easily.

"Explore whatever else you want, but make sure you at least work up what we've discussed." Gillette chuckled.

"No problem, Dave," I replied, rising from the chair and extending my hand. "We'll be back to you within two weeks, gentlemen."

As the taxi darted forward, I stared out the window, though my eyes absorbed nothing. Colleen sat quietly beside me. She chose to ride with me rather than go with the others in a different cab. I glanced at her appreciatively. The whites of her almond eyes glowed against her copper-skinned face.

"I got it," I announced, grabbing her arm with an enthusiastic squeeze. "No meetings or strategy sessions on this one. The cab ride will be approximately ten minutes. That's it. We'll give it ten minutes and whatever ideas we come up with . . . we go with."

"Peter," she countered. "They're paying ten thousand dollars just for the concepts with illustration and production expenses on top. How could you give them ten thousand dollars worth of ideas in a ten-minute cab ride?"

"Easy. One thousand dollars worth a minute. Is what we come up with worth any more if we spend ten hours or ten days on it? We either hit the mark or we don't!" Why not change my whole frame of reference for business, as I was learning to do in those evening classes? Why wait for Tuesday nights to challenge the old formulas? Couldn't I dive in now, without preparation, and see what happens?"

"I calculate we have used up three minutes already," Colleen noted, humoring me.

I leaned back and tried to enter my mind much in the way I had during the class exercises. I searched through a fantasized library, dipping into blocks of cells containing notions on travel, pleasure, freedom and escapism. Thoughts and pictures began to take shape. I whipped out my sketch pad and did thumbnail layouts of proposals. By the time the yellow cab jerked to the curb, ten approaches had been duly recorded.

Colleen reviewed the designs, trying to contain her enthusiasm and surprise. "Hey, hey . . . not bad, maestro, not bad at all."

Once in my office, I fell into the restored antique barber chair, vintage early 1900. I closed my eyes and listened to Colleen's footsteps as she entered the room.

Sitting on the edge of a coffee table, she placed her hands on her knees, bending toward me. Colleen coughed with obvious intent. "Why are you doing this?" she asked. "Not that I disagree. You certainly covered the whole spectrum for Gillette with those proposals. You just seemed so flip about it."

I stared into her eyes. "You're my friend in this dignified jungle," I said, trying to communicate my affection. "As to your question, I'm not sure how to answer," I added. "Gillette, the others—they think we should sweat; so we sweat. Last week I labored over the Endel job for two nights just so the mountains would be perfect. When I delivered it, they couldn't have cared less."

"So are you saying we shouldn't care either?"

"No. If I felt that way, I'd walk," I said. "Maybe there's a more natural way to do all this."

"Like ten concepts in ten minutes during a cab ride," Colleen suggested.

I smiled. "Why not? I don't know if I could do that again. Next time I might be too self-conscious."

"Oh, I doubt that," Maire volunteered as she entered the room. "I'm glad you're back. The calls have been piling up all afternoon."

"I know," I replied. "I'll take them one at a time, but later . . . not now."

"*Salute.*" Maire gestured comically, then hustled out of the room. At forty-seven, she displayed an energy and efficiency that classed her with women twenty years younger.

"I'd better get back to the board," Colleen said as she approached the door.

I stopped her. "Thanks. Really, thanks."

Bowing almost imperceptibly, she left the office. I walked to the balcony. Leaning on the railing overlooking the studio, I noticed a waving hand at the far side of the two-story cavern. "Yes, Dominick," I called.

"Before you go home tonight, could you look at the hospital logo designs? I'm having trouble with the color-key symbols."

Nodding my assent, I continued to observe the activity in the giant studio. This had been a long trip for me—short in the number of years, but extensive in energy and input. I watched the business machine I had set into motion as if I were a stranger, alienated from its mechanics and values. My pilgrimage led elsewhere. My association with Luke wedged an ever-widening gap between my own sensibilities and the cool rush of a commercial art and design studio. Yet this day, for the first time, I bridged both those worlds with my experiment in the taxi. I paid silent homage to the classes again. I realized that I had begun to complete a cycle in my life. One day, perhaps soon, I would walk away from this business, not to escape from pain, but simply to follow a voice within that had become significantly more audible.

A telephone rang. Its persistent hammering echoed from my office. I decided to ignore it. Maire peeked her head out of an adjoining room and called me.

"Tell David I'll call him back in the morning," I said without thinking.

Maire nodded her head slowly, then disappeared again. Several seconds later another call came in for me. Again, I lingered on the balcony and did not respond to my telephone. I had the most pervasive sense of peace as I leaned against the railing.

"Your highness, I'm so sorry to disturb you, but there is another call," Maire shouted.

"Tell Alex the retouching will be finished by tomorrow."

Maire relayed the message and then came stampeding out the door.

"How did you know?" she asked.

"How did I know what?"

"Who was on the phone . . . Peter, how'd you know?"

"You told me," I answered matter-of-factly, genuinely confused.

"No. I didn't tell you who was calling now or the time before."

"Oh, Maire, I don't know. It really doesn't matter."

The telephone rang again. She peered at me, waiting. "Do you think I know who's on the phone?" I asked. Maire folded her hands on her hips. "Okay, I'll play. This time it's Delaney-Sloan about the photographs."

Scurrying into her office, she snapped the phone receiver off the desk. Her eyes opened wide as Delaney-Sloan confirmed delivery of the photographs. Stunned, she mumbled a response. Composing herself, she returned to the balcony. "You were right, exactly right."

I shook my head, surprised. "Coincidence, Maire . . . really!"

Back in my office I felt curiously unattached to the phone. It rang again. I wrote the name "Tom" on a pad and waited. Maire buzzed. She asked me to guess, but I refused to continue the game. She informed me politely that Tom Butler was waiting on the phone. "Tell him I'll call him in the morning," I said, staring wide-eyed at my pad.

I then decided to push at the perimeter of the experience. Although no phone chimed, I recorded the next thought that popped into my head. Airport. My eyes danced over the letters as I wrote them on a pad. I tapped a pencil nervously on the drawing board. While I doodled circles around the word, I watched the second hand jerk spastically on the antique French wall clock.

"Peter, I'm finished," Phil, my production manager, said, entering the office.

Holding my hand in the air like a traffic cop, I interrupted, "Not now, Phil. I'm sorry. I'm expecting an important call."

The older man, a veteran designer and letterer, shrugged his shoulders and left. The silence became thick. My pulse seemed more pronounced. I jumped from my seat, startled by the ring of the phone. A minute later, Maire charged into the office with a pile of papers.

"Listen, Pete, sign these two forms and I'll send Allen to the airport. They called to say the sample books from France just cleared customs."

After she left, I paced the room, circling my clear Lucite drawing table. Feeling claustrophobic, I walked onto the balcony.

Most of the people had departed. I noticed Colleen laboring over several page layouts. I started to tell her to go home but stopped myself. I admired her ambition. Checking my watch, I thought of Jamie. As I headed back to my office, she appeared.

Throwing a kiss, Jamie climbed the stairs to the second floor with Rachel snugly contained in a pouch in front of her chest.

"Jamie, hello," Colleen called from behind her drawing board.

"Hi. Does that slave driver still have you working?"

"No. This is my choice," she replied.

Turning into my office, Jamie embraced me.

"A good day?" she asked.

"A fascinating day," I replied, lifting my daughter from the sling to nuzzle her. Rocking Rachel in my arms, I related my escapade with the telephone calls. Jamie listened quietly. I knew she wanted the experiences in the classes to remain contained, instead of spilling over and intruding into other areas of our lives. Jamie had come to accept Luke within a very confined context and although she, too, was fascinated and charmed by his inscrutable manner, at times she found him unknowable and definitely unnerving.

"Here I go again, right?" I smiled. "It really doesn't make any sense. I didn't ask to know who would be on the phone and I certainly don't see how it matters."

The phone rang again. I moved to answer it and then paused.

"Aren't you first going to tell me who's calling?" Jamie joked.

"I'm not sure I want to," I replied.

"C'mon anyway," she persisted.

"Okay, it's . . . it's Jack Egan," I said as I picked up the receiver. "Yes," I said quietly, staring at my wife blankly, "I don't want him to touch the plaster before it's dried. Okay. Okay. Yes. Thanks, *Tina,*" I ended with special emphasis. "Uh, huh. Good night."

Jamie remained silent, relieved and yet disappointed.

"I guess it's over," I mumbled.

We wrapped Rachel back into the cloth cradle and left the office. As we were about to exit the building, the telephone rang again. We grinned at each other.

I moved hesitantly to the wallphone. Rattling off my words in quick succession, I muttered, "Yes. No. Yes. No. Yes. Okay, one more time. It's, um . . . Rene." After the brief exchange, I replaced the receiver back on its hook. "Wrong again," I declared, knowing that I had guessed and that must have made the difference. On the other occasions, the names had floated into my awareness. Now, in searching for more proof as if I disbelieved the experience, I fished with skepticism, a bias I knew would short-circuit the process. God has no bias, Luke once told me in all seriousness. I laughed. Who was he to think he could quote the ultimate power of the universe with such authority?

15

Wings flapped against the airborne bodies of sea gulls glid-ing only inches above the water. Spotted ducks strained their necks in search of bread crumbs. Blue-brown water rimmed the lake. Two boys rolled down a small, grassy incline as an athletic fourteen-year-old struggled to launch his kite. Little girls giggled secrets as they watched an old woman arrange pieces of popcorn at her feet. Her tiny brown paper bag rested limply on the ground. A dog barked in front of a sign that read, NO DOGS ALLOWED.

A series of man-made lakes and pools tumbled down the hillside in the park near our home. Known locally as the Duck Pond Park, this planned oasis amid the hustle had become one of my favorite retreats. Having just dropped Terry at the train station and shopped for groceries at the market, I honored myself with a break in what had become a busy Saturday afternoon schedule.

I scanned the landscape lazily as I sat alone in the center of a large field. Faces smiled at me from among blades of grass. Strollers drifted by, hand in hand. A pause. At least that had been my intention in stopping here. But somehow I couldn't resist the pencil and pad in my pocket. I designed a woman's body designed into the form of a ques-tion mark. The dot below her anatomy became an eyeball leering playfully at the legs above it. A perfect logo for an entertainment product my company had been recently assigned. "Magritte, you'd be proud of me," I whispered, paying homage to the twentieth-century master of the

unexpected and the surreal. I had sweated to free myself
from the realism that had confined my drawings for years.

The laughter of a little girl drew my attention back to the
park. I slipped the pad into my pocket, concentrating now
on the panorama in front of me.

Then, without warning, a huge, three-dimensional image
ripped in front of me like an explosion. For several seconds
it obliterated the park. I saw only Rachel's face. It flashed
before me like a frozen phantom. Her eyes bulged open in
terror. Her face appeared so frightened, so real. Adrenaline spewed into my bloodstream as the muscles in the back
of my neck snapped tight. A coolness rippled through my
arms and legs. I tried to control the reactions of my body
but couldn't. My breathing became shallow and rapid. I
dug my fingers into the earth beside me, trying instinctively
to ground myself. I squeezed my eyelids tightly together.
Although the full image of my daughter disappeared, the
outline of her face still registered in my vision like the fading imprint of a sunspot.

I rubbed my eyes with the palms of my hands. What the
hell was that? The question made me dizzy. Ignore it, I told
myself. As my body regained its balance, I focused intently
on a group of grade school boys playing soccer. I needed
something solid to concentrate on.

"Rachel's fine," I murmured, unable to stop the inner
dialogue that ensued.

Rather than fight myself, I let the thoughts flow. Frag-
mented images materialized, floating before me like cut
sections of film: the rounded silky bottoms of my month-
old daughter's feet; the tiny, wrinkled hands with gracefully
tapered fingers, curious replicas of my own; her intense
baby eyes, wide open and absorbing. Even her wispy cooing
played on a tape echoed in my mind.

The tension left my hands. The back of my neck relaxed.
I inhaled deeply just as a red Frisbee glided into my lap.

"Hey, mister, would you throw it back?"

I winced at the formal address. I coddled the child within, never fully acknowledging that the aging process had long ago stripped my face of adolescence. I smiled through my beard, curling the edges of my mustache with my fingers, then tipped my head. Max, at forty, I assured myself, had to be more of a "mister" than I. And yet, twenty-nine years had left a definite imprint in the crevices of my forehead and in the skin around my eyes. Without altering my position, I snapped the plastic wedge through the air easily, directly into the hands of a waiting youngster. Smiling, the boy flashed his okay sign.

Then as if a bullet had slammed into my brain, I grabbed my head when a loud cry suddenly hammered in my ears. Jamie screamed my name in the vast arena just behind my eyes. Again and again and again. My body went cold— colder than before.

"Jesus, Jamie . . . what's happening to us?"

Trying to contain my burgeoning hysteria, I searched the park for my wife quickly, hoping my ears, not my thoughts, had carried her voice. But I couldn't find her amid the meadows and people surrounding me. The drone of chatter and the sparkle of laughter heightened my anxiety.

The panic level rose so quickly that I couldn't remain seated. I sucked in a long, deep breath and bolted from the ground. Get home. Now. Come on, move! My legs carried me in a dead run up the side of the hill toward my car. My tingling hands fumbled with the shiny silver keys. I moved outside of every standard frame of reference. Nothing seemed familiar, not even my own body.

Sliding into the front seat, I realized I had lost my agility. With great effort, I inserted the key into the ignition slot and turned it. The starter whined over and over again without making contact.

Let it rest. Easy. Turn it and start it again. "C'mon, car, turn over. Please start!"

Rachel's face rose out of the fog again and danced

before me. Her beautiful, dark, inviting eyes were glazed
and frozen . . . intense yet almost lifeless. Her lips were dis-
colored. Her mouth stretched open as if she had been trying desperately to say something.

"Rachel," I screamed, trying to catch her with my voice.
Immediately she disappeared, leaving me alone and dizzy
in the dampness of my body. I could feel myself losing control.

Again I closed my eyes. In the blackness, her face reappeared. For a second I peered intently into her eyes, feeling myself being pulled. I thought about Luke, about
Jamie's terrible dream, and about the uncanny accuracy of
my little game with the telephone.

I've got to get out of here. Now. I jumped from the car.
Seven blocks. If I ran, I could be home in a couple of minutes. Throwing myself toward the sidewalk, I lunged forward, frantic and charging like a stampeding animal.

Jumping from the curb between two parked vehicles, I
collided with a slowly moving car. Flesh against metal. The
thud of my body hitting the fender had a hollow ring.
Brakes locked. Tires screeched to a halt. Breaking the
impact with my hands threw me off balance. Tumbling over
twice, I paused for a moment, dazed. As people rushed
from their cars, I climbed to my feet. Pushing them aside, I
forced myself to keep going. Soon my body carried me into
a full run again, though my hands and elbow ached from
the collision. In the distance a man yelled in my direction
as car horns receded into the background.

One foot in front of the other. Stay focused! A pain
developed in my right side, but I numbed it by diverting my
attention to the staccato beat of my shoes slapping the
pavement. Three more blocks. Two more blocks. After
jumping a hedge, I turned finally into my street, barely able
to contain an urgent need to scream as my house came
into view.

After racing across the lawn, I jumped five stairs, then

shouldered my way past the front door. As I charged into the hallway, Jamie came running down the stairs. She held the baby in front of her like a porcelain doll. Rachel's eyes swelled out of their sockets. Her mouth opened as if calling for help. Her arms extended fully in front of her as if grabbing for air.

"She's not breathing," Jamie said in a deadly quiet and controlled voice. Her words hatcheted the air between us.

Oh, God, her face is blue, I screamed inside. I grabbed my daughter, flipped her upside down and shook her. Holding her tiny feet in one hand, I used the other to search her mouth for some object . . . some obstruction. Her tongue was free. I bounced her up and down, slapping her back, hoping desperately for some magic to jar her system, to clear the passage so she could breathe. Suddenly, the rattling and the pull of gravity had its effect. Rachel began to vomit and cough.

She's alive, a voice within me shouted. She's really alive.

A smile fluttered uncontrollably across my face. Jamie pressed her hands to her chest as tears flooded her eyes.

In delight and relief we fondled our child with a nervous intensity, wanting to erase with our hands the trauma of the past few minutes.

Then Jamie, who now held her, felt the muscles in Rachel's body contract. Again our daughter gasped for air; her eyes opened wide; her pupils dilated. Jamie repeated the shaking procedure and turned Rachel's head to the floor, as I pressed down on the baby's stomach. Once more she vomited.

Ever so gently, Jamie turned her again and cuddled her in her arms. After several minutes, she handed the baby to me.

"I'm going to try Dr. Reese."

Rachel wrapped her tiny fingers around my thumb. As she resumed breathing, I felt my own lungs drawing in oxygen for both of us. Though light-headed, with my pulse still pounding furiously, I started to hum a lullaby. The old, familiar melody had a mellowing effect on both of us.

From the kitchen Jamie negotiated with the doctor's answering service.

A hollow groan surged from my throat as I gaped with disbelief at the weird glint reappearing in Rachel's eyes. Obviously she could instinctively anticipate the blockages in advance. Within seconds she threw her arms out in a reflexive response to expand her chest. Her breathing stopped completely.

"Jamie, forget it. We've got to get her to the hospital right away. There's no time."

Again I turned her upside down and massaged her stomach . . . but this time she didn't respond. Knowing that I had to try to shock her digestive tract so that she could dislodge sludge in her trachea, I drew my hand back to about eighteen inches away from her abdomen. I stood transfixed, poised like a boxer about to deliver a shattering blow. My hand trembled. I froze, unable to move, unwilling to back away.

Suddenly, Jamie appeared just beside Rachel. She pulled the baby close to her own chest and nodded to me. "It's okay, Peter. Do it!"

Tears cascaded from Jamie's eyes. I muttered an apology, then slammed my open palm deep into the soft flesh beneath the baby's ribs. At the same instant, Jamie grunted as if her own body had been assaulted.

Rachel recoiled spasmodically from the shock. The dam broke and mucus poured from her mouth. She drew a first clear breath; the upper part of her torso began to expand and contract in easy, even rhythms.

Keep going, I counseled myself. Move! I turned Rachel upside down as gently as possible, securing her ankles firmly in my left hand. Jamie led the way as we broke into a sprint, running out the front door, across the wet grass, and into her car.

After securing herself in her seat, Jamie took the baby, held her head toward the floor and whispered reassurances softly to both Rachel and herself.

The ignition whined lazily for several seconds before starting. I threw the shift into gear, then floored the accelerator. The speedometer topped ninety as we sped down the roadway, weaving through the clutter of traffic and racing ahead.

Intermittently Rachel gulped a breath. Jamie kept stroking her back with one hand while supporting her forehead with the other, hoping to provide some guise of security, knowing the upside-down position had to feel precarious.

My thoughts bounced from "faster, Peter, faster" to "slow down" as the aging blue convertible swerved, almost out of control, and sped down the curved driveway to the emergency entrance of the hospital. A nurse leaped for safety, tripping in her haste as my car skidded to a halt only inches from the plate-glass window.

The sea of lights and the white-clad bustling people became a blur as we charged through the swinging doors.

"I'm Dr. Marcus," a young woman declared as she eased the baby out of Jamie's reluctant arms.

I stumbled through the story while the physician investigated different parts of Rachel's body, still holding her on an angle toward the floor. She was breathing easily now.

"Stay right here," the doctor instructed. She took Rachel into an adjoining cubicle while an attendant ushered Jamie and me to seats in the emergency room.

"I'll be right back," I mumbled to Jamie as I jumped up from the chair to find the doctor. A nurse put her hand up to bar my entrance to the doorway. Then, obviously changing her mind, she moved aside.

The doctor had laid Rachel down on a large sterile table draped in white. Again I heard the muffled cry of my daughter gasping for air. Her face turned bright red. Dr.

Marcus inserted a rubber device into her mouth. The nurse threw a switch and the room filled with a loud, mechanical sucking noise. A clear plastic tube pulled white mucus from the baby's throat. After several seconds, they removed the machine as Rachel breathed normally.

My face flushed; I strained to push back the tears. Leaning against the wall, I bent forward and rested my hands on my knees. The nausea and light-headedness began to pass.

"Are you okay?" the doctor queried.

"Yes. I'm fine now." Awkwardly I straightened myself and withdrew from the room to find Jamie.

"She's okay, babe. She's breathing fine. Right now, they're just checking everything out."

Jamie did not respond.

"Hey, everything's okay now. Rachel is fine," I repeated.

Although my words penetrated, she offered no acknowledgment. She rose stiffly from the bench and walked slowly to the examination room. She watched through the doorway as the doctor moved the stethoscope along our daughter's chest. Jamie grinned painfully; her hands began to shake. The trembling spread throughout her entire body.

"Jamie . . . look, you can see for yourself, it's really okay," I insisted.

She turned to me and smiled faintly. She bit her bottom lip and squeezed her eyes closed as if to concentrate. For a moment Jamie seemed to relax. As she opened her eyes, her body wobbled slightly. Then her pupils began to disappear beneath her eyelids. I grabbed her as she lost consciousness. With the aid of a nurse, I carried her into the next room and placed her on a bed. The woman elevated Jamie's legs, covered her with a blanket and monitored her pulse. Opening glazed eyes, Jamie jerked herself up, scrutinized my face carefully and then confronted the nurse. "Is my baby really okay?"

"Sure, honey, your little girl is just fine. And pretty too," bellowed the robust lady. "You just lie there for a couple of minutes and you'll be fine."

"Give me a second, Jamie. I'll check on Rach again." I tapped gently on her nose.

I found Dr. Marcus playing with a very gay infant in the examination room.

"She's a real cutie," the doctor remarked.

"Why?" I appealed to her. "Why did this happen?"

"Sometimes," she began as if presenting a thesis, "when a child is very young her capacity to eject particles in her throat is not fully matured."

"And so?" I wanted more.

"Well, if that's the case and the baby is lying down or asleep, food or even milk can back into the throat from the stomach and solidify. Naturally, this would result in blocking the air passages to the lungs," she concluded, turning her back to me. Twenty seconds limped by.

"But if it could happen once, couldn't it happen again?"

The physician's fixed smile changed into a mildly belligerent expression; her voice edged with impatience.

"With a healthy baby like yours, this is really quite a freak occurrence. To ensure it will not recur, make certain you put her on her stomach or her side, not on her back, after she eats. In that way, any food or liquids backtracking up her esophagus will be easily ejected. Believe me, there is nothing to worry about."

"Thanks. Thank you," I mumbled.

For a few seconds my system withdrew from its primitive state of readiness until, like an electrical short circuit, the incident in the park flashed before me. I had almost forgotten. Holding my daughter, I looked directly into her eyes and whispered, "Did you call me, Rach?"

In the car, the hiss of the stereo all but smothered an old tape playing Beethoven's Seventh. The whipping cadence of passing vehicles easily invaded the interior of the convertible. The giggling music of Rachel's voice as she mouthed a Raggedy Ann doll filled the car. Her apparent comfort defied her recent experience.

Perhaps she didn't know about dying, I speculated, awed by her ease. Or if she did, maybe she didn't fear it.

We spent the entire evening tossing and tumbling with our daughter, bathing in the energy of her animated fingers and dancing toes.

Terry, who returned home from the city after nine o'clock, stood spellbound as we told her about the events of the day. She started to cry.

"Poor Rachel. I'm so scared for her."

"Terry, there's nothing to be scared about any more," I assured her. Jamie squinted at me nervously, then left the room with the baby in her arms. Terry, too upset to talk more, excused herself and went to bed early.

After rocking Rachel to sleep, Jamie joined me in the kitchen. She perched herself on a chair and dangled one bare foot over the wooden arm. Her head rested on her other knee. With considerable expertise, she stretched her foot upward, bringing it almost parallel with her head. After lifting each leg ten times in the same fashion, she sat erect in the chair. Her hands began to tremble again, but she hid them under her thighs.

"God, it was so hard to put her to bed," she said. "Peter, I just wanted to play with her forever . . . nonstop." Jamie attempted a smile but couldn't release the frozen muscles in her face. Closing her eyes, she breathed deeply in a slow, practiced rhythm.

Although reluctant to sabotage her very physical technique of calming herself, I whispered, "Do you want to talk about it now?" She remained so fixed in her breathing exercise, so secluded in her concentration, that my words never reached her.

I waited. Admiring her.

My tall, gangly figure hovered over the table like an elongated monkey, all arms and legs. I had spent many years making peace with my physical form. As a youngster, my height had resulted in my being seated at the rear of every classroom, placed at the end of every line. Only as an adult did I begin to appreciate my physicality. Jamie had taught me to respect my body as she respected hers. Previously I had focused on exercising my intellect.

Slowly, Jamie revealed the bloodshot eyes beneath her lids. A frail smile dawned on her face. She grabbed my hand and forced words from her mouth. "I'm ready." A pause. "How'd you know?" she asked. "What's going on, Peter?" She held herself in check, sighed, then continued. "You were right there at the exact moment I came downstairs."

"The whole experience . . . it's more than just weird," I replied, pulling on my beard self-consciously. "I decided to stop at the park . . . oh, which reminds me, not only do I have to get the car, but the groceries are still in the back seat." I groaned my exhaustion. "Anyway," I began again, "I couldn't have been there more than a couple of minutes when I saw Rachel's face as clear as I see yours now. I couldn't block it out. Her expression duplicated the one she had when I got home. And then I heard you call me— clearly. I didn't just think it, Jamie; I actually heard you scream my name. I just knew to come home."

She turned away from the intensity of my gaze, tucked her legs underneath her body, then grabbed my hand again.

"It's okay, honey," I said. "We're home. The baby's home. Everything's okay." I kissed her gently. "Tell me about you."

"When I saw Rach lying there, all I could think of was 'I'm alone.'" Tears started to pour down her face, but her voice remained steady. "I was so scared I wouldn't do the right thing. I just kept wanting you to be there. Inside, I guess I did scream your name." She paused, her face pale and drawn. "I had just finished a chapter of Bach's book when I felt something change in me. A chill ran through my body. A queasy sensation." Her lips quivered. "When the feeling didn't go away, I tried to read some more, but all I could think about was Rachel. I just had to check her. I freaked when I walked into the bedroom."

Her voice trailed off to a near whisper. "I kept saying to myself, 'Jamie, stay with it, you have to help her, you're the only one.'" Her face tightened, becoming flushed as she noticed my smile. "Hey . . . what are you smiling at?" she barked.

Her voice jarred me. "Relax, Jamie. I'm smiling at you, at me, at Rachel. You did super; you did stay with it. Today was a great day for all of us."

"Only the ending. The rest was a nightmare. Listen, I'm as aware as you are of what today means. For a couple of minutes, when it really counted, we all somehow talked to each other . . . and yet, none of us spoke a word and you were almost half a mile away. Only God could know how thankful I am for that . . . but it still frightens me; it really does."

"Why?" I asked. "Isn't this the kind of thing we've been striving for?"

"You . . . not me." She eyed me painfully. "I don't want to live my life on the edge of a cliff. Maybe that's excitement for you, but not for me. I want you, Rachel, this house, our life . . . on terms I can understand."

I wanted to find an adequate rebuttal, not only for Jamie but for myself. "All I want to do is remember the positive side of what happened."

"Please don't play games with me," she pleaded. "That's not all you're into. You're like a little kid dazzled by all these inexplicable events." I didn't answer her. "You want to like it," she continued, "well, good; go ahead. I don't want to stop you. But for me, if I had the choice, not in ten lifetimes would I ever want to go through an experience like that again."

Putting my hands around her waist gently and pulling her body into the cradle of my arms, I tried to alter the focus. "C'mon, Jamie, I don't want to do this. Can't we just be thankful for being in touch and leave it at that?"

"Sure . . . but are you willing to 'leave it at that?'" she replied.

"What's that supposed to mean?" I asked, dropping my arms from around her.

Jamie backed away and pushed the words out. "Should... should I say it or should you?"

"Say what, Jamie? I really don't know what the hell you're talking about."

"Well . . . I think you do know what I'm talking about," she blurted, surprised at the aggressiveness in her own voice. She pressed her hands over her mouth.

"Go ahead—say it!" I pushed. "If we can't talk to each other, we don't have anything."

"I, well, I thought eventually you'd attribute the miracle side of our experience to Luke . . . like you do with everything else."

"You're really out on a limb. Why dump on Luke? I never did that to you about your relationship with Max."

"I know," she admitted, turning away. "I don't want to fight you."

"But you are, Jamie, so why don't you get it all out!"

She walked to the window and stared at her reflection on the darkened pane. "Ever since we started with the group, I feel like our lives have been invaded." She turned again but still didn't confront my eyes. "There's nothing tangible. You know I'm no good at presenting proof and evidence. It just feels like we're all flirting with something that's unnatural. Even Luke. He used to be much softer. All I can think of is that weird blue eye of his. I don't want to lose control . . . of us."

"But that can't happen," I said. "Luke would tell you that himself. He's just trying to help us be more aware of what we already know inside. That's all he's ever done."

Jamie sighed. "Oh, Peter, I don't know anything any more. I'm just so scared."

"There's nothing to be scared of." I grabbed her by the shoulders. "Don't you want to understand? Don't you want to grow?"

"Peter, you're hurting me." I released her immediately and stared at my hands, dumbfounded. We both stared at the tremor in my hands. "Look at what you're doing," she said. "Don't you see? You're scared, too."

"He's only taught me beautiful things."

"Well . . ." she countered hesitantly, "maybe that's changing."

Our eyes locked. For the first time I understood what our friend, Max, had meant when he said that Jamie could become a formidable opponent or ally despite her sometimes submissive demeanor. I never wanted to choose between her and Luke.

"I shouldn't have pushed you to join the group," I mumbled. "If you want out, it's okay."

"No, no," she snapped abruptly. Jamie knew she couldn't quit, not now. "I want to stay."

"Then why are you taking swipes at Luke?"

"I'm not. I'm grateful for what he's done for you. But, well, when I'm with him in class, I feel . . . out of balance. I keep thinking . . . maybe, just maybe, if we had never known him, nothing like this would ever have happened to Rachel. Maybe today would never have happened."

"Are you saying Luke had something to do with Rachel's choking?" I asked, gaping incredulously at my wife.

The long silence unnerved us both. "No," Jamie answered finally.

"Good," I said quickly before she could change her mind. "So what about cheering for the happy ending?"

"Okay, okay," Jamie squeezed out, putting her hand up in submission rather than engaging in more verbal combat. She disliked word games, relying on intuition more than logic. I knew she hated opposing me. Arguments were not simply disagreements to her; each one represented a serious threat. Jamie did many things to protect herself and our marriage, as if giving vent to all her thoughts and her inclinations might echo her mother's mistakes and cruelties.

Peeking through the strands of sandy-colored hair that dangled in front of her face, she looked directly into my eyes, letting go of her anxiety.

"I need a little more time with the class," she said.

"Maybe we both do," I mumbled, less confident than before. Usually I fielded her doubts like a tennis pro in the playoffs. This night her fears left their mark. My arguments did not stand up to my own scrutiny. My chest tightened. I suppressed random thoughts, pushing Jamie's premonitions off into the distant mist. In direct contradiction to Luke's teachings, which I stoutly defended, I buried my own developing fears instead of confronting them.

Lifting her chin with my fingertips, I smiled at Jamie's frowning face. I winked and kissed her lightly on the lips. At first she didn't respond, standing limp and lifeless. When I kissed her a second time, her body became animated. She pressed herself against me. Pushing her hands under my shirt, she danced her fingers across my back, then pressed them into my skin. She wanted to lose herself in the embrace, to hold on, to keep the world still, if only for a few moments. For Jamie there were no more solid mountains, just temporary landscapes that threatened to shift from day to day.

"Let's pack it in for today," I said quietly.

We turned off the lights in the kitchen and living room, beginning a silent routine in which we both moved steadily through the house, checking doors and locking windows, securing the domestic hatch.

Somehow this most familiar act suddenly lacked its traditional security. Everything looked different, felt different.

Jamie wandered down the hall alone. She rubbed the surface of the bedroom door, concentrating on her hands and the touch of her skin upon the wood. Something had changed irrevocably. The walls, the floor, the ceiling . . . nothing seemed quite as solid or reliable as it had been the day before.

The room began to spin ever so slowly as she gripped the door for support. Jamie imagined it disappearing beneath her fingertips, envisioning herself falling, stark naked, through some vast nameless expanse. Her momentary fantasy suddenly solidified and seemed real. She clutched her skin as it rippled in response to the cool rush of air skimming the most delicate parts of her body. Although exposed and vulnerable, she was too awed to be self-conscious. Her body fell at a terrific speed. In the distance, just below her, she saw a piercing blue eye floating in a silent sea of blackness. Three familiar yet unidentifiable people stood on the iris. They shouted wildly and motioned for her to turn around . . . to go back. But Jamie, unable to alter her descent, slipped further into the dreamlike adventure, compelled by some force outside herself.

As she glided downward, a thunderous rush of air whipped and whistled past her ears. She fell free, like a sky diver without a parachute.

A rope smoldered off to her right, radiating its own internal glow. It led to a flaming sun thousands of miles in the distance. Jamie tried desperately to stop her plunge by grabbing the rope, but it burned her hands each time she attempted to seize it. Engulfed in the hypnotic gaze of that enormous lifelike eye, she almost drowned in the quicksand of her images.

Forcing the sum of her energy into her hands, Jamie slammed her fists against the bedroom door. It worked. She broke the spell.

"Peter," she called with high-pitched urgency.

I darted from the bathroom to the bedroom. "Are you

okay? What's wrong?"

"Nothing, nothing. I'm sorry. I guess I'm just still jumpy."

Watching her lie down on the bed, I, too, felt saturated by recent events and my own swirling reflections. Ironically, this was something I believed I wanted . . . to know more, intuit more. Yet when I allowed my thoughts to drift to Luke, I felt submerged in a dense and unsettling fog.

I questioned not whether I could rely on Luke, but whether I could trust myself to know . . . when to move, when to stand still or when simply to walk away.

16

The days that followed blurred into one another. Each evening after Jamie, Terry and Rachel went to sleep, I retreated to the tiny library alcove the former owners had annexed to the house. Although I championed my books as grist for the mill, I knew I also used them as a support system when I doubted myself or my situation. My passion to touch base with the printed page had accelerated since the incident with Rachel. Jamie had been right. What had happened with our daughter had been the exact kind of experience I had sought, and yet instead of bolstering my enthusiasm, it had eroded it. I even avoided touching base with Luke. Next Tuesday night's class would come soon enough.

I scanned the most prominent titles on the cluttered bookshelves, withdrawing, of all things, an old, thumb-worn Plato anthology that had been one of my bibles in undergraduate school. Solid. Logical. Ordered. Just the kind of reading experience I needed.

The book fell open to the "Meno" dialogue. I turned to the beginning of that section and started reading. All the major points had been underscored, but the red ink had faded over the years. I ran my finger along the indentation made by the pen. Another year. Another lifetime. I wanted to bury myself in the material, but instead I kept seeing parallels between Socrates' method of inquiry and the questions we asked in Luke's classes.

In the Meno dialogue, Socrates played cerebral midwife to a simple, uneducated slave boy, who under questioning gave birth to the basic theorems of geometry. For Plato this supported his fundamental axiom that we each hold true knowledge within us; learning consists of discovering what we already know.

I slapped the book shut triumphantly. My reading had helped me validate what I had learned in those classes and from digging inside myself. Yet the affirmation was hardly a clear victory; I had relied on someone else's authority, in this case Plato's, rather than my own.

As I reached for the light switch, I noticed Max's little gift on the desk. Crazy Max. He used psychology, physics, even street logic, to explain in a reasonable fashion all the events that had occurred in class. And yet despite his commitment to empiricism and rationality, he had given me a copy of *The Tibetan Book of the Dead*, mentioning it as possibly holding some explanations for the yellow mist we had, apparently, seen around Luke. A smile rippled across my face. Okay, Max, you're on. I fell back into the chair and eavesdropped on a journey recorded thousands of years ago by a group of Tibetan monks.

Most of the sagas of the soul's journey from life to life, or death as we label it, had fantastic mythological trappings. However some stories, more subdued than the others, suggested that passage through a yellow light meant the spirit had encountered its own truth, which inevitably mirrored the truth of all men. Thus the light around one soul could be seen by the others who were open to it. A very heady commentary.

I put the book down, remembering reports gathered by respected clinicians and researchers about people who had died and been revived, during which time they claimed to have experienced an unearthly peacefulness and clarity as they were embraced by a white or white-yellow light. Their descriptions had uncanny similarities to those found in the Tibetans' ancient book of the dead. I left the library satisfied.

Standing at the foot of our bed, I watched Jamie sleep. Her mouth hung slightly ajar. Her full lips curled against the sheet. She embraced the pillow with both arms and wrapped one leg around the quilt; the other fell precariously off the side of the mattress. I bent over, lifted her foot like fine crystal and returned it securely to the bed. I pulled the blanket over her shoulder, then kissed her lightly on the forehead. Had Jamie been awake, I would have thanked her just for existing, just for being in my life. Upstairs, I checked on the baby.

Returning to my bedroom, I slipped beneath the covers and searched for Jamie's hand until I found it. I clasped her open palm gently with my fingers and closed my eyes. But sleep did not take me. Instead, my eyelids kept opening. "You don't make yourself go to sleep," I counseled myself, "you allow it." I stopped fighting my restlessness. Edges blurred. I drifted finally into a restful slumber.

The following evening I returned home late, having worked overtime to complete a presentation. I greeted the sounds of voices in the kitchen with disappointment, my image of a few quiet hours alone with Jamie and Rachel shattered. Expectations never match reality, I mused.

As I entered the room, the conversation stopped abruptly.

"Hello," I chimed, genuinely astonished. After kissing Jamie and the baby, I nodded at the unlikely visitor sitting beside Terry at the table.

"What a surprise! How are you, Fran?" I hoped my voice sounded warm. Jamie's mother, making one of her rare appearances, nodded her head affirmatively. "So," I asked, "do you own half of Manhattan yet?"

"Peter!" Jamie bellowed.

"That's okay, dear," Fran said to her daughter. "It's a perfectly sensible question," she added, now staring directly at me, "but you know, Peter, I like to maintain a sense of humility about my holdings."

A stalemate! One for you, Fran baby, I acknowledged to myself only. "I'm glad to hear that," I said aloud, deciding not to pursue the conversation after glancing into my wife's shotgun eyes. Terry smiled, intentionally interjecting an unrelated thought. The women continued to converse as I withdrew, busying myself by making a pot of tea.

Fran glanced fleetingly in my direction, distracted by my presence. Although she needed eyeglasses, she never wore them. Eyestrain, as well as attitude, had given her a stern expression. Fran's face, only lightly made up, barely betrayed her forty-nine years. A blush of lipstick counterpointed the severity of her hair, which was pulled back tightly in a swirl behind her head. Dressed conservatively, she looked like a mannequin displaying change-of-life clothing at Lord & Taylor. Her fingers harbored the last traces of her femininity. Long and beautifully formed, they embraced the cup delicately. When not occupied with a specific task, Fran had a nervous habit of rubbing the tips of her fingers with her thumbs.

Terry appeared captivated by the older woman's quick city wit and complex stories about herself and her second husband's financial matters. "How wonderful to build a mini-empire with someone you love," she romanticized. In the midst of listening to details about their sizable real estate organization operating in Gramercy Park, Terry cheered enthusiastically when learning that Fran, not her spouse, had assumed the presidency of the firm.

Ambivalent, I watched this lady dominate the two younger women. Jamie, cuddling Rachel tightly against her shoulder, catered to her mother like a Cinderella servant. First she filled her cup with coffee, then she stroked her hand. Her attentiveness distressed me. I wanted to be forgiving, but I resisted. I calculated that the total worth of Fran's twenty-seven years of motherhood would not quite fill a thimble.

Her presence brought the past alive for me. While Jamie

sat in an institution, her mother's second marriage and
career had blossomed. While her child's tears dried on sterile linen, this woman became the queen of Gramercy Park,
eventually purchasing eleven brownstones in the district.
Buildings had replaced people. Lease agreements had
been substituted for love arrangements. Infrequently, when
I permitted myself to perceive her apparent neglect and
cruelty as born of unhappiness, my indictments crumbled.

When Jamie tried to serve some cheese with one hand
while balancing Rachel with the other, Fran shook her
head. "I know you had a scare with the baby a few weeks
ago, but I think you can put her down."

Flustered, Jamie stared at her mother. Regaining her
composure, she placed the baby in an antique cradle by the
door. Although Fran had been right, I wished Jamie had
not followed her mother's instructions so obediently.

When my wife offered to play a Mozart cello solo that she
would be performing in three weeks, Terry and I exhibited
enthusiasm, recognizing fully her desire to share her music
with her mother. Fran smiled politely. Jamie began self-consciously, furrowing her forehead until the moody melody
swept her away. After a few minutes, Fran dropped her
head and surveyed the newspaper on the table as her
daughter continued to play. Terry watched in disbelief. She
wanted Fran to love Jamie at least half as much as she did.
Her admiration for the woman soured.

A couple of seconds later, I noticed Fran's sly diversion as
well. Five minutes! That's all Jamie had asked for! I eyed my
wife, thankful for her total absorption in the music. Most
likely, she would not look up again until she completed the
piece. Rather than leave it to chance, I edged over several
feet and placed my body in the line of vision between Jamie
and her mother.

Later, as we undressed for bed, Jamie had to push herself
to confront me. By her tone of voice, I knew she had
rehearsed her question several times before speaking. "Why

do you always have to goad her, Peter?"

"Your mother does not inspire my finer qualities," I answered flatly. When she stared at me impatiently, I changed my tack. "I guess I want to break through that wall she carries around with her."

"But you know how uncomfortable it makes her," she said quietly.

"Questions don't upset people . . . people upset themselves."

"Oh, no. don't play with me!" No longer able to suppress her annoyance, Jamie bellowed in an unusually loud and strained voice. "If people upset themselves, how come she upsets you, smart ass?"

"Touché," I said, acknowledging her point and surprised by the intensity of her retort.

"Hey, Peter, please." She hesitated. "My mother's hardly ever here, and, yet, each time you have to bait her."

"Jesus, Jame, her interest in you is minimal," I said in a loud voice. Jamie backed away. "Fran looks out for Fran, honey, but you treat her like visiting royalty," I grunted, shaking my head. "You see her and talk to her when you make the move to call her and visit. And then you're sandwiched between a contract signing and two urgent telephone calls. She hardly ever initiates contact with you. Her impetus to play mother is very limp."

"It's enough for me," Jamie answered in a hushed voice.

"Well . . . I know that, but I'm not as forgiving as you. And I'm not talking about the hospital scene when you were a kid. I'm talking about now."

"Peter," she said, her voice quivering slightly, "why can't you accept that it's okay with me? Whatever I have with her is more than I used to. I don't look at what's missing; I value what's here. Does that sound so ridiculous to you?"

I shook my head. "No, Jame. I hear you." I approached her slowly and kissed her nose. "No more insincere questions for your mom, okay?"

Jamie sighed in relief. Winning her point was a lot less significant to her than de-escalating a disagreement. She ruffled my hair, then tapped my head. "It's like beating a brick wall."

"Well, if we keep beating it, maybe it'll move."

We crawled into bed; Jamie turned to me. I wrapped my arms around her. Within minutes, we both fell asleep.

Once again a doorway unlocked for Jamie. She found herself thrown into an all-too-familiar dream. Her legs moved easily as she pranced across the same lush mountain field she had traversed once before. Brisk winds fluttered through her hair. In the distance, stony ridges and tall, squared peaks created architectural designs against the sky. A radiant sun hovered above the horizon.

Her energy peaked and ebbed as she mounted the last plateau. Rachel lay comfortably across her chest in her pouch. Entranced by the awesome beauty of the landscape, she twirled in circles, then knelt to pick strawberries. For several minutes, she rested on a large limestone mound. The mountains glowed, turning blue and purple as dusk approached. In the valley, the white mist developed like thick wads of cotton mysteriously inflated with helium.

Jamie stroked Rachel's face and sang, "Ah ma lady, ah ma lady." She continued her ascent. The winds became stronger and more unpredictable. She closed her jacket and tucked the green plaid blanket securely around her daughter. Looking back, she realized that the mist had completely enshrouded the base of the mountain. A dense fog moved up the hillside, consuming acre after acre. She stopped abruptly, surveying first the area on her right and then the area to her left. Aimlessly, she unhinged the sling and laid it on the ground.

Jamie knew this experience well. Even while dreaming she struggled to pierce the wall of the oncoming event. And yet she went on . . . forced by some internal movement to play it through to the very last act.

The enveloping cloud curtailed her vision to mere inches. She pushed at the fog around her face in panic. When she bent down to pick up Rachel, her body went limp. Her daughter had disappeared. Adrenaline flooded her system. Her diaphragm pushed against her lungs. Dominated by shallow, erratic breathing, Jamie slid into vertigo. Her fingers dug into the earth below. She crawled, directionless, on the ground; a dry thin cry burst from her throat as she called her child.

Once again she felt herself swept out of her body and ejected into the air high above the mountain. White clouds raced against a background of blue space. Jamie peered through the thick and distracting formation. She saw herself alone in the field. Once the fog lifted, she had an unobstructed bird's-eye view. Curiously detached, she watched her own tense movements. Her daughter's name echoed off the tall monolithic rocks. Jamie could see her child cuddled by the folds in the vibrantly electric Scottish blanket. Rachel sat alone on the other side of the peak, apparently unconcerned. She did not hear her mother's cry. Then to her amazement, she noticed Max peek out from behind a boulder. He had a rose in his hand. He smiled, waved to her and disappeared again.

The horse came into view, commanding all her attention. The huge muscular black and white spotted stallion stood on the outside ledge near the highest peak. From aloft, she stared at the mystical creature. Suddenly he began to shift his head from side to side in very slow, graceful motions. He pranced in wide, irregular circles. Jamie felt intimidated by the horse as he turned his head upward and confronted her directly.

A smothered shriek exploded inside her as she stared at its blue watch-eye. Both she and the animal were frozen within each other's vision; then the horse bolted, plunging down the hillside. Jamie's perspective shifted as she felt herself sucked back into her body. Standing about twenty yards away from her daughter, she gaped up the mountain-side, her attention riveted to the charging horse. Mesmer-ized by its power and energy, Jamie stood still as the animal galloped toward Rachel. Pieces of limestone exploded into the air as the crushing hooves thundered down the moun-tain. The lather on the horse grew white and foamy.

The charging animal crashed through the barrier she'd seen at the end of her previous dream. A hot wind rushed past her face as his fury now closed the gap to within inches of a deadly collision with her baby. Jamie awoke, leaping off the bed. This time she caught herself as she slammed against the bureau. Startled, I ripped the quilt off the bed, poised for some unknown assault. Jamie stopped me by putting her hand up.

"The same dream," she sighed. "The horse . . . every-thing. Oh God, the details were exactly the same." Jamie had forgotten about Max. She ran from the room, tripping on the first step of the staircase. I followed after her. When I tried to help her up, she pushed me away and scrambled up the stairs on her hands and knees.

"Jamie," I called, following her. I could hear her crying as she darted across the hall into the baby's room. Breathless and sobbing, Jamie stood over the crib and watched her baby sleep. Her hand trembled as she stroked Rachel's back. Finally she turned away and left the room. When I followed her, she put her arm out as a barrier between us.

"Please, Peter, don't touch me. I feel dirty." Her fists clenched. "I . . . I can still smell the horse's breath."

I watched her crawl back into bed and pull the covers up to her chin like a little girl.

"Jame, do you want to talk about it?"

"We've talked about it over and over again. I know what you believe. You think I've packed the breathing experi-ence with Rachel and my discomfort with Luke's eye into one nightmare. But . . ." She started to breathe heavily.

"But that doesn't explain it for me. Why the exact same dream?"

"Okay," I said, sitting up in bed and nodding my head confidently. "You've got to understand; if you still have the same fears, you could easily have the same experiences . . . dreams included." I took her hands. "Nothing's going to happen to Rachel. As soon as you know that, the dreams will be over."

Jamie tried to listen, but those eyes—the horse's eyes and Luke's eyes—still haunted her. From the darkness, piercing blue searchlights with uncertain portent besieged her. Sweating nostrils exhaled enraged groans. My words couldn't compete with those impressions. Jamie turned away, the sounds of hooves smashing against rocks still alive in her ears.

17

Tiny beads of sweat dripped down my forehead. My feet glided over the oily pavement, cushioned by the innersoles of leather sneakers. I ran in a studied pattern. Four beats to each breath in, four beats to each breath out.

Like the Sioux Indians I had once studied, I maximized my energy flow by altering my slightly pigeon-toed stance so that both feet pointed perfectly straight and moved parallel to each other. And like the runners I had viewed during slow-motion replays of Olympic long-distance competitions, I cupped my hands loosely and lifted my head, visualizing myself filled with helium.

I turned north to sprint along the west side of Central Park. As I paced a city bus belching brown clouds, I increased my speed to stay ahead of the pollution. I grunted at the vehicle, baring my teeth, then grunted a second time to amplify the challenge. Gazing into the front grill, I dipped my head respectfully to my mechanical rival.

A poster, plastered on the side of this ten-wheeler, diverted my attention. The illustration contained a startling, lifelike close-up of an alluring young woman. She beckoned to the viewer, tantalized him. Her mouth curled sensuously, caught in a kiss. A silhouetted section of a suspension bridge protruded from the right side of her head. Several octopus-like cranes attached themselves to the steel girders, their long steel tentacles threatening the people below. Huge metal doors opened in her neck to expose a complex network of support beams beneath the fleshy exterior. A small army of technicians and equipment poured out. Many drove computerized bulldozers, which were ravaging the land indiscriminately. The headline read, DON'T LET HER UNDRESS IN OUR CITY PARKS. Save Our City Committee, the conservation group, had sponsored the advertisement.

This particular billboard, designed to be as garish as a Forty-Second Street peep show, had been my brainchild, the one that had been inspired by the view from the board room in a client meeting with Dave Gillette. I had offered my services and those of my company to the committee. Not only did I supervise the project; I did some of the actual rendering myself.

My pulse grew rapid as I strained to stay neck and neck with the bus. I smiled parentally at the poster. I loved the eyes on the woman's face illustrated on the poster. The right one was a deep, warm brown; the left one was teal blue, electric and penetrating. I had sketched and airbrushed the irises so that the blue one would seem to follow a passing viewer. In fact, I spent several nights perfecting the illusion. My ironic tribute to Luke.

As I ran, Max's distinct form, balancing on the back of a broken bench two blocks away, was easily recognizable. I narrowed the distance between us, noting now the frankfurter in his hand, one of the few staples in his eclectic diet. Although dressed haphazardly, Max achieved the perfect effect in all black: not sinister, but warm, dark and eternal—an image of another era when "beat" took over Greenwich Village and the bohemian radicals sought to resurrect the nineteenth-century intellectual Mecca of Paris in lower Manhattan. I also knew the secret of his woolly mustache and closed-lip smirk. Belittling cosmetic dentistry, he swore allegiance to the mouth that nature and a series of accidents had designed. Thus, instead of repairing his broken teeth, he merely camouflaged them.

As I came to a point parallel to where Max sat, I broke my studied stride and darted into the street. Finally, as I came within earshot of my friend, he saluted with his frankfurter and said, "Here's to the conspiracy of all us rabbits caught in the land of wolves. Fine poster work on that bus, ol' buddy," Max continued. "Curious . . . those eyes. Very curious," he teased, reclining now into his comfortable park-bench slouch.

"Stuffin' yourself with garbage again, eh, Max? C'mon, get off your butt and I'll pace you across the park."

Max licked his lips with the flourish of a connoisseur. "Hey, big boy, I tore myself away from the aroma of the Hudson River just to be here with you. Now, don't you want to pay a bit more respect to an old man?"

I leaned over and kissed him on the top of his shiny bald crown. Eyeing the man who was twelve years my senior, I concluded, "I treat all grandparents the same way."

We sat together, staring silently into the traffic. The midday meeting represented a welcome break in both of our schedules—I, the renegade from the East Fifty-Seventh Street business district, and Max, the West Side psychologist, both of us pausing in our dealings with our respective clients.

"Another long-term patient graduated from therapy this week . . . by mutual consent," Max said. "That's the best . . . or, at least, it's supposed to be. It's always sort of strange for me." He curled his mustache—his preamble to serious talk. He spoke slowly. "You don't plan it . . . it just happens. You get so involved. You get to know everything about them: their loves, their hates, their problems, their passions." He paused, rubbing his broad forehead with the tips of his fingers. "You adopt their lives and their families, if only for an hour or two each week, so you can see it like they see it." He smiled sadly. "You come to love them, and then they leave your life forever."

He could have been talking about Mona and his kids, I

thought. "They leave as happier people, Max . . . happier because they knew you."

"Good line," Max replied. "Not that it's true, of course, but it sounds good." I pushed my friend playfully, almost toppling him from the bench. "Beating on an old man," he whispered. "For shame, for shame." He smiled. "You had lunch yesterday with Luke, right?" When my expression grew unexpectedly solemn, Max added, "Ah, now I know, I have to hear about it."

I didn't want to start, but Max pressed me.

"It's been a week since the choking episode with Rachel," I began, shaking my head. "When I tried to tell Luke about it, he put his hand up and touched my lips. Then he proceeded to describe to me everything about the incident. He didn't miss a thing . . . from the flashes in the park to the stuff in the hospital." I peered directly into my friend's eyes. "I asked him if he'd discussed it with Jamie or you, and he said no."

"I haven't seen or talked with him since it happened," Max confirmed.

"Neither has Jamie," I added. "Sometimes, I get the distinct feeling he's purposely leading me around in circles. I could feel myself starting to boil, so I asked him directly. I asked him how he knew and he didn't flinch." Despite my discomfort about it, I had to smile admiringly. Not once had I ever seen Luke's apparent mellow mood ruffled. "The man just gave me one of his biblical answers," I continued. "You know . . . 'when we're open, our knowing is not confined to the vision of our eyes or the sounds in our ears' . . . and so on."

I rose from the bench with an exaggerated sigh of mock resignation, a sort of breathing version of "can't fight city hall." Max jumped up from the bench, joining me. We strolled into the park, entering at Seventy-eighth Street. A horse-drawn sight-seeing carriage, filled with laughing occupants, sped by us. The driver's old tuxedo flapped noisily in the wind. A plastic flower, one of many decorating the coach's canopy, fell into the street at our feet. Max picked up the imitation rose, grunted quietly to himself and then tossed it into a trash basket.

"Peter, do you want to continue?" Max pressed, trying not to play therapist, but assuming the role nevertheless. Then, without waiting for an answer, he asked, "Do you think Luke had anything to do with Rachel's choking?"

"I don't know," I replied as I kicked a stone along the path in front of me. "Sometimes, he's like a father, a brother, a teacher, my friend—all in one body. I love Luke."

"Do you love him enough to question him?"

I nodded. "Yes, yes, I think so."

"Okay, then. Did Luke have anything to do with your daughter's choking?" Max asked again.

"You don't give up, do you?" He shook his head. "Okay. Then neither will I. The answer is no. No, I don't think he had anything to do with it . . . except, well, teaching us to be more in touch. Jamie doesn't actually accuse him, not in so many words, but I know she has her doubts."

"And how do you feel about that?" Max questioned.

"A little guilty. I wanted this whole thing to be fun for her, an adventure." I sighed noisily. I felt responsible for Jamie's happiness, aware, always, of how much she had suffered. And the baby—God, I thought, the baby's everything to her. "Max, you know what Rachel means to Jamie and how she's always doted over her. Well, now it's worse. The baby's always in her arms."

"Hey, any mother would react that way. Give her time. It'll pass."

As we entered a tunnel that allowed us to pass beneath a main traffic artery traversing the park, I said, "I thought time would make the difference too . . . until last night. She had another dream, just like the one she had before about the charging horse with Luke's eyes." Max stopped short and grimaced. "What's the matter?" I asked.

"Ah, nothing," he replied, taking my arm almost parentally. "Dreams are the way we deal with fears we can't confront when we're awake. The ingredients, well, they're all personal and often jumbled up . . . it's our way of presenting new information back to ourselves in a new form. Sometimes it helps; sometimes it doesn't."

"That's pretty casual, Doctor. How do I present that neat little thesis to Jamie when she jumps out of bed in the middle of the night, with her face soaked with perspiration and her eyes bulging out of their sockets?"

We exited the tunnel and continued walking along the macadam path. We didn't speak for several minutes.

"Do you want me to see her?" Max asked.

"Right now, I think she just wants to be left alone." The chimes from the clock by the Central Park Zoo rang out across the fields. I looked at my watch. "I have a meeting at two-thirty. I've got to go. See you at lunch tomorrow with Luke."

"You're an overachiever," Max replied. He patted my cheeks affectionately. "Sometimes, ol' buddy, I think you try too hard, but, maybe . . . maybe I'm wrong."

I shrugged my shoulders. We hugged each other. "Thanks," I whispered, turning and pushing off into an easy sprint. Four counts in. Four counts out. My legs gained strength as I patterned my breathing to my pace.

After watching me disappear in the distance, Max pulled a crumpled pack of cigarettes from his back pocket. He extracted one bent specimen and placed it between his lips. Searching for a match, his hand came up empty. Smiling to himself, he looked over his shoulder again, staring directly into the sun. Finally, he began his trek back to his apartment.

Lost in thought, he stepped into the street at the edge of the park, with vacant eyes, moving directly into the path of an oncoming bus. The screech turned heads for three blocks. Max froze.

The driver, half off his seat, tugged frantically at the steering wheel. The bus swerved to the left, heaving on its tires and missing Max narrowly. The man opened the mechanized accordion doors.

"You stupid bastard!" he screamed. "You better look where the hell you're going!"

"All right. All right," Max said, shrugging an apology.

The doors slammed shut and the bus lurched forward. Max watched it pass, noticing a Save Our City poster displayed on the rear of the vehicle. The maiden's intense blue eye seemed to track him as he crossed the street.

Instead of going to his own apartment, he found himself standing in front of Celine's front door. Max knocked for a long time.

"Here I come," Celine sang as she turned the knob. "Persistent little kitten, aren't you?" She left the door ajar so he could follow her into the living room.

"You got a couple of seconds? I can't stay."

She ignored his statement and delivered a small Japanese bowl filled with miso soup.

Max took several polite sips, then asked, "Do you remember the reading you did on me about the horse?"

"Ah, so you've become a believer."

He shook his head. "It's a long story." He sighed, embarrassed to pose the next question. "Listen, could you describe the horse?"

She started to laugh. "From a hoof?"

"Well, did you have an impression? Was he big or small, brown, black, or white? What were the colors of his eyes? Anything?"

"You're serious, aren't you? You cute man." Max nodded. "Well," Celine said, "as I told you, it's more like a symbol. I don't think the reading should be taken so literally. I mean, it could be a real honest-to-goodness horse, but . . . but I

don't know. The information was meant for you, not me."
The expression on her face grew solemn. "Why do I keep
feeling something urgent about all this?"

Her last comment disturbed him. Was he buying into the
hocus-pocus? Of course not. After all, he was a psychologist, a scientist of sorts, not a mystic. Then why would the
reading matter at all to him? Why? He never answered the
question he posed.

18

With casual expertise, I backed my car into cramped quarters by the curb. Like an aging buffalo with tuberculosis, it sputtered and groaned even after I switched off the ignition. An artist, balancing a ten-by-ten-foot canvas as he negotiated through the lunch-break river of humanity, passed by.

I consulted my watch and took my pulse. After thirty seconds, I grimaced, keenly aware of the rapid internal drumbeat. The morning's "touch of the flu" had invaded my entire system. Ignoring chills, fever and a raspy throat, I walked into Toby's Temple. I nodded to the stuffed parrot, then maneuvered through the sea of customers waiting for tables. When I arrived at the reserved tatami room, I found it empty. Rather than wait alone at the table, I elected to look for Luke at his home.

Tipsy from fever, my gait sluggish, I turned the corner into Luke's street. As I leaned against a car to adjust a shoelace, beads of sweat bubbled on my forehead. I scanned his building from my position diagonally across the street. No activity in the windows of the loft. Then, to my surprise, two nuns emerged from the front entrance of Luke's building.

I could feel my whole body become rigid. For a moment I held my breath, then I darted into the traffic. A blast from the horn of a delivery truck sobered me. I paused, then made my way more cautiously to the other side of the street. I almost lost my balance when I leaped over the curb. The fever fogged my vision. Centering myself, I stood conspicuously in the middle of the sidewalk and gaped at the approaching sisters.

One nun, very frail and very old, appeared almost hidden within her habit. She wore small circular wire glasses that pinched her bony nose. A black patch covered one eye. Its thin band creased her cheek and forehead. The second woman, perhaps eighteen or nineteen years old, exuded a virginal naiveté, her lips full and alive, her skin unblemished. Her movements coordinated perfectly with those of the older nun, as if choreographed.

The frozen faces, outlined in starched white linen, drew near. I searched their expressions for a message . . . a sign. I stood there, like a drunken fool, staring at them. At first they ignored me completely. Then, detouring around me, the older nun, quite unexpectedly, turned and stared right at me. Her one functioning eye appeared luminous, a clear albino iris charged with a lifeless iridescence. Unbalanced by the intensity of her gaze, I peered back at her during the short interlude, then watched both her and the other black-robed figure continue to glide down the street, their habits fluttering in the wind.

I entered Luke's building a touch dizzy and breathless but regained my equilibrium in the elevator. The doorbell activated Westminster chimes.

Rudy opened the antique metal door. "Hi," he greeted me softly.

We embraced in a hearty bear hug. My inquisitive eyes scanned the opened doorways. "I got to the restaurant a little early, so I thought I'd meet Luke here."

"Well, he's . . . he's busy right now." Rudy eased me quickly toward the door, but not before I caught a glimpse of Luke standing in the living room with Collis, Dan, Deedee, and several others. He appeared to be waving his hand at them, not unlike a minister administering religious rites. "I'm sure he'll be at Toby's soon," Rudy concluded, patting me gently on the shoulder.

I walked for blocks, circling the area several times. I kept associating the nuns with Luke's strange behavior. I had never before questioned his often bizarre and fanciful manner. Then why all the questions now? Had I changed? Had Luke changed? Or was this all because of Jamie?

This time when I entered the restaurant, Lazarus, the gaunt manager, waved to me, pointing to the tatami room. The others had arrived. After I removed my shoes, I climbed into the raised cubicle to embrace Luke and then Max.

The luncheon began in silence. The drone of others eating and chatting in the cafe spilled into our enclosure: a teacup and chopstick environment. Gregorian chants flooded the room. I assumed that Lazarus had changed the music in honor of Luke.

After the entree, Luke drew Max's attention with his eyes. His right hand rose from the table as if possessed. Suddenly, everything he did seemed bizarre to me. Luke extended his index finger and middle finger. He had adopted a similar gesture in class, leaving some of us confused and tense.

Max beamed brightly, obviously amused. The energy between them intensified. Ever so slowly, Luke shifted his body until he faced me. Now he brought his other hand into an identical position, extending his fingers. A charged, nonverbal offering. I nodded several times; a queasy sensation washed through my body. A waiter came into the room, delivered wooden bowls of bean soup and a can of cream soda, then withdrew.

"How do you feel the class is evolving, Luke?" Max asked.

"How do you feel it's evolving?" he asked, returning the question.

"Good!"

"And you, Peter?" Luke inquired.

"You know how I feel. At first, it was exciting, productive, a real adventure. But . . ." I hesitated as Luke drifted in and out of focus. "But since the experience with Rachel, everything has become more tenuous and confusing."

I faced Luke, wanting to be respectful. "For Max and the others, it's been different—little visions and games in class. But for Jamie and me, it's like being suddenly put on the line. Not that we haven't handled it, but, sometimes—well, sometimes, I feel like a sky diver who just jumped out of an airplane without a parachute." I touched Luke's arm. "Why the eyes over my shoulder? Why Rachel? Why are all these things happening?"

Luke bent his head downward and smiled like a little boy; his rounded belly spread over the edge of the table as he leaned forward. "You ask why everything's happening. To that I answer . . . why not? But, perhaps, there is a more useful question. What have you learned from what's happened?" He pulled on his beard, then continued. "The more you expand your awareness, the more you will come to know about who you are and who I am."

Max countered, "Are you saying we don't know?"

"Perhaps it is a question of what you're willing to admit," Luke stated, igniting his second cigarette with the smoldering butt of his first.

"Okay," I said, smiling self-consciously. I would risk saying more. "I look at you and become confused. You're obviously overweight, you chain-smoke, and your apparent addiction to cream soda borders on comedy. Knowing what you know, why would you be this way?"

Luke smiled again, welcoming a question. "When people appear too perfect or too special, we enshrine them . . . keep them at a distance, like the prophets we've talked about in class. When that occurs, we can no longer really hear their words." He paused, allowing his thoughts to reach their mark. "My vulnerability, my shortcomings, are a reflection of everyone. I mirror those around me to be one of them, so they might hear what I say."

"Luke, what are you saying?"

"Whatever you come to hear."

"Forgive me for pushing," I said, "but I'd like to be more direct and have you answer more directly. Jamie and I have had some incredible experiences. I think what disturbs me is that I sense it's escalating. I want to understand why."

"We each have our own lessons to learn," Luke replied. "In a way, we attract our own experiences, ones which give us the opportunity to have such lessons."

"Are you saying we wanted that near miss with Rachel?" I asked.

"Did you?"

"That kind of question doesn't deserve an answer."

"Maybe it does," Luke said carefully. "Not that you specifically thought of your daughter having a breathing problem, but that you wanted to know something, something you may not have yet learned. When we miss the lesson, we continually relive new versions of the same problems . . . like the man who goes bankrupt several times for the same reason or the individual who divorces based on incompatibility only to remarry another person with the identical personality. We meet people who do these kinds of things all the time. I'm sure that each of us, in our own life has many similar examples."

I nodded. Attentive to my reaction, he finished by saying, "When we embrace the fears, defuse them and let them go, only then do we move on. Otherwise, we invite the same kinds of experiences time and again."

"I guess it could be a fatal invitation," I said, "if I extend your theory."

"Oh, it's not a theory, Peter. Theories are games. Let's take an example: breast cancer. Did you ever wonder why, here, in breast-conscious America, women never get cancer of the elbow? A group of reputable scientists are engaged in elaborate studies to correlate certain fears and attitudes with the onset of breast tumors. Theory? For them, perhaps. They need their step-by-step scientific proofs to affirm their own awareness, but there are other, more direct paths. That's why you and I, Max and the others have come together." He paused to scratch the front of his chest. "A light bulb. A thirty-six-thousand-ton machine that flies. A laser beam. At one time, mere thoughts, fantasies... until one person decided to act without the slightest shred of evidence and do what others called impossible. Only when we can't admit and trust what we already know do we search for evidence in order to act."

Luke's eyes glazed as he cocked his head to the left and smiled once again. He had finished. At that moment Deedee arrived. She sat beside Max. I became conscious of my fever again as Luke's smile evolved into an intense wild-eyed grin. His face faded out of focus. A yellow mist interfered with my vision. I looked away.

Without speaking, Luke shifted his attention, locking eyes with Deedee, who smiled at him. Lazarus appeared suddenly at the table, white apron in hand. He bent over, kissed Luke on the cheek, and disappeared as quickly as he had entered. Another minute elapsed. Luke rose to his feet and bowed slightly. Fingering his belt loops, he tugged his pants up, embraced each of us affectionately and left.

I wanted to talk with Max but felt guarded in Deedee's presence. I checked my watch. "I have to get back to the office."

"Are you okay?" Max asked noting my red-rimmed eyes.

"Just a minor case of flu. I'll be fine," I answered. I embraced my friend.

Deedee winked at me. Her lips were wet. "Hey, big boy, how about a hug for me?" When I embraced her, she pushed her pelvis against me.

I tapped her head lightly. "You never give up, do you?"

"Little by little, I'll get you all," she cooed in my ear.

As I left the room, I noticed Deedee lean against Max and slip her hand over his.

19

The little mouth sucked fiercely, drawing the formula quickly through the rubber nipple. Her tiny fingers gripped the soft plastic sides of the bottle. Funny grunts of satisfaction mixed musically with Jamie's humming. The antique rocker swayed back and forth.

Rachel began to suck air noisily, having exhausted the contents of the bottle. Jamie took it gently from her, performed the burping ritual, then placed her daughter carefully on her stomach in the crib. She'll be okay, she argued to herself. You can leave her. C'mon, get out of here. "Sleep tight, kitten," she whispered finally, watching Rachel's eyelids begin to close. As Jamie tiptoed from the room, she heard Robin calling from the kitchen.

"One or two teaspoons of sugar?" her friend shouted.

Jamie hurried to reach the stairs before she answered, "One's fine."

The two women carried the coffee into the living room and then began to exchange their news.

Jamie pushed herself to be enthusiastic, babbling on about the discovery of her ring in the park, an event that had been totally overshadowed by the incident with her daughter. She grabbed her friend's hand many times, either to strengthen her connection to Robin or to accent a thought. Jamie hadn't realized how the easy hugs exchanged by those in the Tuesday night class had freed her to rely on her body more as an instrument of expression.

Robin listened attentively, forcing her smiles. She couldn't decide which disturbed her more: Jamie's involvement with Luke, Rachel's near mishap or the greater looseness she detected recently in her friend's entire demeanor.

They had known each other since college. Jamie had always worn her hair pulled back straight off her face in a rather stately fashion, Robin thought. But now her thick sandy blond hair fell lazily against her cheeks and curled haphazardly over her shoulders. Her blouse, rather than being neatly tucked into her jeans, had been knotted casually around her waist, exposing a thin strip of flesh. If it had been anyone but Jamie, she would not have noticed. Yet even if she admitted noticing Jamie's unmistakable sensuality for the first time, Robin couldn't quite adjust herself to her friend's new burst of physical affection. She scolded herself for recoiling each time Jamie touched her. Between nervous puffs on her cigarette, Robin adjusted her clothing repeatedly.

The phone rang.

"It's your man," Jamie announced.

"My man, huh! I just married him. I didn't create him." She rose from the couch, reassured by her friend's announcement. "Still the country girl mentality: husband, home, till death do us part and all that shit," Robin thought, recognizing her own sarcasm in contrast to the innocence that had always attracted her to Jamie. "I'll take it in the bedroom." she said, cloistering herself automatically in case some "ugly" matter should arise on the phone.

"Want to trade husbands?" Robin asked, returning to the living room. "I'm due for a new model." Jamie smiled sadly at her comment. "No matter, Jame. You mentioned on the phone that you had another dream."

Jamie sighed and stared at her friend pensively. Suddenly, distinctive knocking at the side door interrupted them. "Come in, Cleo," Jamie called.

"No one knocks like that one!" Robin said.

Cleo charged into the room wearing an outrageous mirror-studded poncho. Her heels slapped the floor. A soldier's gait.

Jamie smiled, but Robin winced at Cleo's aggressive masculinity.

"Did I interrupt ladies' talk or real talk?"

"It depends on your point of view," Jamie quipped.

"Knowing your interests, Cleo, we were talking real talk," Robin volunteered.

An awkward silence. Cleo flopped into a chair, rubbing her hands together. "Great, I'm ready."

Jamie stared at her enigmatic friend. From her tightly-cropped hair to her leather boots, this woman oozed raw power. Cleo fascinated her. When others attacked her mannerisms as abusive, Jamie supported her individuality quietly. Despite the pose, the garb and the apparent strength, Jamie connected easily with the more vulnerable person beneath the facade. Cleo protected Cleo. And Jamie refused to judge her.

"We were discussing what has now become my recurring dream," Jamie began.

"Unbelievable!" Cleo exclaimed. "I've been thinking about your dream all morning." The two women shared a smile. "The dream and that terrible experience with the little princess . . . and, oh, Terry's yellow light. How come all this stuff began when *you* started with Luke?"

Jamie became defensive suddenly. "Cleo, Peter's studied with Luke for more than a year. What if I tell you that strange, chubby man is actually charming?"

"Charming like a rattlesnake," she snapped. "So he's gotten to you too, huh?"

"That's not true," Jamie countered. "You don't understand. I have to go to the classes. Peter's so involved."

"What does that have to do with you?" Cleo asked.

"Everything. I have to do all that I can to keep our marriage strong. Sharing our—our experiences is part of that."

Jamie grimaced. "Look, you've never met Luke."

"I don't have to. Just listening to you is enough to scare the hell out of me. This guy has taken the deep plunge over the edge, beyond the beyond. If it were me, I'd get as far away as possible. And I wouldn't walk, I'd run."

"I guess that's my feeling as well," Robin added, almost embarrassed to support Cleo's position.

Jamie looked away. "Listen, maybe if it weren't for the well, the awareness we had, maybe we wouldn't have been able to save Rachel."

"Come off it, Jamie, that's Peter's rationale," Cleo stated. "You're giving in to him. It's as clear as the nose on your face. This guy is off the wall."

"But I don't know that," Jamie said, polarized by her friend's position. "Cleo, when I was a kid in a wheelchair, with all my braces and metal back support, I looked . . . weird, and the other kids avoided me like the plague because I was different. Well, so is Luke—different. I don't want to do to him what everyone once did to me."

Cleo leaned back in shock. She couldn't believe Jamie's defense of a man that she herself had viewed with considerable discomfort only a few short weeks before. "You mean you buy his whole act now?" she asked.

"I'm just trying to understand, to be open," Jamie insisted. "After all, Peter has been involved with Luke for over a year."

"Correction," Cleo chimed. "We're not just talking about Peter. Now, you're involved."

Her observation irked Jamie. How could she ever look for guidance from a person who scared her? Initially, most of her comments had been to counter Cleo's attack. But now her own views confused her. Had she become more a part of the group than she realized?

Bolstered by Cleo's frankness, Robin added, "The whole situation sounds a little cultish to me."

Jamie whipped her head around. "I'd like to change the subject, okay?"

The other women agreed. Cleo poured herself a cup of coffee and began to talk about the inequities of her job.

Robin asked her questions, but Jamie drifted in and out of the conversation. She had become inexplicably hypersensitive to her breasts. The pores of her skin bristled. Forcing herself to participate, she asked, "Cleo, do you think your bosses understood you in the first place?"

The answer barely penetrated. Jamie's focus had turned inward again. She imagined a hard lump deep inside. Unable to remain seated, she excused herself.

Locking the bathroom door, she stared at her face in the mirror. Her body tensed. Slowly, she removed her blouse. Working her fingers behind her back, she released the catch on her bra.

From the living room she heard Cleo's voice. "Whatever you're doing, try to make it quick. I have to be at work before noon."

Jamie lifted her arm toward the ceiling and began to examine the right breast slowly. Her fingers kneaded the soft flesh. Starting from under her armpit, she worked her way deliberately around the perimeter and under the base of her bosom. No lumps or hardness.

Dropping her extended arm, she lifted the other and repeated the procedure. Her fingers probed nervously. Tiny beads of perspiration dotted her lips.

A deep sigh escaped from her throat as she finished; she had not found any irregularities in either breast. Cleo's voice intruded again. Jamie wet a washcloth and quickly removed the thin film of sweat from her face. As she dried herself, she saw her mother in the mirror. The image startled her. The older woman stood there, naked and dumbfounded, clutching her breasts. Then Fran's expression turned to one of rage. Her fingers trembled against her skin. Jamie gasped and the mirage disappeared.

When Jamie returned to the living room, she couldn't camouflage her discomfort. Cleo pressed for an explanation, finally eliciting a complete description of her experience in the bathroom. Robin shook her head and left rather abruptly.

Cleo leaned across the coffee table. "The wheels of the gods turn slowly for you, don't they? Can you see, Jamie? It's continuing to happen? What can I say to you? How do I move you?"

"Don't worry about me, please," Jamie pleaded. "I'll find my way."

"I'm not convinced of that. I can't just sit by while something happens to you. If you won't help yourself, I'll have to do it for you."

Later that evening, at home, Jamie sat on the edge of the mattress. "Peter, are you up to talking?"

"Sure, I'm all yours." I smiled, looking up from my reading. I had come home earlier in the day to nurse my cold.

"Something happened," she said, her voice communicating clearly the gravity of her remark.

In exact detail she described the incident with her breasts and her mother's image in the mirror. As Jamie concluded the story, she cleared her throat apprehensively. "Did you hear what I said?"

I nodded. I couldn't believe the subject matter of her experience, remembering my lunch earlier in the day with Luke and his reference to breast cancer during our conversation.

"It's so crazy," she continued. "Cleo believes the more we're open for it, the more it's going to happen." Jamie stopped. "But to me it feels like it just happens."

"But suppose" . . . I began.

Jamie, unaware of my words, cut into my sentence. "This whole thing is so—so unnatural."

"Listen, Jamie, I'm not at all clear on everything either,

but maybe it just feels unnatural because it's different from the kinds of things we're used to. After all, why does it matter how we get our information?"

"It gives me the creeps." Jamie hesitated, then blurted out her next comment. "Cleo thinks Luke's controlling us more and more."

"Hey, honey, you're not Cleo; you're Jamie."

"Well, maybe I think the same thing," she countered, suddenly reversing the position she'd taken earlier in the day. Yet, as soon as she made the statement, she knew somehow that she really did not want to quit the class. Deedee pampered her, helping her feel at home. Hera confided in her, sharing discomforts not too distant from her own. And Max—well, Max made everything seem safe. But she knew she couldn't ignore Luke's presence, or the altered-state experiences that had come with increasing frequency. It was almost as if she had to run headlong toward the very things she feared.

"If my mother really has a tumor," she said, "what good does it do for me to know that?"

"Jamie, I can't answer that, really . . . only you can."

20

As he approached Columbus Circle, Max smoothed the edges of his mustache with his fingers. The gurgling in his stomach surprised him. He could no longer fool himself with the casual quality of his walk. His destination had been clear from the outset, though he acknowledged it only as he neared the section along Central Park South where he had first seen the black and white spotted horse. Although he viewed Jamie's second dream as nothing more than a neurotic fixation on her fear of losing her child, the character and description of the horse, combined with Celine's tea-leaf reading, pushed him to look at the animal one more time. Luckily, he mused, he kept his private aberrations to himself.

The long line of carriages unfolded in front of him across Fifty-ninth Street. The first horse was as black as the coach behind it. Brown hair covered the second and third animals. He could not see the others parked beyond them along the curb. Would the horse buck again if he tried to pet it? And would the coachman mutter and groan if he asked more questions? When the fourth horse, a ragtag palomino, came into view, Max quickened his step, crossing the street hastily. In less than a minute, he passed all the coaches. No black and white spotted horse. No gleaming watch-eye to stare at him. He watched the carriages come and go for almost an hour. In addition to the old coachmen, several young women drove the ancient vehicles. Max marveled at their faces, often tough and unsmiling. However, one girl, her top hat decorated with plastic red roses, talked to passing pedestrians.

"How about it, mister?" she said, grinning seductively at a young man walking arm in arm with a female companion. "Romance and a ride. Twenty-five bucks buys you thirty minutes—the only bargain left in the city besides the Staten Island Ferry. No kidding! Hey, don't go," she pleaded. But the couple passed beyond the reach of her voice. She shrugged her shoulders, then noticed Max looking at her. "Hey, how about you?" she asked.

"No, thank you," Max called back to her.

"Suit yourself," she mumbled, returning her concentration to those who passed within close proximity of her coach.

Max approached an ice-cream stand. "Two vanilla cones," he said, laying his money down. After pocketing his change, he walked toward the young woman's carriage slowly, aware that she was watching him out of the corner of her eye. Her black hair framed her face haphazardly, the long curls twisting in front of her cheeks and covering one eye. "Here," he said, smiling. She didn't move. "Go ahead. I just thought you could help me with some information. Kind of a trade." He paused, but she still did not answer. "You're going to have to decide real soon about the ice cream before it melts all over my hand."

"Okay."

He handed it to her. She smiled, brushing the hair out of her face. Max calculated her age at sixteen. "I'm looking for a coach with a black and white spotted horse," he said. "The driver is an old man. He wears tuxedo tails. Do you know him?"

"You just described twenty coachmen. Sure don't want a ride in the park?"

Max shook his head. "No, thanks. This, uh, horse—it's got a weird eye, sort of human, blue in the center."

She nodded suddenly. "Everybody knows that horse. A

real lunatic. I don't think the driver's much better." She pointed to her head comically. "He's an old-timer—none too nice and a bit wacky, if you ask me."

"Do you know where I could find him?"

"You sure you want to?" she asked.

"I think so," Max said tentatively while munching on his ice cream.

"It's your neck, mister. That horse is the spookiest animal I've ever seen."

"I know," Max admitted. "Where can I find him or the driver?"

"The old man, Jude—he's an independent. He doesn't work the park that often. Try the licensing bureau on Lafayette." She pointed to the document pinned to the side of the coach as she licked her cone and smiled. "Anyone that drives has to have a license." She also suggested that he look by the other three stations around the park.

"Could you tell me where they're located?"

"Boy, you sure want a hell of a lot for your ice cream."

Nevertheless, she told him where to find the other stations. While she talked, she twirled her hair with her fingers, a habit identical to that of Max's youngest daughter. He thought about asking her if she needed a father but knew she would find such a question offensive. Instead, he handed her twenty-five dollars. "Thanks for the ride," he said playfully. She gaped at him, barely returning his smile as he began to leave.

"Wait!" she shouted, withdrawing one of the plastic roses from her hat. The young woman threw it to him and winked. "Nice doing business with you, mister. Good luck with that horse."

Max nodded appreciatively, toying with the stiff petals in his hand. He spent the next four hours at the other stations talking to other drivers. Everyone knew Jude. His horse, or at least its rare and foreboding blue eye, had become legendary among the other coachmen. Yet no one had seen them lately. One man said that Jude had died, another claimed that the horse had been killed, while a third insisted, sardonically, that an animal with a watch-eye never dies.

Abandoning his search, Max cut across the playground and headed home. As he neared the street, he heard the sound of hooves beyond the next horizon. He waited at the curb, half expecting the huge black and white spotted horse to rise above the crest of the road. Instead, a mannerly dapple-gray appeared, pulling a rather garish red and yellow carriage. Max stared at the rose in his hand. He remembered the one that had fallen off another coach. That time he had thrown the rose away; this time he would keep it.

21

She sat in the foyer, jiggling her feet busily beneath the chair. Her long hair, entwined with beads amid braids and curls, twisted exotically over her shoulders. Hera pulled her blouse down over her Indian skirt, hiding the frayed band as well as the small roll of flesh protruding above it. Besides participating in the Tuesday night class, she came to Luke for private counseling.

Her appointment had been scheduled for 3:30. Having waited almost twenty-five minutes, she jumped to her feet, exasperated, and walked nervously into the living room. It appeared austere without the music and people. She eyed Luke's empty chair, the cushion hollowed from the weight of its most frequent occupant. Uncomfortable with being alone, Hera moved into the kitchen in search of a familiar face, but the room was unoccupied.

She scanned the hallway, then turned the doorknob to the bathroom. A strange whine seeping from a back room diverted her attention. Hera tiptoed farther down the hall, justifying her impulse by construing a slightly ajar door as an invitation.

Luke squatted in the center of a brown athletic mat. Opposite him sat a woman whose back faced the door. Hera scrutinized her closely cropped hair and safari jacket. The woman began to rock back and forth. Her throat emitted a strange sound.

Then, quite suddenly, she lunged toward Luke, punching him wildly about the chest and shoulders. He sat perfectly still, never once lifting his own hands. He turned his head to the side in an apparent attempt to shield his face, but his expression, which confused Hera, remained oddly passive. Rudy and Dan, who must have been waiting at the side of the room, became visible through the crack of the opened door. They tried to restrain the woman.

Deedee joined the others. Standing behind the squirming figure, she put her hand gently on the woman's shoulder. Luke stood up and took her hand. Silence. Hera held her breath. The whimpering subsided.

Working energetically, Deedee then massaged the other woman's neck and shoulders artfully. She stroked the woman in a peculiar, circular fashion, but since one woman stood behind the other, Hera could not see what now transpired. Heavy breathing filled the room, then a deep sigh. Deedee disengaged. She stood still in front of the woman.

Hera backed away from the door. In the midst of taking her first step toward the bathroom, she froze. She couldn't turn away. Once again, she peered into the room. Only Luke and the strange woman were visible now. He leaned forward with that peculiar grin on his face, then stared at the woman, his luminous blue eye holding her like the headlight of a car that has mesmerized a deer in the middle of the night.

Luke returned to his half-lotus position. His lips mouthed indistinguishable words. Hera concentrated, finally able to decipher the name *Cleo* spoken several times.

The door whipped open to reveal Deedee standing full figure in front of her. Hera gasped, startled by the exposure, unnerved by the peculiar smile on her classmate's face.

"Hello, dear, dear Hera. No need to explain. After all, you know how it goes . . . everything we come to know enriches us." Tweaking her cheek, Deedee added, "I do hope you've been enriched. Ta-ta." Without further explanation, she closed the door.

In the session that followed, Hera declined to ask Luke about the incident, embarrassed by her own role. As she sat opposite him on the floor, she drew uncomfortable parallels between herself and the woman in the back room. But her fears dissolved when Luke lowered his head humbly and patted her hand gently.

"How can I help you today?" he began.

22

The chimes rang several times. No response. When the baby began whimpering again, Jamie adjusted the papoose slung across her chest. "Okay, honey," she crooned. "Mama will have that wet diaper off you in just a few more minutes." She tapped her daughter's nose. "Yes, Mama knows what you want."

The door opened finally. Rudy eyed the visitors with an enormous grin. "Oh, hello, Jamie. And, of course, little Rachel. Sorry I took so long, but you're a little early."

"Is that okay?" she asked.

"Of course. C'mon in."

As they entered the living room, Jamie looked. "Do you mind if I change her here?"

"Sure, go ahead. No one will be here for a while anyway." He touched Jamie's arm affectionately. "I'll tell Luke you're here."

"Oh, no, don't bother."

"No bother," he said matter-of-factly, then disappeared from the room.

Jamie spread the papoose out on the rug and used it as a blanket on which to place her daughter. Working quickly, she disrobed Rachel and changed her diaper. She could feel a certain tension begin to constrict her own body.

"Hello," a voice bellowed from behind.

Jamie started, then turned her head around.

"I'm sorry," Luke said. "I didn't mean to frighten you."

"Oh, well, no, you didn't." She laughed self-consciously.

"Yeah, okay, I guess you did."

"Here, why don't I take that for you?" He picked up the soiled diaper and marched toward the kitchen. Jamie returned to the business at hand—dressing her child.

In a few seconds, Luke returned.

"Rudy and I discussed accommodations for Rachel during the class. You can put her to bed in one of the bedrooms upstairs or, if you'd like, you can keep her here."

"Um, upstairs will be fine. I can keep checking her, to make sure . . . to see if she's covered."

Luke cocked his head to the side and smiled. "Still a little nervous?"

Jamie's eyelids fluttered nervously. "Still a little. Sometimes, more than a little."

He nodded his head as a response. "Well, do you want to try her in the room now?"

"Yes, sure."

"Why don't I carry her upstairs for you?"

Jamie pulled Rachel close to her chest. "I can do it."

"Okay," he said quietly, a little-boy smile lighting up his face. "Come, follow me."

The dim lighting on the second floor added to her discomfort. Nevertheless, she accompanied Luke into one of the forward bedrooms. Together, using bolsters from a couch, they built a small barricade around the outside perimeter of the bed.

"There," Luke said. When Jamie placed the baby on the mattress, Rachel began to cry. Before she had a chance to grab her daughter, Luke scooped her into his arms. "Well, well, little person," he whispered softly. "This is a wonderful room for you. Rudy lives here, you know." The baby stopped crying almost immediately and stared into the man's eyes. She lifted her hand up toward his blue one. "So you like my blue eye, huh? Well, that's my favorite, too." He lifted her toward his head so that she could touch his face. She poked at his eye socket with her fingers. Jamie tried to intercede. "That's okay," he said, "she has no intention of hurting me." When Rachel pushed her little thumb into his nostril, he laughed. Jamie couldn't believe his ease with her daughter. He's different when he's alone, she thought to herself, and so gentle with Rachel. That's what Peter must have seen in him.

Deedee passed by the door of the bedroom and stopped short. "Oh, hi!" She entered the room quickly and hugged Jamie, then peeked over Luke's shoulder. "Oh, Jamie, she's so beautiful." Deedee returned to Jamie's side and slipped her arm around her waist. "You're early and that's nice for us. And I'm glad you brought Rachel."

"I'm glad, too," Jamie replied, hardly believing her own words, which bubbled so easily from her. All the tension had dissipated. Their apparent delight and caring for her daughter made a dramatic impression on her.

After Deedee left, Luke and Jamie waited by the bed until Rachel fell asleep.

"You don't have to stay," Jamie said in a hushed voice.

"Oh, I know that," Luke answered.

Without much of a preamble, Jamie found herself suddenly telling him about her experience with her breasts and the image of her mother in the mirror. He listened attentively. "I don't know what to do," she concluded.

"Why not?" he asked quietly.

"It's silly," she whispered. "It's scary, too." Jamie could feel her body tense again.

"Do you love your mother?"

"Sure, of course I do."

"Okay, then would you want to help her if you could?"

Jamie nodded her affirmation. "But, well maybe the whole thing was sort of an hallucination. You know, when people get scared they see all kinds of strange things."

"Were you scared before you went into the bathroom?" he asked.

Jamie shook her head. "No. I was only scared afterward. I

never realized that before." She paused. "But I still don't understand. That's why I don't know what to do."

"Do you have to understand something fully in order to act?"

She thought of the incident with Rachel. "No, I guess not."

His left eye drew her toward him.

"Then what do you want to do?" he asked. Jamie wasn't ready to make a decision and Luke knew it. "Maybe, instead of needing a completely logical rationale, you could trust your inclination about how you want to react to your experience. Try it. You might be surprised." He rose from the bed and took Jamie's hand. The baby was sleeping soundly between the bolsters. "We can go now."

"Thanks," Jamie whispered, genuinely touched by his concern and caring.

I arrived early for class, expecting to find Jamie already there. But apparently she had not arrived. I hugged Lady Claire, Paul, Jessica, Collis and the others. Hera waved to me from the couch. Max never lifted his head up, engrossed in a conversation with Deedee. Rudy distributed ashtrays to the smokers in the class.

The rumble of footsteps coming down the stairs from the second floor attracted my attention. I half expected to see the nuns. Instead, to my amazement, I watched Luke and my wife, holding hands, descend the staircase. Jamie had a strange, glassy-eyed expression on her face. For a moment, she looked so different. I watched her hug Luke and thank him. Her lips seemed fuller and more sensuous than usual. I didn't want to be jealous. And certainly I didn't want to feel excluded. After all, wasn't a closeness between my wife and Luke something that I had promoted constantly?

When Jamie saw me, she broke from Luke and walked directly toward me. Uninhibited, she threw her arms up, hugged me rather aggressively, then kissed me squarely on the lips in a display of affection that she had reserved previously for the privacy of our home. Although I knew we were being observed, I sensed Jamie didn't care.

"I'm so glad you're here," she said, taking my hand and holding it tightly to her chest. "Luke helped me put Rachel to sleep upstairs. He's wonderful with her." She smiled.

"Well, you look great," I commented.

"Where's my hello?" Max intruded, holding his arms out to Jamie. When he embraced her, he closed his eyes for just an instant. Deedee rushed in, swung Jamie around playfully and kissed her. The two women laughed. Within seconds, Hera joined them. I tried to catch my wife's arm, but Deedee intercepted my motion by stepping between us. When my hand landed accidentally on her breast, she smiled victoriously. I withdrew my arm instantly, hoping no one had witnessed my blunder.

"How would you people like to sneak a peek at the meditation room?" Deedee asked. "It's just about finished."

Before I had a chance to protest in order to extract my wife from the group and talk with her alone, Jamie took my hand, then Deedee's, and said, "Lead the way."

The five of us walked down the hallway, past the kitchen, the bathroom and the back den to a ladder mounted on the wall. One by one, we climbed to the next floor, arriving in a tiny vestibule.

"If you feel angry or unhappy, please don't come in," Deedee instructed. "No kidding. The vibrations are very important." She winked suggestively at Max. In single file, we entered through a narrow passageway into a black cavity. Our feet sank several inches into the soft foam-rubber floor.

"Could you slide the door shut behind you?" Deedee asked Hera, who obliged quickly.

As soon as the latch clicked, I realized that the room had no windows. All light had been extinguished. The darkness enshrouded us completely. No noise from outside could penetrate the soundproofed walls, ceiling and floor. The sensory deprivation relaxed Max, but Hera had to sit to ground herself against the onslaught of vertigo. Jamie tightened her grip on my hand.

Suddenly, a match ignited. Deedee lit a candle in the center of the room. "Neat, isn't it?"

"Very professional," I replied.

"Rudy got all the research from Duke and Harvard," Deedee said. "The perfect meditation room." She smiled proudly.

Max touched the walls, surprised to find them spongy. I stared at the candlelight flickering across Jamie's face. Was there something different about her?

Hera backed away from us and lay flat on her back. "Maybe I'll do my living room like this," she declared. We all laughed.

"Why don't you guys stay for another couple of minutes?" Deedee suggested. "I'll meet you downstairs." She squeezed Jamie's hand affectionately and left.

"Do you notice how flat our voices sound?" Max asked.

"Yeah," Jamie answered. "Almost like the walls absorb our words. I like it."

Jamie's remark seemed out of character to me. She maintained that same smile I had noticed when she first appeared on the stairs with Luke. As we joined Hera, squatting around the candle, I addressed Jamie. "Hey, how'd your little meeting upstairs with Luke go?"

"Oh, Peter," she crooned, arching her back into one of those near-impossible yoga stretches. "You make it sound so formal. I told you that he helped me put Rachel to bed." Completing the sentence, she closed her eyes and twisted her head in a circular motion.

"What did you guys talk about?" I asked.

Jamie peered at me, then glanced at Max and Hera. "Nothing really. You know how he is."

"Positively inscrutable," Max chimed in authoritatively.

Jamie nodded her affirmation. "When he gave me his—you know, his look," Jamie said, addressing everyone, "I didn't freak. For the first time, I just looked back at him. I guess this might sound silly, but I felt good."

Max stretched out his arm toward Jamie and patted her knee. "I'm glad you had time with Luke alone. I always thought you two would like each other." He twisted the corners of his mustache thoughtfully.

"We'd better go downstairs," I suggested.

"Uh, can I say something first?" Hera blurted spastically. "You know, I don't really understand everything that goes on in class," she admitted as we all rose to our feet. "Two weeks ago, I thought . . ." She stopped talking and turned white as the blood drained away from the skin covering her face.

Max noticed immediately. "Hera, what is it?"

Her attention focused on an area just above my left shoulder. For a moment, her lips formed a snarl and her eyes narrowed like the eyes of an animal about to do combat with a more powerful adversary. Then, like a quick cut in a television commercial, a delighted half-smile came over her face.

Aware that his words had not penetrated, Max asked again, "Hera, what is it?"

"I can't tell you," she said, throwing her hands over her mouth.

"Sure you can," Jamie added. Several seconds passed. Hera remained silent, still fixed on the area above my shoulder.

"Hera," I whispered, "you can tell us." I knew I didn't want to hear the answer I anticipated.

"Well, I . . . oh, God, I can't believe this. It's so clear." She shook her head in amazement. "I can see two eyes over your shoulder, Peter." She sighed, her voice quivering. "Two eyes. One is blue and the other is brown. Just like Claire and Sandy described them."

I wanted to protest. Why over *my* shoulder again?

"This is, wow, the first, the very first time anything like this has happened! It's happening to me!" Her breathing became more rapid. "It's what I wanted, but it still frightens me."

"Why?" Max pushed, slipping into his therapist role.

"I . . . feel . . . out of control," Hera answered, her face chalky and drawn.

"What do you mean? Could you describe it?"

Max's question fell to the floor unanswered. Hera's eyes bulged open as she drifted further out of contact. She seemed to have stopped breathing. Jamie put her arms around her.

"What's happening, Hera? Tell us. What do you see now?" Jamie asked with an air of authority that I had not seen very often in our years together.

Hera addressed herself to me. "The eyes. They belonged to Luke or—or they became Luke's. He stood in this room with us, right there, behind you. I could see his face, like he was really here . . . in the flesh. He touched your left shoulder several times, sort of tapping it. I guess you didn't feel anything."

I rubbed my left shoulder, disoriented by an apparent warmth in the area.

"And he didn't speak," she continued, "but he made a sound . . . a funny snort."

After we rejoined our classmates in the large group room, Hera had difficulty maintaining her focus on the exercises Luke presented. She kept looking at his face and hearing an echo of the utterance she had heard in the meditation room. When she identified finally the origin of the strange snort, she denied her conclusion. Impossible, she mused. If she didn't know better, she would have said that Luke, or his apparition, had sounded like a horse.

23

She ran her fingers along the bars of the black wrought-iron fence that enclosed the park. Every two inches, flesh encountered painted metal. Antique lights studded empty macadam paths. Lonely swings swayed aimlessly in the wind. No children laughing. No lovers pausing. No senior citizens exchanging teacups of gossip. Gramercy Park in repose, on permanent display.

Jamie loved this neighborhood, with its delicate, feminine air. She absorbed its ambiance like a sponge, although she thought it peculiarly lifeless, like a movie set awaiting its cast of characters.

A black Cadillac cruised the streets slowly. An isolated pigeon waddled on the roof of a parked car. Jamie paused at the stoop outside her mother's building. She admired the brocaded façade with its New Orleans flavor. A small, funereal bronze plaque, discreetly placed, designated the occupants: ZERCON, WALTERS AND ASSOCIATES. Jamie enjoyed the irony, remembering the months of battles between her mother and stepfather. Not only had Fran refused to adopt his surname in business, she had insisted on top billing for herself.

She slid her hands along the polished railing as she ascended the steps. Once she was inside, the frenetic activity in the office almost disoriented her. Behind the reception area, twenty people, crammed into close quarters, answered telephones, stood up, sat down, turned around, twisted and chewed on pencils. Everything happened in fast motion, as in an old Laurel and Hardy movie, complete with shirt sleeves rolled to the elbows and wide neckties dangling from the sides of chairs.

The receptionist tapped her long black fingernails on an oversized coffee table. Her face bobbed over the keys of a jet-black computer. In an icy but polite voice, the receptionist inquired, "Good morning, may I help you?"

"Yes, please," Jamie responded softly. "I'd like to see Fran Zercon."

"Do you have an appointment?"

"Yes. At eleven."

Jamie withdrew into the outer lobby and waited. Chiseled beams in mint condition crisscrossed the ceiling. She sat on a two-hundred-year-old deacon's bench imported from Great Britain. Jamie thought about the warning she wanted to convey. Would she find the words? And how would she begin?

The whine of the elevator filled the chamber. Oiled walnut doors opened to reveal Fran's sculptured smile.

"I'm so glad you're here, darling." Fran thrust the side of her face toward Jamie for a kiss; whenever possible, she avoided contact with other people's germs. Her daughter's were no exception. Equally sensitive to etiquette and outward appearance, she turned to the receptionist. "I don't believe you've met my daughter, Jamie." Unimpressed by the news, the young woman conjured up a forced smile not unlike her boss.

When Jamie and her mother exited the elevator at the third-floor executive suite, they were greeted by a ringing telephone on top of a curved mahogany desk. Though Fran signaled that she would take only a moment, her long-winded responses fueled the conversation for several minutes. Then in rapid succession, she answered a second, third and fourth call. During this time, a small parade of people rushed in and out of the office using sign language to indicate they wanted Fran's signature. Her mouth never stopped moving.

Jamie recalled my remark; her mother did sandwich her between phone calls and meetings. Twenty minutes and a multitude of interruptions later, Jamie walked to the door and opened it.

With one hand on the receiver, Fran shouted to her daughter. "Hey, wait a second, honey. I'll be off in less than a minute." Jamie stopped and waited at the doorway.

After completing the call, Fran began, "Jamie, dear, I know you're angry with me. I'm sorry; these calls just can't wait."

The phone rang again. She asked the caller to try back later, but within seconds she slid into the conversation fully, swept away by her own command performance. In contrast to personal relationships, Fran functioned much more comfortably in business, where she understood the risks and the rules. Jamie turned and entered the elevator. "Peter, you're right," she mumbled to herself in the empty cubicle.

The elevator doors opened on the ground floor. The receptionist blocked the front entrance. "Jamie, your mother asked me to stop you. Relax; she'll be down in a minute."

One more time Jamie sighed to the wind. Back on the deacon's bench, she wondered what she had hoped to accomplish by coming here. Her fantasies about tumors had to be just that—fantasies. Yet her experiences with her own daughter and with her ring and her conversation with Luke provided a new impetus, an increased willingness to make more of an attempt to act on her intuition.

Fran walked out of the elevator as if nothing had happened. Taking her daughter's arm, she drew her to the door. "I decided, love, the only way we'll be able to spend some time is if I get out of here. You have no idea how demanding a business can be."

The moment they descended the front steps, a white private taxi pulled to the curb. Tipping his hat, the driver said courteously, "Good morning, Ms. Zercon." Her mother nodded, involved in the ritual.

Jamie stepped into the cab, trying not to be impressed. At times, her mother's pretension offended her. But now she noticed the woman's quivering lips, which betrayed discomfort beneath the slick, efficient facade.

When she took her daughter's hand, Fran's eyelids fluttered nervously. "I had a brainstorm," she volunteered. "We're going to the carousel in Central Park. You remember, darling, I used to take you there when you were a little girl."

Touched by her mother's unusual gesture, Jamie warmed up to her instantly. She searched for childhood recollections of trips to Central Park. None came. Only the memories of rows of empty beds and the bulbous face of Mary-O surfaced.

The taxi entered the park with its silent occupants, passing a long line of horse-drawn carriages waiting at the curb for their next customers. A panel truck slowed in front of them. The cabdriver veered into the next lane and accelerated impatiently. Just at that moment, Jamie noticed an old man, dressed in weathered tuxedo tails and a top hat, step off the curb with a pail of oats in each hand. Jude trudged across the black macadam, holding court with himself, unaware of having put himself on a collision course with the approaching vehicle. Jamie shouted, alerting the driver, who swerved recklessly to the left, narrowly avoiding the coachman. Twisting in her seat, she gaped out the back window. The tattered driver, having dropped one pail, waved a clenched fist and shouted what Jamie supposed were obscenities. A sigh of relief escaped from her throat. In contrast, Fran, who appeared unmoved by the incident, encouraged the driver to continue speedily on his way toward their destination.

The cabbie dropped his passengers near the old carousel. Wooden horses glided up and down gracefully,

their carved bodies speared by metal posts. These whimsi-
cal caricatures had glittering eyes highlighted by garish
combinations of paint. Metallic honky-tonk music belched
from an antique organ with a miniature steam engine for
its heart. Despite the hour, the carousel had many riders,
adults as well as children.

"Let's go on," Jamie suggested gaily. She thought of her
own child and how much she would have wanted Rachel to
be with her now. Jamie had left her for the day with Terry,
the first time she had done so since the choking incident.
She had wanted to direct all her attention to her mother.
Jamie pulled Fran by the hand and laughed.

"Don't be silly," Fran shrank.

"I'm not. I'm perfectly serious. You didn't just come to
look at it, did you?"

"Well, to tell you the truth," Fran offered, "I never
thought about what we would do when we got here."

"So then, c'mon."

Backing away from the carousel, her mother reiterated,
"No. I'd rather not. If you want to go, then go. I'll be glad
to wait for you."

"Maybe it would break the spell of hard work and no
smiles."

"I'm not interested in breaking any spells, thank you,"
Fran replied. "I enjoy my work. And I smile enough, I'm
sure."

Her mother's face hardened. Jamie couldn't look at her
any more. The expression matched the one she remembered as a child when Fran drove her to the institution.
What compelled her to keep trying? Why? Why? Jamie
never could find the answer. Everyone had counseled her
to walk away, but this was her mother, and despite the past,
she loved her. Period. At one time Jamie had believed that
she needed a reason to care about Fran; but lately she had
accepted the mysterious, undeniable bond that tied her
to the woman who had borne her. As she approached the

ticket booth, Jamie fought the emotional numbness that enveloped her. She knew she had to obliterate the old memories; otherwise, she would withdraw from Fran. Searching her pocket, she retrieved some money. Suddenly, her face wrinkled in a mischievous smile. Jamie purchased two tickets.

She delivered one into the hand of her mother and then mounted a horse. Fran, disoriented in the world of little people, withdrew to a park bench. Jamie motioned and called to her mother. The huge platform eased into motion. Music blared as the mechanical orchestra came to life. Completing the first full revolution, Jamie looked for her mother, waving her arms excitedly. Fran did not respond. Instead, occupied with business again, she made entries into her notebook, her hand jiggling nervously.

Jamie sank into herself, burying the little-girl voice that had almost surfaced. Images of breasts and mastectomies haunted her. The mannequin-like woman on the bench never once looked up at her daughter.

As the wheels ground to a halt, Jamie lingered on her varnished stallion. Vaulting suddenly from the carousel, she stepped right in front of her mother.

"Ah!" Fran jumped, startled. "Jamie, dear, would you like to go to P.J.'s for lunch?"

"No, not really. I only have an hour. Could we just walk?" Fran smiled at her, consenting weakly.

The small man-made lake at the lower tip of the park had turned brown, contaminated by nearby subway construction. As the two women circled the muddy water, their conversation rose and fell, marked by long silences. Several times Jamie tried to introduce the subject of multidimensional experiences. In each instance, Fran cut into her remarks, guiding their talk in other directions. She invested much energy in keeping their interaction light and flowing, devoid of significance as well as problems. Her mouth spewed polished trivia, the caviar of a well-bred woman.

In response to her mother's avoidance of intimate contact, Jamie stopped rehearsing her lines about breasts and
tumors. She dismissed her own visions. She would not tres-
pass into her mother's guarded world.

Fran hailed another taxi and they headed back to
Gramercy Park. "I almost forgot. I want to give you something for Rachel. Just a little doll. I thought it would be
nice." Noting Jamie's hesitancy, she ventured further.
"Please, come up. We can have a quick bite together."

Two sandwiches arrived with coffee and doughnuts.
Jamie found herself eating alone. Fran neglected the neatly
wrapped meal as she negotiated a lease with two parties on
different wires. A one-woman circus.

Jamie decided to give herself one more opportunity to
communicate with her mother. As soon as Fran disengaged
from the calls, Jamie began, "In the course Peter and I are
taking with Luke, we've—"

Fran interrupted her. With only marginal interest, she
asked, "Who's Luke again?"

Her question hit Jamie like a hammer punctuating the
distance between them. For more than two years Luke had
been a significant part of their lives. Jamie reminded her by
relating specific instances that she knew she had shared on
past occasions. Again the telephone rang, leaving her story
interrupted and untold. Finally, Jamie decided to leave, but
when the phone rang again, she whipped around, brushed
by her mother and picked up the receiver.

"Hello. Yes. No, Ms. Zercon is in conference. I'll have her
call you back. Yes. Thank you." She jotted notes on a pad.

"Young lady, what do you think you're doing?"

Ignoring the question, Jamie put all the phones on hold.
She marched over to the door and flipped the latch.

"I want five minutes, that's all! Five uninterrupted minutes," Jamie stated. "Please, let's sit down."

"I prefer to stand." Fran folded her arms in front of her
bosom.

"The visions I was telling you about . . ." Jamie began.

"Yes. Yes," Fran acknowledged as she lamented the critical telephone calls she might be missing.

"Mother, will you sit down?" Jamie insisted, pulling her into a chair. Her own aggressiveness frightened her, but she had to continue. "Do you have your breasts examined?"

"What?" her mother asked, dumbfounded.

"I know it sounds like an absurd question, but just answer me."

Begrudgingly indulging her daughter, she responded, "No . . . not really."

"I want you to have them checked. Actually, there's a technique for examining them yourself."

"And why, may I ask, do you want me to do this?"

"I don't know, I just want you to," Jamie pleaded.

Rising from her chair, Fran spat her words at Jamie. "If you're finished, I'd like to get back to work."

Upset and concerned, Jamie digressed. "I'm not doing this to upset you. I love you. I just want good things for you." Jamie could feel her strength fading. "Please don't be angry."

"I'm not angry," she hissed. Fran snapped the latch open. She turned and kissed her daughter on the cheek. Jamie hesitated. "Look, I don't want to harp on it, but would you check them? Get a mammogram," Jamie reiterated.

"No, young lady, absolutely not . . . until you tell me why."

Leading her mother back into the interior of the room, Jamie told her mother about her experience in the bathroom. Her mother listened, visibly agitated. Cutting Jamie short, Fran said, "Okay, okay! Are you finished?" Jamie eyed her mother sadly, searching for some hint of warmth or at least an opening through which to reach.

Without waiting for her reply, Fran continued her offensive, "If you're finished, I'd like you to leave."

"What do you have to lose by listening?"

"What do I have to lose?" Fran hissed. Her voice soared out of control as her face flushed. "You have the nerve to ask me that? You kids are all alike. Do you hate me that much? I know you still want to get back at me. All these years and you still haven't forgotten."

"No, Mother, don't." Jamie's voice broke.

"I did what was right for both of us. I just wasn't cut out to be a slave to a disabled kid. I didn't have any choice but to put you in that hospital." Fran paused, her hands trembling.

"I know. That's over. What I said has nothing to—"

Cutting in again, Fran exclaimed, "If you want to frighten me, you've succeeded. Congratulations! Now will you get out!"

Jamie spoke softly. "Mom, I'm not trying to hurt you. I want to help."

"I don't want to hear it. Do you understand me?" she shrieked. Marching back and forth in front of her desk, she growled to herself, "What kind of weird kid did I get cursed with?" Facing her daughter, she said, "Please go. I don't want you here any more."

Taking her by the arm, Fran led her to the door. "You think about what you just did. You need help. How dare you say I have breast . . . " Fran could not use the word.

Jamie had tapped the unthinkable.

The door slammed behind her as she walked to the elevator. Several people from the other offices lingered in their doorways. Fran's loud voice had penetrated the walls.

Jamie leaned against the railing beside the elevator. Tears cascaded down her cheeks, wetting her lips. An office boy watched from afar. He walked over to her timidly and offered a tissue. She refused, but he insisted she take it. Jamie thanked him as she boarded the elevator and watched the doors close.

At the corner of Third Avenue, she found an unoccupied phone booth. Jamie waited several minutes until her breathing became normal again. Finally, she dialed the studio.

"Maire, can I speak with Peter?"

"Jamie, he's not here. Do you want me to have him call you back?"

"No, that's okay. Thanks anyway." She hung up the receiver, left the booth and hailed a taxi. Jamie gave the driver Cleo's address.

24

I had wandered through the haunting dream scenario many times with Jamie. I walked the hillside with her. I touched the veil of fog that she described. I stared into the eyes of the lunging horse. But for the first time, Jamie's dream had come alive for me during my own sleep the night before; I had entered her world on top of the mountain. My preoccupation with her story had taken root, I assumed, which resulted in my having a similar dream.

As I sat in the privacy of my office, having just returned from a series of meetings, I searched each aspect of my own dream for insight. Stumbling through it, I forced myself to concentrate. The escapade played over and over and over again.

Jamie stood near the highest plateau. Strange linear rock formations soared into the sky. Little Rachel sat alone on the other side of the huge peak. Then the thunder of hoof-beats exploded in my ears. The hot breath of an enraged animal perfumed the air. Jamie froze, a spectator to the impending impact that threatened our child. Just before the force slammed into the baby, I awoke.

My dream differed from Jamie's in one very essential way. I never saw the horse or its blazing watch-eye. Despite the rush of power and implicit threat of violence, the charging animal was conspicuously absent. The tall grass and bushes quivered from the impact of an invisible force. Dirt and limestone shards flew into the air. I calculated the movement by the deep indentations crushed into the ground. The animal had danced before me, definite, yet invisible.

During an early morning conversation, Max had suggested that since I could not face the loss of my wife and child, I conveniently obliterated the horse, an apparent symbol of both those possibilities. I objected to Max's psychologizing my dream. I had wanted something more from our discussion, but I didn't know what.

I began to dissect the images again, but the buzzer interrupted me. Like a person awakened abruptly from a deep sleep, I reoriented myself to my office. I picked up the receiver.

"It's Jamie on line two," Maire informed me.

Pushing down on the blinking button, I began, "Hi, babes." No response. "Jamie—are you there?"

"Peter," she whispered into the phone, her voice filled with tension.

I pushed myself away from the drawing board and held the phone with both hands.

"I can't talk. Call you back in a minute," she concluded.

The line went dead. I moaned as if someone had sat on my chest. I glared at the receiver for several long seconds before putting it back on the hook. I stared at the phone, my only connection to Jamie. I waited. And waited. I dug a pencil into the soft mat covering the drawing board. Caught in the quicksand of phantoms and fantasies, I begged Jamie to call back.

Suddenly two phones rang at once. Without waiting for Maire to answer, I intercepted one call. The moment I heard a man's voice, I jumped to the second line.

"Jamie?" I asked urgently.

"I'm sorry," she answered.

"Christ, Jamie," I exclaimed, relieved to hear her voice. Afraid to ask but wanting to know, I threw my question at her. "Are you and Rachel okay?"

"Yes, yes. Peter, I'm really sorry I had to hang up. Right

now, I'm in Cleo's apartment. I stopped off on the way home from the city. I didn't want her to know I was calling you before. She's been drinking some wine, but that's not it. I can't put my finger on it, but she's acting very bizarre." I sighed my relief as I listened intently. "I mean . . . almost like she's out of her mind. I'm so scared for her."

"What's she doing?"

"Nothing. It's what she's saying. She keeps going on about Luke and Rachel and me. And Peter, her voice doesn't sound normal. When she laughs . . . God, it's like an old lady."

"I don't want to make light of it," I replied, "but Cleo does an awful lot of crazy things. Maybe it's just the wine."

"This is different," Jamie said, her voice cracking. "Please, I hate to ask you, but could you come over? I'm afraid to leave her . . . and somehow, I'm a little afraid to stay."

I glanced at the clock, nodding my head. "Okay. I have to make two quick calls and then I'll leave."

"Please come now, Peter. Right now. Please!"

"Okay, I'm on my way," I responded, the urgency in her voice propelling me from the office.

Once I was out of Manhattan, the traffic eased despite the heavy showers that pelted the city. In less than an hour, I drove into the circular driveway in front of Cleo's building. I trotted through the rain into the modern high rise. The elevator climbed twelve floors rapidly. I ran to the door, knocked several times, then pounded my fist. The door flew open. Jamie grabbed me by the arm.

"Thank God you're here!" Jamie blurted, hugging me quickly. Her rain-soaked hair lay flat against the sides of her face, accentuating her strong and graceful features.

"Where's Cleo?" I asked, searching the living room with expectant eyes. The wind whipped the curtains by an opened window. A small puddle formed on the floor below the window.

Without speaking, Jamie guided me toward the wall of glass. I felt the blood drain from my arms and legs. My mouth went dry. Visions of Cleo's body splattered on the cement terrace below bombarded me. As I drew closer to the window, I heard the eerie whinny of a horse. Jamie and I looked at each other momentarily.

I leaned over the windowsill to scan the network of paths crisscrossing below.

Cleo was standing alone in the rain, between this building and the structure facing it. She raised her fists, threatening an imaginary companion, then paced within a limited area as if caged. Several people, disturbed by the noise of her outbursts, yelled at her from their windows.

Seeing me at the window, Cleo shrieked, "You're stealing my friend away from me . . . you bastard!" Her voice reverberated throughout the canyon of glass and bricks.

Choosing my words carefully, I replied, "Cleo, please . . . come on up. We'll talk about it. Whatever you want. No one wants to steal your friend."

Laughter belched from her throat. She threw her right fist into the air. "Don't sucker me," she screamed. "I know your game."

For a moment, I experienced Cleo's anguish rippling through my own body. We had to bring her in. Just then, near the flooded playground, I spotted two dark forms. I gasped. Jamie wedged herself beside me and peered out the window.

I pointed as I spoke. "Look about one hundred feet directly behind Cleo, just to the right of the playground." She focused on the two figures. "Jamie," I continued, my voice thin and strained, "they look like nuns!" Meanwhile Cleo spun around and shouted at the robed women.

"We've got to get her out of there before she gets locked up," I said, shaking my head, confused by the presence of the nuns. I quickly exited the apartment.

Jamie called to her friend. "Cleo, we're coming down."

No response. She ran after me. "Peter, this whole thing seems so unreal. What does this all mean?" I didn't answer. I pulled my wife into the elevator.

She grabbed my jacket and began shaking me. "What's happening to all of us?"

I held her hands gently until she stopped pulling on my garment. "It's okay, Jamie. Cleo is hysterical. We'll help her. You'll see."

After racing out of the elevator into the corridor on the ground floor, we ran across the patterned carpet. I threw the rear lobby doors open. Instinctively, I braced myself for an assault. Jamie followed behind, her hair flying wildly in the wind. We saw Cleo at the same time.

As Jamie approached her, I searched for the nuns by the other building. I caught a glimpse of them walking in the opposite direction. Without thinking, I ran after them, sprinting across the wet cement terraces, jumping over small brick ledges and treading through beds of flowers flooded by the rain. My heart pumped frantically as I drew near the figures. I jumped directly into their path and blocked their way with my arms. Inspecting their faces, I sighed aloud. The "nuns" had been two building porters draped in long black ponchos. They had come out in an attempt to bring Cleo inside.

Trotting back to the women, I sensed the presence of an audience. I gazed upward into the silhouetted heads of residential voyeurs peeking out of open windows in both buildings. As I approached, Cleo threatened, "Stay away from me. I warn you, stay clear of me." I stopped about fifteen feet away from her.

Jamie pleaded, "It's me, Cleo. Come with me. Please trust me. I promise no one will hurt you."

Cleo's chest heaved. Holding her hands out in front of her as if to ward off a blow, she cried out, "I know you won't listen, Jamie, but it's him and his friend. They're strange; they're dangerous. You have to get away."

"Maybe you can help us, Cleo," I interjected. "I want what's best for Jamie and Rachel. If you can help us, please do it. We want to listen."

"Bullshit. You just want to gobble me up."

Jamie countered the accusation. "Cleo, I wouldn't let anything happen to you. C'mon up." Her fingers reached out to touch her hands. Cleo allowed the contact. Jamie gripped her firmly and began to lead her back to the building. Water dripped off them like an open faucet. The wind whistled. The downpour continued. Careful not to disturb their movement, I paced myself, staying twenty feet behind.

Without warning, Cleo ripped her hands free. She bolted from Jamie and raced across the lawn. I ran after her. She leaped over the terrace wall. When I caught up to her, she threw a wild punch, which missed its mark. I begged her to stop, but to no avail. I threw my arms around her as we reached a small hill. My forward thrust threw us both off balance. Our bodies careened into the air, then plunged into the wet grass, uprooting it. We came to rest in a slick of mud. Recovering from the fall, I tried to help Cleo. She did not resist my efforts. Her eyes became vacant. Very slowly, I helped her until she stood on her own feet.

"Cleo, I'm going to take your hand and we're going to go up to your apartment. Jamie is coming with us." Walking tall as if to demonstrate her inner power, she followed me. Even in her stupor, spitting out obscenities, she displayed a graceful, long-legged elegance. Jamie took her other hand as we entered the building.

Several people waiting for the elevator gawked at us, astonished by the spectacle of mud and rain-soaked clothing. Two women walked away quickly. The doors parted. We stepped inside. As the elevator moved noisily upward through the cavity, water, dripping from our clothes, accumulated in a large puddle on the elevator floor. No one spoke. Jamie and I avoided each other's eyes.

The doors opened on the eleventh floor. Cleo stood

rigid, refusing to get off. I held the doors as the buzzer began to ring.

"Come on, Cleo. Come on," Jamie said evenly. Finally releasing her body from its catatonic grip, Cleo walked stiffly through the corridor.

In the apartment, she stalked over to the red felt couch and seated herself.

"Cleo," Jamie advised, "let me put a towel under you."

"Jesus, Jamie," Cleo jumped. "That's a classic example of how your mind's turning to shit. I'm talking about life and death; you're still doing the housewife routine, worrying about the damn sofa." I knew the comment embarrassed Jamie. In an attempt to minimize the implications of Cleo's actions, she had focused purposely on something trivial.

"When will you believe me?" Cleo asked in a loud whisper. She clasped her hands between her thighs and began to rock.

"Believe what?" I questioned.

"That what you are doing is wrong, dead wrong. You're fucking with nature. Just like all the others, you're corrupting the balance. Only God can do that." Her words amazed Jamie, who in seven years had never once heard Cleo utter God's name in any context.

Doodling with the mud on her clothes, she continued. "You want to be God."

"No, Cleo," I answered. "I want to help you. Please let me help you, Cleo. Trust me."

Jumping from the couch, Cleo assumed the aggressive pose of an untrained boxer. "Well, then, you overgrown baboon, here's another piece of information to mix with your rattles and warm bottles. You're going to lose your wife or your daughter. Maybe both. There are many signs. Luke doesn't give. Luke takes." Enjoying her own commentary, Cleo smirked.

"That's not true," Jamie said softly. "He has helped, he—"

"No, no, no!" screeched Cleo, clasping her hands over

her ears. "I can't listen any more." She squeezed her eyelids tightly shut. "That's not Jamie talking. Jamie wouldn't say that; she couldn't!"

"Cleo, honey, it is me. I'm just not scared any more," she countered gently, but her friend ignored her.

"Why are you so upset, Cleo?" I asked gently.

She turned to me and smiled sadly. "Because I love Jamie. Because I care more than you do." Cleo put her hands out to me, in a reconciliatory gesture, then shook her head. She strutted over to one of the lamps and began to unscrew the shade. Jamie and I watched her, trying to anticipate her mood changes and movements. Removing the shade, she ripped the cord from the wall socket and raised the ceramic column over her head. Holding it like an ax, she inched toward me. Jamie jumped in front of me, putting her hand out to Cleo.

Tears filled her eyes as she pleaded with her friend. "Oh, Cleo, please give me the lamp. Please, I love you."

I eased Jamie to the side. As I faced Cleo, I spoke in the softest voice possible. "Cleo, when we get confused and scared, we all want to strike out. I've felt that way many times. Maybe . . ." Snapping my arm, I pushed my wife out of range and ducked as Cleo swung the lamp like a bat. Crashing into the wall, it shattered into a hundred pieces, leaving a jagged rupture in the plasterboard partition.

Springing back to a full stance, I faced her again. Dried mud flaked off her hair. Cleo laughed. She moved methodically to the duplicate lamp on the opposite side of the couch and began to unscrew the shade. I moved behind her quickly.

"Cleo, you want us to stop with Luke? Okay, let's discuss it," I said. She continued to manipulate the cloth lampshade.

"Cleo, if you take the shade off, I'm going to have to hold you," I warned. "If you leave it alone, I'll walk away."

"Okay," Cleo agreed, moving casually away from the

couch. When I turned as promised, I encountered a frightened expression on Jamie's face. Swiveling, I lunged toward Cleo, who had already seized the lamp like a club. We both fell to the floor. Her weapon split apart on the edge of the table. Biting and punching, Cleo twisted unpredictably. Surprised by her strength and snakelike movement, I scrambled for her wrists. Finally, I pinned her.

Cleo opened her eyes wide, looking not unlike Luke in one of his trances. Her throat gurgled as if she were about to vomit. Sensitive to her distaste for men, I wanted to remove myself as quickly as possible. When I freed her hand, however, she slammed her fist into my head. I grabbed her wrist again. She spat in my face. For several minutes, she struggled furiously under my grip.

Hissing her message into my face, Cleo yelled, "Luke wants to dominate us, take us over. He's begun with you." She laughed wildly. "And then, you dumb fuck, he'll get his claws into your wife and, finally into your child." Her tongue wagged loosely, as if disconnected. She turned to Jamie, sobbing again. "Please, Jamie, don't let him do this to me."

Jamie knelt beside her friend. "Cleo, Peter doesn't want to do this. We don't know what else to do. Please, just relax and he'll let you go."

I felt the tension leave her muscles. Her clenched teeth parted as the strain on her face eased. Jamie stroked her hair. Very slowly I began to release my grip. Cleo remained passive. After pulling myself to my feet, I grabbed a pillow off the couch and put it under her head.

"She's beginning to really relax." Jamie sighed, stroking her hair. "What are we going to do?"

"Let's try to get her composed and then we'll decide. I just hate to have some doctor come and arbitrarily give her a shot. Maybe she'll just pass through it. I hope so for her sake."

Cleo's mouth moved in an infantile sucking motion.

Jamie stayed by her side, stroking her forehead.

"No one's going to hurt you . . . or me. And I'll be here as long as you want me to. You won't be alone." She began to hum a lullaby that both she and Cleo had sung to Rachel. Jamie kissed her friend and at that moment remembered Mary-O kissing her.

Removing my mud-caked jacket, I walked into the kitchen to wash my face, then ran cold water over my wrists. When I heard a rumble in the living room, I darted back quickly. Cleo, now on her feet, spoke in a shrill voice. "I'm fine now, folks. If you're finished, I'd like to go."

"Go where?" I asked innocently.

Whipping her head around in anger, she replied, "Go to the goddamn bathroom."

"Sure, Cleo," Jamie answered. "We'll wait for you." Strutting indignantly down the hall, Cleo swaggered comically. Jamie accompanied her. When she realized she was being followed, Cleo lurched forward, charging down the hall into the bathroom. With a slam, she locked the door.

We listened at the door. The water began to run in the sink. "Cleo, do you need any help?" Jamie asked, soliciting an answer . . . any answer.

Cleo started to cackle. "I know what kind of help he gives, dearie. The hard kind that gets jammed between your legs." The toilet flushed. "I'll never let old watch-eye get me. He almost did it when I saw him."

"What?" I exclaimed to Jamie, who shrugged her shoulders, bewildered.

"Cleo, did you meet Luke?" I asked. I listened carefully, but Cleo did not answer my question. How could I differentiate between her hysterics and events that had really occurred?

She rambled on about Luke's blue eye and the strange gestures he made when he talked. I knew Jamie had described him to her many times; yet the accuracy with which she described the man and his mannerisms was astounding.

Unexpectedly, I noted a definite change in the quality of her voice. I listened carefully to her words, all of which seemed to be filtered through a suppressed groan. My mind bounced to one specific image.

"Move away, Jame." I leaned my back against the opposite wall. Bracing myself in a fashion I had once observed in a movie, I lifted my leg to the height of my waist and slammed it full force into the door. The doorjamb cracked apart from the impact. Within, a startled Cleo gaped at us angrily; one arm dripped with blood. She held a razor blade to the other wrist. She responded to the intrusion by striking out against me with the blade, catching me superficially on my shoulder as I grabbed her wrist and disarmed her. Again I brought her down to the floor.

Jamie lifted her arm. "Thank God she missed the artery," she sighed as she made a tourniquet with a towel.

"Jamie," I panted, "I don't know what to do next."

The doorbell rang. Jamie and I shuddered. Composing myself, I whispered, "Don't answer it." The bell rang a second and third time. Suddenly Cleo screamed at the top of her lungs. Fists banged on the door. A voice announced the presence of the police. Jamie scrambled to open it.

Two policemen pushed their way into the entrance hall. "What's going on here?" one asked. He did not wait for an answer. "We received numerous calls about a woman screaming and acting crazy in the courtyard. The lady just across the hall identified her as"—he paused and consulted his little black pad—"Cleo Lawrence. Are you Cleo Lawrence?"

"No, I'm not. Cleo is my friend and she's had a bit too much to drink. Everything's under control." Jamie attempted to ease them out the door. The taller officer refused to move.

"I'm sorry, lady," he grinned, "but we'll have to see Miss

Lawrence in order to straighten this out." A small portable walkie-talkie barked from his belt. The polished wood handle of his gun poked conspicuously through his coat.

"It's impossible. She's in bed."

"Who are you?" the other policeman asked.

"I told you before . . . I'm her friend."

"What's your name?" he persisted, his voice stern and irritated.

"Jamie. Jamie Halsted. Is that it, sir? Do you have enough?" Jamie asked.

"No, ma'am, I'm afraid not. We either have to speak to the lady who lives in this apartment or a relative . . . and since you're neither, then . . . "

Jamie interrupted him. "Listen, she's alone in New York. Her family lives in Ohio. Please. Everything is okay now."

At that point, a scream burst from the hallway. Cleo shrieked, forcing me to release her rather than attempt to explain my holding her pinned to the floor.

Running into the living room, she gaped angrily at the policemen. Her shirt had stiffened under the dried mud. The bloodstained tourniquet had begun to unravel. "Get the fuck out of here!" she screamed. The policemen looked annoyed. Jamie moved in front of her friend, not quite sure whom she protected. I entered from the side hall, my clothes also stained brown and red. I had covered the cut on my shoulder with a hand towel.

"Officer," I began, not fully cognizant of the absurd picture I presented. "This lady has been under great strain." Sensitive to their eyes on her wrist, I added, "She even tried to hurt herself. We appreciate your response and concern. I don't think you'd want to see her further humiliated. I think we can handle it from here." My stomach knotted. I knew if she made just one more insulting remark, we would completely lose control over the situation.

Once again, Cleo leveled her shotgun mouth at the police. "Yes, you assholes, we can handle it from here."

"I'm sorry, but at this point we have to make out a report. I also think we should call an ambulance and make sure she's okay. That's a pretty nasty cut on her wrist."

"Call an ambulance?" Cleo said, shocked. "How about asking me?"

"Lady," the taller officer began, his tone tinged with anger. "We think you need a doctor. It's for your own good."

"Fuck you, you creep. How the hell would you know what's for my own good?" she retorted. Jamie marveled at her vulgarity as well as her apparent coherence. Cleo turned away.

One officer asked for the location of a telephone. The other pulled a pad from his back pocket as he moved farther into the apartment. Cleo jumped from behind Jamie and pounced on the man, throwing wild punches. She connected with a right hook to his head. I grabbed her arm, separating her from this hapless victim. The other cop pushed me aside.

"Okay, lady, take it easy," he shouted angrily as he wrestled with her.

"You'd better cooperate, miss. We don't want to hurt you." The officer held her wrists. Cleo tried to kick him, narrowly missing his crotch. Finally, he managed to slam a set of handcuffs on her. Jamie began to cry.

"Hey," I barked, "you didn't have to do that."

"Listen, mister, we'll be the judges of what to do," the cop scolded. "There is something very wrong with this lady. What we did is for everyone's good, including hers." He returned to the telephone in the kitchen, shaking his head.

Cleo started to whimper. Then she stopped, laughed and spat at the surrounding people. I walked her into the living room. One policeman followed. They shuffled through the broken ceramic pieces spread over the furniture and floor. Jamie sat next to her, clasping her hand.

I doubled back into the kitchen to confront the other officer. "Who did you call?"

"Bellevue Psychiatric, but they're jammed now. So they're sending an ambulance from St. Paul's." Noting my grimace, he said with unexpected kindness, "Don't worry, mister. We've been through this a thousand times. She'll be okay."

Two more policemen entered the apartment.

"I'll need identification from everyone," one of the officers declared. "And a full statement. I'll call this in to my supervisor. We might require you and the other lady to come down to the station."

The man's pen wiggled across the pages as I rattled off the requested information. Words fell from my mouth lifelessly. The pathetic figure of Cleo captured and bound distracted me from the task.

Suddenly, the room came alive with the arrival of three more people, obviously the ambulance crew. After consulting with the officer in charge, one of the paramedics knelt beside Cleo. "I'm going to give you an injection to relax you," he said, motioning to have the handcuffs removed.

Panic flooded Cleo's system. Her aversion to medication almost matched the intensity of her aversion to men. Sensing an impending confrontation, I moved toward them just as Cleo jumped off her chair onto the couch.

"I want you all out of here this minute," she cried. "Do you hear me? This is my house . . . you bastards are polluting it!"

"C'mon, lady," one policeman shouted at her. "Get down off the couch; we're just trying to help you."

Jamie interrupted. "May I talk with her?"

The officer shook his head, declining her request. The paramedics interceded. "We'll handle it, ma'am."

The three emergency medical technicians, their uniforms expertly pressed, surrounded Cleo. One of them removed a white garment from a black satchel he had been carrying. The dangling straps identified it.

"Wait!" I said. I placed myself in front of her, protecting her from the oncoming assault. "Let me talk to her."

"Listen, pal, unless you want to be taken in for obstructing a police officer in his duty, I suggest you move away."

Pushing the cop almost to the edge of his patience, I asked again, "Just give me two minutes." The officer finally acquiesced. I faced Cleo, who looked at me blankly. "They only want to help you. Please, Cleo, sit down."

At that moment, screaming in desperation, she leaped off the side of the couch. Two medics tackled her while a third administered an injection into her shoulder. She squirmed for a few seconds; then her body went limp. Her words became garbled. The ambulance attendants put her quickly into the restraining garment, tying her arms criss-crossed in front of her chest. They fastened the cords dangling from the ends of the sleeves to cords behind her back.

Swooning from the effects of the drug, Cleo lifted herself laboriously to her feet. Dumping words out of her mouth half-formed, she stumbled across the room toward the door. One of the officers intercepted her limping form. Reacting to the harshness of his interference, she bolted in the opposite direction, colliding with one of the medics. Trapped between them, Cleo fell to her knees and sobbed. Jamie hugged her and tried desperately to comfort her while tears flooded her own eyes.

The other two medics, who had left the room, returned with a stretcher. They loaded Cleo onto the portable bed with professional indifference. They strapped her into it, looping the nylon belts around metal hooks.

Cleo glared at me. "Luke can't silence me. I know. You tell him I know." As they carted her down the hall, she babbled something about Rachel and the blue watch-eye. At the elevator, she cursed her captors. Then her voice trailed

off in heavy sobbing. "God help . . . please. Help me. Someone please help me!"

Jamie stroked her arm as they carried her into the elevator. "I'm going with her in the ambulance," she told me.

"Sure. I'll close up the apartment and meet you at the
hospital." The elevator closed its door rudely, muffling my
last words.

25

The scars of the battle littered the apartment—the remnants of anger and anguish. The waterlogged curtains stuck to the wall. Mud stained the red couch. The debris of the broken lamps were sprinkled over the room. A light rain sprayed the floor as the wind whistled through the opened windows. "Luke can't silence me. I know. You tell him I know." Cleo's words echoed in my ears despite her absence. I brushed the mud off the felt pillow, trying to restore some order to the living room. Bending down, I winced, suddenly aware of the burning slash across my shoulder. I stood up and remained absolutely still for a few moments; the pain eased. As I shut the window, I heard Cleo's voice reverberate in my head again. "You tell him I know." I picked up a broken ashtray. "You're corrupting the balance. Only God can do that." I could not escape her commentary, nor did I try. "You're going to lose your wife or your daughter, maybe both. There are many signs."

Drifting into the kitchen, I noticed a small snapshot. A fourteen-year-old Cleo in pigtails beside an old red tractor. With baggy pants gathered at the waist and boots caked with mud, she stood tall and flashed a proud, carefree smile for the camera. I could not explain it to myself, but this night I had grown to love her.

Mechanically, I continued to clean up more of the debris, sweeping up the broken glass, then laboring to remove jagged splinters from the chairs and couch. The blood that had spotted the bathroom sink and tile floor washed away easily, but the stubborn red blotches on the wallpaper would not wash away. Exhausted, I lifted my jacket from the floor and stared at the crater in the living-room wall. "You tell him I know." Cleo's words accompanied me as I left the apartment for the hospital.

In the corridor, waiting for the elevator, I had the most peculiar impression. I kept visualizing a spoked wheel rolling down the hallway. Despite its substantial speed, it never reached me. I rubbed my eyes, fighting my apparently overactive imagination. When I looked again, the wheel was gone. Then I thought of the photograph of Cleo near the ancient tractor. Suddenly, I remembered some old farm equipment in the background. That had to be it, I concluded, recognizing the effects of a traumatic afternoon. Yet when the doors of the elevator opened, I checked the corridor one last time before leaving.

St. Paul's had been a parish rectory before the turn of the century. The original three-story building, austere and Gothic with a chiseled limestone facing, had been set back on a park-like acre bordering the East River. The construction of a major highway, the decline of the bordering neighborhood and a fire that left the church, a block away, partially destroyed, persuaded local parishioners to abandon the property and rebuild farther uptown.

For twenty years, the rectory had remained empty, its ornate shutters fallen to the ground and its pipes broken and its windows shattered by local vandals. Then the Sisters of Mercy established a residence for severely retarded and mentally disabled adults at St. Paul's, refurbishing the structure.

In the 1930s its reputation as a humane haven for an unwanted segment of the community's population resulted in a city-sponsored building program. A sprawling sixteen-story hospital, which developed the open land between the rectory and the river, was placed under the combined administration of the Sisters of Mercy and New York's Joint Hospital Agency. Successive administrations and the encroaching dominance of the medical services resulted in the sisters' unpublicized retreat back into the old parish building, where they could still maintain the gentle ways that had brought St. Paul's into the public eye originally. Yet the hospital complex, which surrounded them, offered the standard array of sanctioned medical tactics for its psychiatric patients—drugs, electric shock, isolation rooms and the like. In 1962 St. Paul's, with the exception of what had become known as the Sisters of Mercy rectory unit, became an overflow facility for the city's vast network of public hospitals. Cleo had been admitted to St. Paul's as part of a Wednesday night overflow.

Why did they paint everything gray? I asked myself as I entered the elevator. Three nurses, a nun, a woman in a green uniform wheeling a tray of drugs and an orderly squeezed into the steel cubicle before the doors closed abruptly.

I made my escape from the elevator on the seventh floor. My eyes scanned the anonymous gray partitions that beckoned me to follow the black arrows leading down a dimly lighted corridor. At first I hesitated, thinking of the little girl in pigtails beside the tractor. But then my feet shuffled forward as if drawn by the graphic directions stenciled on the walls. As I turned left and entered a vast rectangular chamber flooded with fluorescent lights, I saw Jamie immediately, her disheveled form leaning against one wall. We embraced, lingering for several minutes while rocking back and forth in each other's arms. We held hands without speaking, even after seating ourselves on a hardwood bench. I stared at the thick metal doors at the end of another corridor. Each one contained a small window in which heavy wire mesh had been sandwiched between thick plates of glass.

"Is she in there?" I indicated with my head.

Jamie's body still trembled, unable to relax in surroundings that were all too familiar. "They have her in an intake unit. They said I can't see her any more today." She sighed. "Peter, you're not going to believe this, but they can keep her here for thirty days."

"Why?"

"I don't understand exactly . . . something about it being a court matter, since the police delivered her here. They listed her as an attempted suicide."

I sighed, gaping at the unforgiving steel doors that faced us. "Jamie, I wish there were more we could do for her tonight, but there isn't." She winced at my comment. "Cleo's a survivor," I declared in an attempt to reassure my wife as well as myself.

"First thing in the morning, I'll get Bob Seldon on it. I'm sure one of his lawyers can handle this." I paused. "Jame, what about her parents?"

"Been taken care of. I called Cleo's mother in Ohio. The poor lady sounded like she was going to have a nervous breakdown." She sighed. "Anyway, both her parents will fly in tomorrow morning."

"Do you want to go now?"

Jamie began to cry. "How can . . . how can we just—just leave her?" She stood up slowly and leaned against the wall. I knew she had to be thinking about her own incarceration as a child when her screams, like Cleo's, went unanswered. "She was so scared when they brought her in," Jamie said. "God, if she could have just seen Luke with Rachel and talked to him, none of this would have happened." She grabbed my sleeve. "One of the medics, well, he—he said something in her must have snapped. He kept calling it a—a psychotic episode. But why, Peter? Why is this happening all around us?"

I looked at her, unable to answer. I could legitimately have called her friend unstable, chronically hostile, even hallucinatory—certainly, by even minimal standards, a

good candidate for a nervous breakdown. An understand-
able conclusion. Sensible. A neat package. And yet Cleo's
references to Luke still haunted me, as if her words had a
life of their own. I knew I no longer fully trusted him, a fact
that I found exceedingly difficult to admit.

26

The Arizona loomed like a fortress along Riverside Drive. Three pointed towers protected its imaginary flanks. When refurbished in the mid-thirties, art deco doors, window-stones and trim had been blended curiously into a Gothic motif. High-relief metal flourishes greeted visitors at the main entrance.

Although some dismissed the building as garish and antiquated, I loved its grotesque charm and individuality, the perfect place for Max to reside.

A bulletin board listed, in bronze lettering, all of the professional tenants in the building. Several doctors, psychologists, a dentist and a chiropractor displayed their names with appropriate symbols. The most incongruous listing presented: MAX R. SORENSON, PERSON. He lived on the seventeenth floor in one of four apartments that contained outdoor terraces formed from the recessed ledges of the building.

I rang the buzzer several times before I heard footsteps approaching. I knew immediately that they were not Max's manly thuds. The door opened very slowly, revealing the small but shapely figure of Deedee.

"Well, well . . . you've arrived," she said, feigning a light Southern accent and wiggling suggestively. Barricading the two-inch opening with her body, she teased me with a mocking grin.

"Am I going to be invited in," I countered, "or have you taken possession of Max's apartment?"

"My, my . . . am I being rude? Please come in." Deedee put her arms around me and kissed me directly on the lips while assaulting my thigh with a pelvic thrust. I disengaged immediately, trying to neutralize my displeasure with her tactics.

"A little shy?" she kidded, wetting her lips but knowing not to push further.

"Isn't Max here?"

"No, honey," she replied, pausing for effect. "Don't look so worried. He just ran downstairs to get you some food."

The interior of the apartment matched the ambiance of the building. Brown walls, perpetually in shadow, embraced a large decorative fireplace housing at least a year's accumulation of ashes. Seedy furniture, old antiques and a small library of books thrown together haphazardly. Two discount tickets to an all-Beethoven evening at Carnegie Hall were taped to the telephone. Max's abode . . . neither elegant nor sophisticated, but like autumn, somehow warm, cultured and involving.

"Would you like some tea?" Deedee offered.

I nodded my head. "Yes, I'd love a cup. Thanks." As I turned to leave the room, I added, "Do you serve on the terrace?"

"For you, Peter, a-n-y-t-h-i-n-g. You do understand, don't you? Anything." She grinned.

Shaking my head like an indulgent parent, I left the room through the glass doors leading through the garden solarium and onto the terrace. The Hudson River mirrored the lights from the Jersey shore. Apartment buildings housing thousands of people glowed like illuminated beehives atop the Palisades cliffs.

Deedee joined me, bowing slightly as she offered the cup of tea. She had unbuttoned the top of her blouse and her staged act of humility caused her breasts to be exposed. Trying to ignore her rather rambunctious display, I tipped my head quickly, then turned to face the river. Deedee took my hand, but I withdrew it.

"You know," I said, "underneath all your games, you're a very special person. You don't have to come on to me or the others all the time."

Despite the softness of my voice, Deedee recoiled. "You think you're so smart, don't you?" She began to button her blouse. "I've seen you with your little pad and pencil . . . Jamie talks about it all the time. You like to use pictures to relate to the world, so they call you an artist. And I like to use my body, so they call me something else. Only it isn't the same, is it? Just because we talk in different languages, you're distinguished . . . and I'm dirt!" She turned to leave the terrace.

I touched her arm. "Wait. I never meant that. I . . ." The words disappeared. I smiled, almost to protect her from my own judgments. "I don't pretend to understand and I'm sorry."

Deedee grinned like a little girl and kissed me lightly on the cheek. "How's that?" she asked.

"Better." I laughed.

"Good," she continued, turning and facing the river, "but you have to understand; that may be on your terms, but it's not on mine. You're very, very attractive . . . and so is Jamie."

I stared at her.

Deedee smiled at my reaction. "People are people, silly boy," she added. "Luke says we're all the same; we share the same spirit. So if he doesn't differentiate between a man and a woman, a saint and a sinner, why should I?"

She shrugged her shoulders and smiled awkwardly, her face resisting the sincerity of her expression. Suddenly she seemed genuinely attractive.

"You see that war memorial," she said, pointing north, "well, believe it or not, when I used to play hooky from school, I'd go there and watch the boats along the river." Her eyes glowed. "And you know what?" she said, pushing her finger into my shoulder. "On that memorial, carved in the center of those rectangular pillars, are the names of Civil War generals and battles. To keep myself from getting bored, I memorized them. And that was at least ten years ago."

I smiled warmly at Deedee, more receptive to her in these moments than at any previous time.

She turned to me like a schoolgirl. "You want to hear some of the names?"

"Sure."

"Well, here goes," Deedee warned, touching her fingers to her teeth. "Mind you, I'm not going to tell you all the names or even the famous ones, just the ones I liked." She giggled. "Okay. Cedar Creek. Kennesaw Mountain. Chickamauga. Cold Harbor. Five Forks." Deedee paused, delighted with her recall. "Here's more. Bull Run. Fair Oaks. Roanoke Island. Aren't they beautiful names?"

Loud clapping signaled Max's return. He was carrying two small waxed paper bags. "Very good," he commented, applauding and embracing Deedee. Then he wrapped me in an enthusiastic bear hug. "Hey, ol' buddy, I'm glad you're here. In your honor, I have purchased some of the finest sushi in the city."

"Fantastic," I replied.

Max radiated affection, always remembering the significant events as well as the little delights in everyone's life. "Dee, do you want some too?" he asked.

"No. No way," she said. "You two cannibals just go ahead and enjoy yourselves. I prefer my food cooked. Besides, I have to meet Luke downtown."

"Suit yourself . . . be deprived," he joked, kissing her on the nose. To me he proclaimed, "The chef requires only ten minutes!"

After Max disappeared, Deedee poured herself some juice and said casually, "Max is going to move in with us at Luke's loft."

"What?" I exclaimed, visibly shocked.

"I thought you'd get a charge out of that. Don't judge him either; only God can do that . . . and God doesn't. Besides, he'll be well taken care of." She winked. "Max might tell you it isn't true, but don't believe what he says."

I stared directly into her eyes. "Congratulations."

She smiled at me seductively while massaging the rim of her glass. "For what?" she asked, now playing the game her way.

"I guess Max represents another notch in your . . . futon?"

"Very fanciful, Peter," she countered. "Do I detect a note of jealousy?" she questioned, enjoying the conversation thoroughly. I didn't answer. "No, perhaps *jealousy* is not quite the right word," she continued. "I think you're being overprotective of a single, middle-aged man. Don't underestimate him, or me." My continued silence annoyed her. "Okay, big boy. You're one of the few holdouts. One day, I'll be coming for you." She burst into laughter, amused with her pun.

After Deedee left, Max and I squatted at the redwood table. Using chopsticks, we consumed the food in silence. As we completed our exotic snack, I began, "Are you moving in with her at Luke's?"

"No. Of course not."

I eyed my friend. I wanted to believe him, but Deedee's words stayed with me. Would Max lie?

"You're sure now," I pressed.

"Well, almost sure," he admitted. "That's one of the things she's been lobbying for, but I'm fine here. Besides, I'm too old and too conservative for group living . . . I think."

When I pushed my plate to the side, I noticed what I would have surmised as unthinkable in my friend's apartment—an artificial flower. I picked up the plastic red rose and twirled it in front of Max. Both of us stared at it without saying a word. Finally I said, "Definitely out of - character."

Max grinned. He cleared his throat self-consciously before responding. "Believe it or not, that's a gift from a very attractive young lady."

"Ah," I sighed, putting the rose back on the table with exaggerated care. "Think we should water it?"

Max shook his head. I concurred, smiling absentmindedly as I focused on another issue. "Is this something new with Deedee?"

"New for me." Max wiped the sauce neatly from his mustache. "But she's been after me for a long time now." He smiled happily. "Why do you ask?"

"Why not?" I countered.

"Listen," he said, putting his arm over my shoulder, "as much as you try to make all these questions sound casual and neutral and all that, I hear other stuff in there."

"It's very funny how things work out. I guess I would never have figured you with Deedee—not that I'm judging either of you. She does her thing and…"

"Hey," Max interrupted. "I'm not exactly a blind school kid. Nor am I making anything more of this than it is. I have fun with her; she's a delight. You have to live all you can while you're alive. Who knows what's around the corner?"

"If I didn't know you better, I'd say that sounds pretty cycnical," I observed.

"Not cynical, Peter—realistic."

"Well, anyway, the whole thing strikes me as strange."

"What do you mean 'strange?'" asked Max.

"I don't know exactly. Deedee's like a lure on a fishing line . . . sucking everyone in sexually. Every time someone gets involved with Deedee, they become more . . ." I searched for the right word, ". . . more subservient to the group."

Max started to laugh. "You build quite a case, don't you?

I can't believe you're so skeptical . . . of Luke. What happened?"

"Nothing," I replied. I couldn't admit to myself, any more than to Max, that the pedestal I had built beneath Luke had begun to crumble.

"Oh, I almost forgot. Follow me, my friend," Max said, changing the subject. "I want you to have my first watercress of the season, grown with fresh mountain spring water." Like a proud papa, he handed several sprigs to me, which I downed promptly. "Good. And try some of my bok choy." His eyes glazed over nostalgically. "You know, the kids always used to like my bok choy." The deep crow's-feet by his eyes crinkled almost painfully.

"Anything doing with them?" I asked.

"Well," he began, exhaling noisily, "I called Julie last week. It was her nineteenth birthday, but she wasn't home. Asked Mona to have her call me back collect." He stared into space for a second. "But she never did."

"Maybe she didn't get the message," I countered. Max smiled weakly. "Hey, Julie doesn't really know you," I said. "Neither does Kathy. If you could just get them to stay here for a while, I think everything would change."

"Maybe it's not meant to happen in this lifetime."

"Well, whatever happens in this lifetime, Jamie and I and Rachel will always be your family."

"I know, Peter. Thanks."

As we returned to the living room, I said, "You know, something happened the other day which keeps coming back to me. It's silly, but . . ."

"But what?"

"I, um, had this, uh, I don't know what to call it. Not a vision, not something concrete—just a thought, almost like a fantasy or a daydream with pictures. Do you know what I mean?"

Max eyed me curiously. "Don't tell me anything specific, just tell me the general subject area of your 'daydream.'"

"I don't want to make this into a game of charades."

"C'mon, humor me," Max countered.

"Okay. Something to do with transportation."

Max's eyes opened wide.

"What's the matter?" I asked.

He smiled, putting his hand in the air and simulating Houdini as he touched two fingers to his forehead and began. "A wheel, turning yet standing still. Like one of those old wagon wheels. Wood spokes, wood rimmed with a metal covering— right out of an old western."

I gaped at him, excited and uncomfortable. "That's exactly what I saw. Exactly."

"Did you figure out what it means?" Max asked casually.

"No. But I don't understand. Did you have the same . . . impression?"

"I guess so," he said quietly. "There have been cases of spouses, parents and children, even friends, transferring thoughts to each other. You know, like the sort of mental telepathy they're experimenting with at Duke and the University of Chicago. Perhaps, ol' buddy, I'm picking up your channel."

"Maybe it's your TV set, Max, not mine."

He nodded, affirming the possibility. Max stood up and walked to the window. The lights of the George Washington Bridge flickered in the distance. As he stared at them, his face tensed. "I was going to talk to both you and Jamie together. But, maybe, I shouldn't wait?"

"Wait for what?" I asked.

"I don't know. When I met Deedee yesterday," he began, cocking his head backward and looking at the ceiling, "I picked her up from Luke's loft. I kept thinking about Cleo, especially her babbling about seeing Luke. Well, ol' buddy, I asked him."

"You wonderful son of a gun. Always pitching."

Max put his hand on my shoulder. "I want to tell you, Luke said he *did* see Cleo."

My mouth fell open.

"Wait," Max insisted. "I know what you're thinking. But Deedee was there at the time. Apparently Cleo phoned Luke. She asked for a meeting, using her friendship with you and Jamie as her calling card. He agreed to see her." Max stopped, twirled his mustache and made a clicking sound with his mouth. "They met for about an hour. As described to me, nothing very dramatic occurred . . . well, at least almost nothing."

"What do you mean?" I pressed.

"According to Deedee, both she and Rudy left the room," Max replied. "When they returned, Luke and Cleo sat on the floor together cross-legged, facing each other. Luke did his thing, that funny smile . . . you know. She said Cleo began to tremble. Luke put his hands out to her. In response, she screamed. Then, without explanation, Cleo ran out of the building."

"That explains why Cleo's descriptions were so accurate, but what the hell scared her so much?"

"Hey, the lady is pretty unstable," Max countered. "Anything could have set her off—his weird smile, his blue eye. If she came to see him already uptight, it wouldn't take much."

"I'd like to believe that, I really would." I thought of how frightened Jamie might be if she knew about Cleo's visit. Despite my ambivalence about her relationship with Luke, I knew I couldn't tell her. Max laughed, drawing me back into the conversation. "Are you saying you don't feel good about my explanation?"

"I'm . . . reserving judgment," I answered evasively. Consulting my watch, I said, "I really have to leave. Just one last question—why do you think so many people find Luke frightening?"

"People get frightened when they don't understand something—or someone." His voice dropped. "Listen, plenty of people threw rocks at Christ."

The reference surprised me. What the hell was Max implying?

We walked toward the door in silence. Passing his desk, I noticed several books on horses. One title, *The History of Ancient Breeds,* caught my eye. "A new hobby?" I asked, pointing to the books.

"Sort of," Max replied.

"Well," I sighed, standing in the doorway. "Enjoy Deedee, really, but be careful."

"Yes, Father," Max countered with a grin.

I hugged my friend and left.

27

The music of the carousel permeated the air. Behind the green wooden benches, two boys tossed a football. A white-haired lady, supporting herself with a cane, hobbled along the path. A teen-ager negotiated a turn on his skateboard and whizzed by the older woman.

This human zoo provided Jamie with an endless smorgasbord of people to watch. But then the passing of a Franciscan monk diverted her attention. His smile reminded her of Luke. More and more things in her life seemed to have his imprint on them. She stared at the carousel with its dancing horses gliding around and around. Her mother had insisted on this meeting.

The well-dressed woman strutted toward her from a distance. Jamie spotted her immediately. Fran's arms hung stiffly at her sides rather than swinging with the cadence of her legs. Her head seemed riveted to her shoulders in a military posture. Jamie hardened herself to what she imagined might be another assault, remembering her last encounter with her mother at this exact location. Fran smiled weakly as she approached, her hand lifted to shield her reddened eyes. The exposed vulnerability surprised Jamie. She had never seen her mother cry since that infamous car ride to the hospital. The intimacy touched her, yet she maintained her guard.

Fran kissed her in the usual curt manner. Her lips quivered as she fumbled through her pocketbook. Her hands moved spastically. Without speaking, she pivoted away from her daughter and walked toward the ticket booth.

After buying two tickets, Fran approached her daughter, the tension in her face growing more pronounced. One side of her mouth curled in a smile, but the other side, which could not let go, stiffened as if paralyzed. Holding up the tickets like a lottery prize, she spoke in a husky, strained voice. "This time, Jamie, would you join me?"

Jamie bowed her head affirmatively, fighting back the tears that threatened to flood her eyes. Fran led the way.

Walking a few feet apart, the two women entered the giant gazebo and waited for the circular platform to stop spinning. Jamie stared ahead, unable to look at her mother. The merry-go-round creaked to a halt. Fran climbed awkwardly onto one wooden statue and sat sidesaddle; Jamie swung atop its neighbor.

A Viennese waltz issued from the antique band-organ. A tottering attendant, chewing on the end of an unlit cigar, leaned on a giant lever. The carousel began to move. Fran gazed off at an indeterminate point, avoiding eye contact with her daughter. Jamie stared at the stranger sitting beside her.

Four minutes later, the old man pulled the lever toward his chest. The carousel lost its momentum as the motor disengaged. Ever so slowly, it glided to a halt. Fran dismounted quickly and left the enclosure. Jamie closed her eyes for a moment, biting her bottom lip. She slid agilely off the wooden saddle.

She joined Fran on the path. They walked together along the cracked black pavement. Their gait echoed the underlying tension.

The clasp of Fran's pocketbook snapped open. Trembling fingers removed an initialed silk handkerchief. Dabbing her eyes, the older woman cleared her throat noisily. Her index finger rubbed against her thumb.

"This is all very new to me," Fran said, her voice soft, yet strained with years of harshness. "I wanted to see you to apologize. But there's so much more." Shaking her head and breathing heavily, she paused. "Why it took this to make me . . ." Her voice broke. Fran fought to deliver her soliloquy as planned.

"You don't have to," Jamie volunteered.

"No, I do have to. Don't make it easy for me. You've been doing that all your life."

The awkward silence returned. They hiked up a small incline, assuming an easy pace. As Fran regained her equilibrium, she looked into Jamie's eyes. "First, and I guess you know what I'm going to say . . . I have breast cancer."

Jamie gasped. A shudder of fear whipped through her body. Turning away, she rolled her eyes toward the sky.

"But I thought . . ." Fran stopped. Confused by her daughter's reaction, she said, "Last week, when you told me to have a breast examination, somewhere, deep inside, I believed you knew what I certainly didn't want to hear."

"It's so . . . so frightening sometimes," Jamie offered. "I usually have hollow dreams. I never really know whether what I feel or think or see is true or not. Oh, God, Mother, I'm so sorry."

"Well, don't be," Fran snapped. "It's not like you had anything to do with it!" For an instant, a fraction of a second, she questioned her own assumption, as did Jamie. Their eyes met. Quickly, both women looked away, avoiding the half-born notion before it rooted.

"Young lady," she said, exasperated with herself. Softening her voice, Fran started once again. "Jamie, they said they caught it early . . . very, very early. Chances are I will not even need radical surgery. And you did it for me. I never would have known or thought to look until it got so bad that it didn't matter any more. Jamie, you saved my life." She paused to touch her daughter's face affectionately. "Why is it that you have to confront your own mortality before you dare consider what it is you're living for?" Fran reflected. "It's not that I have been a terrible mother; I haven't been a mother at all."

Jamie slipped her arm through her mother's. She felt Fran's muscles tighten instinctively. She maintained a closeness nevertheless. They strolled together. "You don't have to go any further," Jamie said. She had received more than she ever dreamed possible from this unapproachable woman.

"I want to," Fran continued, disengaging from her daughter self-consciously. "I'm telling you what's true, only I could never admit it before. Now that I can say it, it doesn't seem to matter any more. Just words." Her eyes filled with tears, smearing her mascara. "I'm not very good at any of this."

"You're doing just fine," Jamie reassured her.

"What's gone is gone, I guess," Fran observed. "You can't patch old wounds. I'm a realist, not a philosopher. I can't change overnight." Her voice became more brittle. "Affection never came easy for me. I'm not one of those 'touchy' types. Frank bitches about it all the time, but if he wanted a nymphomaniac, he married the wrong person." She shuddered. "I don't feel it. I just don't feel it." Hiding her head against her shoulder, she began to weep for the life she had never enjoyed.

Jamie began to cry, too. She hugged her mother for the first time in twenty years. A young man stopped to ask if he could help. They shook their heads. As he left, Jamie smiled through her tears. Fran pulled away, regaining her composure. Again they walked side by side. Another period of quiet elapsed.

"Mom, may I suggest something?" Jamie asked.

"Of course. Please."

"Okay," Jamie sighed. "Peter and I know a nutritionist who works with alternative treatments for cancer. I can't tell you he knows more than the doctor with the knife, but I know it's worth exploring. Before you decide to do anything, I'd like you to consult him."

Fran drifted for several seconds before answering. "I will."

Jamie nodded. "I'll call you with his number tonight. If I can, I'll go with you to see him."

Looking at her watch, Fran interjected, "There's a big closing today at the office. I have to get back. I just wanted to begin. You're a special young woman. I know that now."

When they reached Fifth Avenue, they turned to face one another. Jamie reached to embrace her mother, who retreated automatically. Fran pushed her chin forward, exposing her cheek for the acceptable kiss, her body still stiff and unforgiving. For a moment, Jamie felt cheated again, but when she gazed into her mother's eyes, she saw a difference.

Aware of her coldness, Fran murmured to her daughter, "I can't promise I can be more than I am. But I do want to try." Fran spun around and scurried down the street.

Jamie leaned against a tree. The receding figure of her mother with its distinctive mechanical stride chilled her. She knew Fran's rigidity was more deadly than the cancer that grew in her breast. But perhaps now she had a chance. At least they could face it together. The word dazzled her. Together!

Jamie knew she would never have had the strength three years ago, even three months ago, to follow her intuition and confront her mother. So the Tuesday night classes had made the difference, she thought.

As Jamie left the park, Peter's favorite poster greeted her, plastered on the side of a bus. The eyes of his surrealistic maiden stared at her. Though months of display had weathered the advertisement, the blue watch-eye appeared more brilliant than ever. The eerie pulling sensation she sometimes experienced in Luke's presence rippled through her body.

28

Brown pillows decorated the black walnut furniture. An ornate wood mantel exposed a modest fireplace outlined in old Belgian tiles.

Jamie had just finished rolling on the rug in the living room with Rachel, alternately tickling and stroking her. Now she presented her daughter with a little furry yellow duck. When she turned a key under its belly, the duck waddled, making sharp staccato quacking sounds. Mother and child watched in fascination. The duck became progressively more lethargic in its movement, taking its last step in slow motion. It raised its right leg, paused momentarily, and fell over. Jamie made a sad clown face. Holding the tiny creature in her hands, she rewound it and set it back into motion to Rachel's delight.

The bathroom door opened and Robin rejoined the duo in the living room. Her make-up appeared unusually sparse, but her silk slacks and almost transparent shirt had obvious style. Robin arranged her pants carefully before she sat down.

"Jamie, I've been thinking about what you said about having that same dream again last night. It seems to me, dreaming something many times doesn't make it any more valid than dreaming it only once."

"I know, Robin. Sometimes I think if I could be more at ease inside when they occur, maybe they'd just disappear."

"Yeah," Robin agreed. "I'd be for that."

Alone in the kitchen, Terry closed her art history book.

Robin's voice distracted her. She slouched back in the chair, scanned the room, then peered through the scalloped curtains. The sun, hanging low on the horizon, splashed into the kitchen. Terry squinted, readjusting her vision. Distant trees snapped into focus. They outlined the hilly acre on which the house had been built. Toward the rear of the property, a small rise obscured a low plateau, which had never been cultivated. A rope hammock, strapped to hundred-year-old oak trees, showed the only intrusion of the human hand.

Half mesmerized, she stared into the gentle rocking motion of a figure in the cord cradle. She noticed the strain the body put on the rope. "You're getting heavier, Peter," she mumbled aloud. Rising to her feet slowly, she walked over to the cabinet and selected a small glass. Before she closed the door, her attention focused back on the hammock. The cord cradle, weighted by its load, drifted back and forth in the hazy afternoon sunlight. The hammock and the surrounding trees melted into a yellow mist. Terry withdrew a second glass, then filled both with cherry soda.

Holding one of the small tumblers in her hand, she went outside. As she stepped down the hill, she glanced toward the occupied hammock, smiling to herself.

A large black bird gliding over the yard drew her attention. She discontinued her ascent for a moment to admire its graceful plunge. It soared down toward the trees. A flurry of activity rocked several branches as it disappeared suddenly in the thick foliage.

At the top of the small rise, Terry stopped abruptly. The hammock, radiating the sun's yellow rays, was empty. The indentation from its recent occupant remained. Her muscles tightened as she scanned the yard. Her fingers pressed hard against the glass in her hand and then unconsciously released it, dropping it to the ground. Her thoughts fired like small explosions. Remembering the yellow light that once hovered in the bedroom, she turned and walked rapidly toward the house. Jumping up the stairs two at a time, Terry vaulted past the kitchen door, slamming it behind her. Several minutes passed before she strolled into the living room, jittery yet trying to appear casual.

"Is anything wrong?" Jamie asked.

"No . . . well, I don't know. Where's Peter?"

"He went out about an hour ago. He should be back soon."

Terry began to tremble. Jamie placed Rachel in the playpen and steadied Terry by the shoulders.

"What's the matter?" Jamie solicited. Terry told of her experience in the yard. Even little Rachel's occasional giggle did not dispel the enveloping mood. Robin actually backed away from the other two women in the room.

Jamie stroked Terry's arm soothingly. "Come," she said, leading her back to the kitchen. "Did you hear the stories about people in deserts who see . . ." The words faded. She, too, saw the figure swinging gently in the hammock. The sun bathed him in soft, muted yellows. His motion mirrored the leaves.

Terry turned away.

Robin peered through the window and stared impatiently at an empty hammock gliding in the wind. "What's going on?" she asked, genuinely confused.

After scrutinizing the figure, Jamie faced Robin. Questioning her own perception, she spoke quietly. "Rob, don't you see someone in the hammock?"

"No. Of course not," she replied.

"Look again," Jamie instructed.

"Nope. Zero. The hammock is quite definitely empty," Robin reported.

Jamie told Robin that both she and Terry saw a man in the hammock. Robin's half-laugh increased the tension in the room.

"I'll be right back," Jamie announced. She checked the

garage for the car. It was gone. Back in the kitchen, she peered out the window. "Terry, the shape in the hammock looks more like Luke than Peter."

"I kept thinking he looked awfully heavy," Terry recalled. "Let's call the police."

"No. No. It might be Claude from next door. Come on, we'll go together and greet our guest." Terry shook her head. "Okay, then I'll go without you."

"Wait," Terry snapped. "I'll go."

Robin remained at the window.

The sun glared at them from behind the trees. They inched down the incline holding hands. Jamie's fingers grew cold. A lump developed in her throat. By telling herself to focus on the figure in the hammock, she managed to keep the lid on her own panic.

From this distance, the figure appeared more visible, although still indistinct. He sported a beard and had a large girth. His arms were outstretched. The energy he expelled soothed her in spite of the mystery. She thought it peculiar that his body formed the shape of a cross. They hesitated to move forward, knowing they would lose sight of the hammock as they descended into the small hollow in the yard. As they walked down the incline, they noticed an object balanced on the stomach of the reclining figure. Terry recognized it as a top hat.

The two women walked quickly across the depression in the yard. When they walked up the other side, they stopped short. The hammock was empty, yet the ropes remained molded to the now-absent form.

"I'm sorry. I can't stay out here," Terry said, turning around.

"No one's here," Jamie argued weakly. "There's nothing to be frightened about."

"I'm sorry." Terry ran for the house.

The wind whistled gently through Jamie's long hair. The warmth of the sun danced on her skin. Trees bled orange and yellow. Jamie jumped with a small yelp when a squirrel scurried across her path. She walked toward the hammock. Touching the sun-drenched cords, she felt an unexpected warmth. Suddenly she spun around, sensing somebody behind her. There was no one there, although she felt the presence of someone or something. The heat of the sun tranquilized her. She experienced an "end of the world" peace. Her eyes closed. Her body stood absolutely still. For an instant, her presence extended beyond her fingertips, as if her awareness had expanded to encompass the trees, the grass, and the surrounding sunshine. Her throat released a soft, sensuous sigh.

The flapping wings of a crow startled her. The tension returned. Jamie withdrew from the area and walked back to the house.

Inside the kitchen, Robin sat stiffly at the table, sipping tea. Terry stared out the window like a marble statue. Her eyes focused on the hammock.

"Did he say anything?" Terry questioned Jamie as she entered the kitchen.

"Did who say anything?"

Exasperated, Robin chimed in, "What is going on here?"

Terry faced Jamie. "Who was it?"

"You were out there with me," Jamie insisted. "No one was in the hammock."

Terry gasped, sinking into a chair. "Jamie, when you were there, I saw the man on the hammock next to you. How could you not have seen him?"

Jamie whipped around to the window and caught the now familiar image of the man in the hammock. The muted sunlight silhouetted the top hat that still rested on his stomach.

"Was he there all the time? Terry, for God's sake, tell me . . . was he there all the time?"

"Yes. All the time."

Possessed by a flood of energy and anger, Jamie charged

across the kitchen and out the door. Leaping into the hollow behind the house, she tripped, tumbling over a small rock. She scrambled to her feet; her fingers dug into the soft grass as she pulled herself up the incline. On reaching the top of the small rise, she confronted the empty hammock from a distance of about ten feet. She turned and searched for Terry in the window. Her house guest nodded a silent yes; she could still see the man from the kitchen. Yet when Jamie spun around, the hammock remained empty. She experienced a lightheaded sensation again, almost as if she had been released from her body and placed into a safe and peaceful womb. The crisscrossed ropes glowed from the intense sunshine. They had a distinct luminous quality. The yellow hues became almost blinding.

"Luke, is it you?" she whispered, taking her first step forward. "I can handle it now. Let me see you."

Terry watched from the window, wide-eyed. She couldn't believe Jamie's persistence. She screamed as her friend climbed into the occupied hammock. Robin stared ogle-eyed at Terry, then gawked at a very commonplace scene outside. Nothing made sense. She grabbed her pocketbook and fled.

Terry hyperventilated. Cupping her hands over her mouth helped her to regain control over her breathing. "Jamie!" she called out the window. "Jamie, please come back in. Jamie! Answer me! Will you please come back? Jamie, can't you hear me?"

No one answered the call. A bird chirped loudly. Leaves fluttered. And the hammock, with its two reclining figures, swayed in the gentle breeze.

"Can we talk?" Terry asked somberly. It had been three hours since Jamie had returned from the backyard and continued her chores as if nothing had happened.

"Sure," Jamie answered. "Just let me make a call to my

mother first. I have to give her a telephone number." When she returned, she noticed Terry's dress, rather formal for an evening at home.

"Going out tonight?"

"Well, that's what I want to talk to you about."

"Shoot," Jamie said playfully.

"I'm . . . I'm leaving."

"You're what?" Jerking her head, she gaped at Terry, who turned away, unwilling to look into her eyes.

"I really am leaving."

"Oh, Terry . . . why?"

No words came. A soft sobbing filled the room. Jamie embraced Terry. "Hey... c'mon, we'll work it out." Stroking her hair, she waited until Terry regained her composure.

Hugging Jamie, Terry said, "I love you, Jame."

"I know that," Jamie answered.

"And Rach is like my own baby; I don't want to leave."

"Then it's settled . . . you don't leave."

Terry pulled away. "It's just all the strangeness in this house. And today . . . my God!"

"What about today?"

"Jamie, you—you climbed into the hammock with him."

"Don't be silly. No one was in the hammock. I just felt tired and wanted to rest for a few minutes. That's all, really."

Terry shook her head. "What about your mother? Doesn't that confirm it?"

"Confirm what?"

A long period of silence followed the question. "Jamie, maybe it's about time you really looked at it. You know, you just have this 'premonition' about your mom getting breast cancer... and bang, within the week, she has breast cancer."

Scared to even ask the question, Jamie pushed the words out. "Are you saying my thoughts did it?"

"I don't know what to think. The whole bit with Luke, his breast cancer example—"

"Well? Go ahead. Finish! What were you going to say?"

"Nothing."

"Nothing?" Jamie questioned. "Nothing, but you want to run from this house."

"Okay, okay. I just promised Peter I wouldn't mention it to you."

"Well, break your promise."

"Jamie, I'm sorry." Terry began to cry again.

Her pain softened Jamie, who said, "Honey, forget it . . . you don't have to tell me. Forget it."

"Maybe you should know," Terry advised. "Remember the day you had that thing with your breasts, when you saw your mother in the mirror. Well, Peter said that the same day Luke spoke specifically about breast cancer. He thought it was an amazing coincidence."

"Well . . ." Jamie said, thrown off guard. "Luke's very . . . special that way. Anyway, like Peter said, it probably was a coincidence. Why don't you come to class with us? Luke isn't anything like you imagine." She took Terry's hand. "And you'll meet Deedee and some of the others. I know you'd like them. This Tuesday, you'll come . . . okay?"

Very discreetly, Terry moved away from her. "I can't."

"Sure you can," Jamie countered softly with a smile.

"I don't want to hear about it. Please, Jamie, stop talking about Luke and that class."

"Okay, okay. But please stay. I need you. Besides, you're Rach's second mommy."

Terry ignored the plea. "Every night I lie in bed wondering whether it's going to come back . . . the yellow light. Or this time, maybe it'll be blue or red. From now on, every time I pass a back window, I'll shudder, always glancing at the hammock to see if anyone's there. And then there's Cleo. Maybe I'll get it, too. I'll flip out."

"You talk as if it's catching."

"Isn't it?" Terry retorted. "If you—"

"Wait a minute," Jamie interrupted. "Before you go any

further, Cleo is very emotional."

"I'm not talking about Cleo," she shouted. "I'm talking
about you. Don't you see how much you've changed?" A
deadly silence followed. "Suppose your next premonition is
about me. Then what? Does that make it my turn?"

Jamie couldn't reply. The question of whether her premonitions heralded coming events or in fact caused them
had crossed her mind several times. If Terry's suspicions
had any validity, then what about her own dreams . . . what
about her and Rachel?

"Jamie."

"Yes," she answered, distracted from her inner dialogue.

"I'm really scared." She paused. "I can't stay here any
more, not even for Rachel. The thing with your mother just
. . . You do understand, don't you? Jamie? Jamie?"

"What?" she asked, her voice flat and distant, her eyes
staring.

"You do understand?" Terry asked for a second time.
Again, no answer. She watched Jamie place her hands protectively in front of her breasts. Frightened, Terry moved
toward the door. "Well, I have to go now. A friend of mine
will be picking me up in a couple of minutes." Still no
response. "Jame, take care of yourself."

"Did you tell Peter?" Jamie asked, almost absentmindedly.

"No. I hoped you'd do that."

Jamie sighed, giving in to the inevitability of what was
unfolding. "I'll . . . I'll miss you very much." She wanted to
hug Terry, but the other woman left the house abruptly,
leaving her very much alone.

29

"Maxy, did you find him?" Celine asked.

"Find who?"

"You know—your horse." Max shook his head and chuckled. "Don't you laugh now," she cautioned. "This is serious business."

"Oh," he whispered, feigning innocence.

"You think I didn't see the books on your desk. Why are you playing with me, Max?"

"I'm not playing with you; I'm just cautious."

"Oh, I see. The psychologist-as-scientist role. Very admirable. Come, I have something to show you."

Max followed Celine into the kitchen. She seated him at the table and presented him with an envelope postmarked from San Antonio, Texas.

"So," he said, without opening it.

"You never told me that the horse had two different-colored eyes."

"How'd you know?" Max asked.

"You forget Terry lives with your friends . . . or 'lived' might be more accurate."

"She left?"

"Last night. Smart girl. From what she described, things are getting very strange indeed at that house."

Max tried to organize his thoughts. "What does this envelope have to do with all this?"

"Everything," she said. "I found out about the horse's eyes almost a week ago. I asked Theadora—you know, my friend the medium— if she could help."

"Oh, no," Max countered, putting the envelope down and getting up from the chair.

"Please, just read it . . . for me."

He hesitated, then dropped back into his seat. Max pulled the pages through the slit already made in the envelope. Theadora, apparently a student of archaeology, recalled a certain fetish for a horse by a pharaoh in the Old Kingdom and then again by one or two rulers in the New Kingdom. She wrote endless little commentaries on the Eighteenth, Nineteenth and Twentieth Dynasties in Egypt. Max whizzed through the descriptions of their tombs and temples. The ram's head of Amon had been a repeated symbol of power. The crowned bull appeared often as the sacred animal of fertility. The phoenix, the bennu bird, the cat, even the vulture, found places of importance on the painted reliefs found in the burial chambers. Not once did Theadora make another reference to a horse.

"Listen, I've read enough," he said to Celine finally.

She looked over his shoulder. "No, you haven't. Now, she's coming to it."

Max sighed and continued reading. "So, dear Celine, I went to the library in Houston and checked the microfilm. They have a marvelous section on Egyptology. And just as I thought, in one of the photographs taken of fragments at an excavation site, a horse, rather smashed and mangled, could be seen on one of the stones. Apparently, all the statues and art had been vandalized. More faceless and armless figures than I've seen anywhere, my dear. What a sight! Very violent."

Max looked up at Celine, who reread the letter from a position over his shoulder. He wasn't quite sure whether he wanted to go on.

"Now comes the good part, " Celine whispered. "The trance."

Max shook his head. He felt hypocritical reading another

word. This had absolutely no credibility in his world. Nevertheless, he lowered his eyes and continued.

Theadora's handwriting changed, as did her perspective. It seemed as if she had begun to read something. She prefaced the passages by saying a spirit guide was reading from the diary of a famed Egyptologist that had been lost in 1883. Therefore, the information had not been included in any of the literature available in libraries and museums.

"Sure," Max murmured. "How convenient."

Celine whacked his hand. "Don't be an ingrate!"

He sighed and continued reading. In 1881, one of the workers on a dig led Emile Brugsch, an assistant to the director of antiquities in Cairo, to a newly uncovered shaft on the south side of Hatshepsut's temple at Dar el-Bashri.

With the help of others at the excavation site, the man shimmied down the narrow shaft and entered a long tunnel. Crawling on his hands and knees with only candlelight to illuminate his way, he found a gallery filled with alabaster and bronze vessels, painted coffins, mummies and the funeral tent of the queen-pharaoh herself, Hatshepsut. He gaped at the names on the coffins: Ahmuse, Thutmose II, Seti I, Ramses II and Hatshepsut. Apparently the remains of these rulers had been removed from their respective tombs ages ago because of looting, and placed within this unmarked cavern.

For the first time, the hieroglyphics revealed a horse form, but only on the funeral tablet depicting the reign of Hatshepsut. The researcher noted the horse with little interest, but Gaston Maspero, the antiquities director, claimed that the animal substantiated a legend written on a leaf from the Papyrus of Ami, the Eighteenth Dynasty holy scroll. The document described the coming of the godhead within every historical period. Such a presence would take the form of a living creature: a man or a woman. According to the prophecy, this power would be balanced by the appearance of a counterforce, namely a four-legged animal with a human eye, which would live as long as the godhead remained alive.

Max stopped at the notation about a human eye. He pictured the horse in the park, then shifted his attention back to the letter.

When Queen Hatshepsut's mare gave birth to a horse with one brown and one humanoid blue eye, the high priests proclaimed Hatshepsut as the only true godhead. She gave the horse royal quarters within the temple and had symbolic depictions of the animal carved on all her statues as she ascended the throne as the sole sovereign, deposing her young brother. The horse, although always subdued in the queen's presence or the presence of her priests, had supposedly trampled several grooms and escaped from captivity on numerous occasions. During one such incident, the animal killed the queen's favorite niece while the guards scrambled unsuccessfully to confine it. Nevertheless, Hatshepsut refused to give anyone the right to hurt or destroy the horse. Her reign of peace and learning differed dramatically from the tyranny dominant during all the other dynastic periods.

When the queen died, her younger brother emerged finally to take his place as Pharaoh Thutmose III. He ordered the horse slain and tried to destroy all signs of his sister's rule. Systematically, his lieutenants defaced all of his sister's monuments, including all references to the animal in the famed temple of Dar el-Bashri in Thebes and in all other provinces, thereby leaving little or no traces of the horse's place among the sacred animals of Egypt.

Although most experts dismissed the story about the ancient queen and her horse as pure speculation, Howard Carter, a renowned archaeologist during the early part of the century, found the story curious and compelling. Theadora switched voices again, now writing supposedly from Carter's point of view.

The royal name for the queen had been Makare by direct translation, but the more ancient interpretations of the hieroglyphics gave her the name of Christiana. She preached love, an unlikely perspective for an Egyptian ruler. At the bottom of a sketch of one of the queen's demolished statues, Carter, according to Theadora, had written the following: "Christiana = Christ?"

Another bizarre notation supposedly from Carter: The archaeologist acknowledged a letter, dated July 2, 1907, from a Catholic priest living in Jerusalem. The cleric described what had been revered as the first statue ever made of Christ, actually carved and painted within weeks of his crucifixion. The representation, which had been destroyed in a fire in 1902, depicted a man on a cross with two different colored eyes.

Max stared at the last entry in her letter. What an incredible concoction, he told himself. And yet, on some level, Theadora had gotten to him. Celine smiled at him triumphantly.

The next morning, Max Sorenson took to the streets again. Dumb! He repeated the word over and over, even while he checked all the appropriate locations, failing to locate any traces of Jude and the black and white horse. At the licensing bureau, Max pushed the registrar to recheck his files twice. No record of any such coachman existed.

Perhaps, one clerk suggested, the man was a gypsy driver, acknowledging a problem no longer confined to the taxicab industry in New York. Yet Max's description of the watch-eye did elicit a response from the department's deputy director, who had overheard his inquiry.

"Leary's Livery on Eleventh Avenue had such a horse, but the animal was destroyed years ago after stomping a stablehand to death. A dirty business," the man muttered. "There's no controlling a horse with a watch-eye. In forty-seven years, I've only seen one, that one, and it had to be put down. I don't scare easily, but that horse rattled my bones."

Max crossed through Central Park on his way home from the bureau office. He hated himself for staring at every horse-drawn coach that passed him. What would another therapist do with him, he considered, a man who kept expecting to see a supposedly dead horse come trotting by him?

30

As we entered Luke's building, I peeked comically around several darkened corners. I addressed Jamie in my best Bogart, "Listen, sister, I don't think we have to concern ourselves with the appearance of the nuns tonight." She pantomimed an exaggerated smile. We rode the elevator in silence. I hesitated at the door to the loft.

"Anything wrong?" Jamie asked.

"No. I just realized that I don't know what I want from this meeting."

"Why don't we go in and see." She smiled, approaching her life now with considerably fewer rehearsals than I. Her calm accentuated my own lack of ease. I knew she had come to pay homage to Luke, while my own increasing skepticism led me to see duplicity everywhere. We had reversed roles without admitting that fact candidly to ourselves or each other.

The button set off the Westminster chimes, sending them through two complete cycles before any one answered the door. Deedee, instead of Rudy, welcomed us with the traditional embrace. Her hug oozed with a genuine affection, but she still flaunted her body, jiggling her breasts against my chest. Afterward she wrapped her arm protectively around Jamie, who reciprocated, then ushered us into the living room. Rudy waved to us from a chair, remaining seated while gesturing to his foot from which his shoe and sock had been removed.

"Just five minutes ago, I missed the bottom step in the

hallway and twisted my ankle." He began to roll up his pants and winced. The swelling extended slightly up his leg.

"Can I help you?" I asked.

"Luke will be down in a couple of minutes. I'll make it till then," he replied, "but thanks." His face broke into a huge grin that expressed his delight with my offer.

"Can I get you something?" Deedee asked. Both Jamie and I declined.

Predictably, a record of Gregorian chants was playing on the stereo. Incense burned in ornate holders. All the ashtrays on the tables sparkled. An empty soda can lay on the floor beside Luke's empty chair.

The round, monkish man made his entrance finally. His head hung low above a body wrapped in a green and yellow polo shirt. A burning cigarette dangled from between the fingers of one hand while with the other he carried a large pan filled with steaming water. A towel had been thrown over his shoulder.

"Hi," he said pleasantly as he placed the metal container in front of Rudy and extinguished his cigarette in a nearby ashtray. "Rudy evidently wanted to try his hand at flying but didn't trust himself," Luke added, kneeling gracefully before his friend and smiling. His strong, meaty hands gently rolled Rudy's pants farther up the leg to a point below his knee. His fingers massaged the calf tenderly, slowly working down toward the ankle, kneading the muscles below the injured joint and extending his strokes expertly underneath Rudy's arch and along the bottom of his foot. Luke kept scrutinizing his friend's face to ensure that he was not exerting too much pressure and causing any pain. Finally, he dipped his hands in the hot water, in which he had mixed a combination of herbs, and slowly doused the leg with the potion. His hands never stopped moving, as if he knew from moment to moment exactly where to place his fingers to bring relief to the swelling ankle.

Jamie watched, mesmerized. I couldn't help but notice how captivated she was by the process. I wondered to whom Jamie would go were she hurt. And yet as I watched, I became absorbed also by the uncanny expertise demonstrated by this man. I could fantasize easily brushstroking a watercolor of a chubby little boy repairing with great delicacy the wing of a fallen bird. Suddenly, I short-circuited my awe. Perhaps Luke had staged this whole display. Perhaps this was merely another calculated ingredient in his sophisticated crusade to lure Jamie and me more solidly into the fold. When I saw my wife kneel down beside Luke and offer her assistance, I almost jumped out of my seat to grab her by the shoulders and return her to the chair. But I stopped myself, begging my face not to betray my feelings.

With Rudy's leg sufficiently warmed, Luke and Jamie lowered it into the water. The swelling had been relieved noticeably. "Ah," Rudy sighed.

After wiping his hands fastidiously on the towel, Luke rose and embraced Jamie, smiling, holding her body tightly to his. She actually had to bend at the waist to conform to his shape or otherwise risk a gouging by his belt buckle. When Luke began to relax his grip, Jamie squeezed tighter, rubbing his back as she did often with Rachel, thereby perpetuating their embrace. Luke nodded his head affirmatively, although no one spoke. I waited impatiently, then withheld my affection when I greeted him. I cursed my own stiffness.

"I'm glad you're here," Luke told us, his eyes jumping playfully in their sockets. "Come, let's sit together." He guided Jamie to a place beside him, displacing Deedee from her traditional position. She stared at her mentor and Jamie, then begrudgingly took a seat opposite them. I sat next to my wife. Rudy and Collis joined, completing the small circle. Facing each other in the center of the rug, we held hands in silence. Luke's blue eye focused on Jamie. She blushed. Grinning wide-eyed, Luke turned to me. We

looked directly at each other. His left eye seemed so compelling. I probed its pupil, but I could not see the torch
some others claimed to see.

As soon as the ritual ended, Jamie enthusiastically
poured out her story about her mother. She patted Luke's
hands several times while she talked. Several "ahs" saluted
her last sentence. I listened halfheartedly, alienated from
what had once been a cocoon for my own metamorphosis.
Nevertheless, in turn, I addressed Luke, cataloging all our
most recent experiences: my dream and Jamie's dream, my
"daydream" of a wheel and Max's identical impression, the
hovering eyes and the yellow mist. I withheld talking about
the nuns purposely, but I wasn't sure why. After almost fifteen minutes of continuous talking, I rested my case.

"Everything is there," Luke stated casually. A three-word
response to an encyclopedia of events. He's either unbe-
lievably naive or very shrewd, I thought. I opted for the lat-
ter assessment. I pressed Luke for more specific answers.

"The lesson is in what you allow yourself to perceive and
know from all the experiences you've described," he counseled. "There are no mysteries, only denials. Perhaps it is
only a question of removing the blinders . . . in this case,
your own fears." He extended his hand toward me, cocking
his head to the side. He beamed like an infant exploring
his world in awestruck delight. "By the nature of who we
are, we attract certain experiences. You might say we invite
them. But we've talked about all this before, Peter. You
could cut it off any time—the dreams, the impressions,
what you've allowed your eyes to behold—but both you and
Jamie are here because you choose to be here, because I
choose to have you here. You keep coming back because
you know to choose that, too."

"I understand all that, I really do," I responded, not
wanting a lecture on free will. "But the meaning within
each experience we've been discussing and their connection to our classes isn't clear."

"Not being clear is just a form of unhappiness."

"Luke, you're not direct. I think you use insight quips to be evasive. You refuse to be on point, therefore your words don't have real meaning."

"They do for those who listen," he replied.

"Well, damn it, I'm listening." My anger surprised everyone except Luke.

"A man who listens with only his ears does not hear all that is said. Although it is only a metaphor, a man must listen with his heart too. Are you happy, Peter? Right now?"

"The answer is obvious, isn't it?" I whispered, taking Jamie's hand and holding it tightly. "I want to figure out what the dreams mean and how they relate to you . . . in spite of how I feel."

"Those are your questions, not 'in spite of how you feel,' but because of it."

"Does that invalidate the questions?" I asked, remembering that Jamie had once raised the same point.

"No, Peter, but certainly the questions are not so useful to you as you imagine. If I give you the answers, I have given you nothing." Luke paused, nodding to himself as if responding to some internal dialogue. "Would it be that you would then come back to me again and again with your questions, enslaving yourself needlessly?"

"Of course not," I insisted. "You've always been my friend—no, much more than that. But . . . but there were no games before."

"There are no games now," Luke replied. "You talk as if I have your answers. You look to me for what you already know."

Somehow I knew something in my own questions was a cop-out. Finally I withdrew, but my reassessment of Luke continued. He never allowed anyone to reach beneath the coolness of his demeanor. Over time, his apparent warmth seemed quite impersonal. And yet, pieces of what he shared struck a resonant cord deep within.

Jamie's lack of participation throughout the conversation surprised me. Had she no more questions? What about her nightmares? What about her concern for Rachel's safety? My thoughts rattled me. Had Jamie's relationship with Luke and those in the class diminished her clarity and concerns about her own family?

When Luke rose from the floor, Deedee clamped his hand possessively, wedging herself between him and Jamie's seated figure. Collis left the room, then returned with a can of cream soda for Luke. He seemed uncharacteristically subservient. I leaned over and whispered in my wife's ear, "I want to leave now." Before Jamie could answer, a telephone call came for me.

After I left to answer the phone, Rudy brought Jamie into the music room and played his latest composition on the piano for her. His fingers danced on the keys of the baby grand. Totally absorbed, she didn't notice Collis slip behind her. He bent over as if to hug her, but instead kissed her on her neck.

Jamie pushed him away. Startled and offended, she moved quickly back into the living room and found herself face to face with Luke. He smiled wide-eyed at her. She smiled back at him uncomfortably, wondering whether he had observed Collis' action. Was Luke trying to be reassuring . . . or smug? She wanted him to have the best of intentions and, thus, concluded he did.

Moments later, I returned to the living room. Jamie and I were lured back to the circle on the floor.

The door chimes resounded through the loft. Rudy excused himself, limping toward the door. Whispered voices filtered into the room. I listened to the muffled conversation self-consciously. Garbled phrases melted together. Why was everything around here so secretive lately? My eyes jumped from poker face to poker face, coming to rest on Luke's visage. Nothing seemed to alter or erase the smile on Luke's face . . . or even arouse his curiosity—not the doorbell, not the whispers. So why did I remain so alert, so hypersensitive and now so cautious about all the events taking place around me?

Suddenly an image flashed before me. I saw a withered man with a pocked face wearing a tall top hat. When I closed my eyes, hoping to obliterate the impression, it lingered behind my lids. The man's mouth opened wide, his teeth caked with old food. The middle of his tongue lunged up toward the roof of his palate, leaving the tip of his tongue shaking against his gums. His lips, pulled back by the clenched muscles of his jaw, stretched paper thin. A hideous, frozen scream without any sound. I had to leave before my face betrayed my growing inner turmoil, before Luke refocused his attention on me.

In another part of the city, unbeknownst to me at the time, Max, during an evening therapy session, saw the same old, semiarthritic man in a black top hat. He, too, searched the bizarre face in the vision. Despite the distortion of the open mouth and bulging eyes, something about the man appeared familiar to him. The image faded for both of us simultaneously.

I ended the evening with Luke moments later. Deedee smirked at me. I prepared for her good-bye embrace by folding my arms across my chest. She gave me a laughing Boy Scout salute. Then, squeezing against me, she murmured into my ear, "Don't worry, smart ass, you're safe from me . . . for now."

Jamie and Rudy embraced, but when Collis advanced toward her, she moved away. Deedee grabbed her seductively, pushing herself against Jamie, who broke away from her embrace off balance and obviously embarrassed. She then hugged Luke quickly and exited.

Once in the street, we walked briskly toward the car. I thought I saw someone familiar duck behind one of the two moving vans parked in front of the building. After helping Jamie into the car, I reversed direction and approached the trucks. Their cabs were empty. Moving to the rear of the second van, I discovered Lady Claire and Dan huddled behind the truck beside two uniformed moving men.

"Hiya, Peter." A flustered Lady Claire smiled. Dan nodded.

"What's going on?" I asked.

"Moving day!" Dan responded.

"No more of your beloved Brooklyn Heights?" I pointed to Luke's loft. "You moving up there?"

"Uh, huh," Dan grunted.

"You, too, I suppose," I said, motioning to Claire.

"Yes, uh, me too," she answered. "Traveling from Riverdale was kind of a pain, you know."

"I guess," I said. "Well, best of luck in your new abode."

The ritualized physical greeting had been conspicuously omitted on all sides. No husky embraces. No sturdy handshakes. I walked back to my car. So those were the whispers at the door, I concluded. My concern shifted abruptly to Max. Would he be next? And what about my own wife? Had she, too, become inextricably entangled?

Jamie never commented on my discovery, nor did she share with me at that time the incident with Collis. Instead, she scolded herself silently for not telling Luke, believing that he would never permit such occurrences in his house. She pondered the origin of Collis's action. Somehow Deedee's undisguised sexuality at the end of the evening had been less offensive to her. Jamie decided that she did not feel as outraged as she thought she should. Therefore, she could not bring herself to discuss her experiences with me—not now, she concluded, and maybe never.

Though waves of exhaustion washed over her, Jamie managed to clean the dishes left in the sink by the babysitter, change Rachel's diaper without waking her, repair

the latch on the crib noiselessly and beat me to the procedure of checking windows and locking doors. The vivid
memories of the previous evening with Luke kept her mind
razor sharp despite the fact that the hour had long since
passed midnight. In an effort to keep busy, to avoid any
in-depth conversation with me and to exhaust herself so
that bed would mean sleep rather than hours of tossing
and turning, she tried to conjure up other tasks. Even
retrieving the mail suited her escapism until she discovered, amid bills and advertisements, a strange envelope
without a return signature. The address on the front had
been written in a peculiar, almost spastic style, as if the
writer had been inebriated or drugged or perhaps stricken
with some debilitating muscular disease. In the kitchen,
Jamie recognized the remnants of Cleo's handwriting within the jagged lines and erratic scribbles.

Dear Jamie:
   I know your next visit isn't until Thursday, but I
couldn't wait to tell you. Acey, that funny bird who
works the chow trays, also works for—guess who?
Luke. He told me himself. Everyone is connected.
Even Peter's lawyers—I'm sure of it. You've got to
get the little princess out. Please, Jamie, you're the
only one left who knows and who's not under his
spell.
   Dr. Delany put me in solitary last week so you
couldn't see me, but I know Luke was behind it.
Why haven't they reviewed my case yet? Why? Don't
you see that's proof? He'll try to destroy anyone
who threatens him, but I'm going to survive ʰis
because I hate the cocksucker. Jamie, I think I'd
already be crazier than a bedbug if it weren't for the
two nuns who visit me all the time.

Jamie felt her pulse quicken. Impossible, she mumbled
to herself.

Sister Catherine and Sister Agnes promised they'd help me get out. I don't know if they can, but it makes me feel good anyway. They call themselves Sisters of Mercy. They really care about me. They're wonderful, especially for nuns.

Please come on Thursday, please.

Love, Cleo

"Anything important?" I asked, startling Jamie as I entered the kitchen.

Instinctively, she put the letter behind her back, but then reconsidered her action. "It's a letter from Cleo . . . you know, one of the usual."

"Oh," I said. "Do you mind if I read it?"

Jamie hesitated, then handed the sheet of paper to me. She watched me consume it, line by line. When my jaw fell open, she knew I had arrived at the section about Sisters Catherine and Agnes.

"I know what you're thinking, but it's crazy," Jamie said. "There's thousands of them. They can't be the same nuns you've seen near Luke's." She shook her head adamantly. "Not the same nuns."

I did not counter her assertion. I wondered whether she had become as protective of Luke as Deedee or Dan or any of the others. Maybe Cleo had been right that terrible night when she said Luke had already gotten to Jamie.

31

"Say it, Max. C'mon, get it over with!"

"Peter, I don't have anything to say. Really. No announce-ments. I just wanted to have breakfast with you, pure and simple. Okay?" He stretched his arm across the table and held out his hand. I stared at it. "You know," he said, "I think Jamie took Terry's abrupt exit a lot better than you did."

"You would think that!"

"Hey, hey, buddy, that sounded like a swipe."

"Sorry," I said in a hushed voice. "Terry packs and leaves without any clear explanation. She didn't talk to me, and Jamie said she didn't talk to her either. That's so out of character."

"Celine also said she wasn't too talkative when she got home," Max added matter-of-factly. "I guess she got scared."

"Maybe," I countered, "and maybe this connection might not be relevant, but those in the class who dropped out during the past several weeks didn't share their reasons with anyone either. From the original eighteen, we're down to twelve."

"All groups have natural filtering systems. Only those who really get involved stay. Like you and me." Max twirled the end of his mustache playfully.

"Are you moving in? Tell me before I start eating my eggs," I insisted.

Max laughed. "You're really serious, aren't you? Peter, if I were moving in, I wouldn't hide it. I've considered it, but for now, I'm okay where I am."

One of Max's former patients surprised him at the table, interrupting our exchange. As she and Max conversed, I leaned back and closed my eyes. Suddenly I found myself staring at a dented wire garbage can being overturned on the sidewalk. It flew five or six feet into the air and ricocheted off a brick wall, splashing its contents over thirty feet. Slivers of glass bounced on the cement. I whipped my eyes open. The images stayed with me.

Max's conversation continued, but he appeared distracted, glancing at me from time to time with the most bizarre expression. After the woman left our table, he turned to me, wide-eyed. "A . . . I couldn't concentrate with her talking, damn it, but it looked something like a metal can, a—a garbage can, yeah, that's it!"

My mouth dropped open. "Then you saw it too," I whispered. He nodded his head. "Max, what the hell does all this mean?"

He twirled the corners of his mustache. "I wish I knew." The edges of his mouth curled for a moment, betraying a slight smile.

I banged the table with my hand. "Max, you're playing this like a game."

"And why shouldn't I?" he replied in a soft voice. "I have an idea. Why don't we both concentrate and see if we can produce another 'image' or 'impression'?"

I threw my head back and sighed noisily. "Okay, I'll play." I closed my eyes and peered into the darkness beneath my lids. After several minutes, I opened my eyes again. Max sat erect with his eyes closed. I waited several minutes more until he opened them.

"Well?" I chimed.

"You go first," he countered.

"Nothing, Max. I didn't see a thing."

Max shrugged his shoulders. "Neither did I. I kept drifting, you know, thinking about Mona, the girls. Even found myself remembering the first time I went sailing on Sebago Lake in Maine. But no images."

Obviously we couldn't force whatever was happening.

"Maybe," Max suggested, "you should take this up with Luke."

"Why me?"

"Somehow, I see them as your impressions."

"Thanks," I said.

"Hey, Peter, everything has a rational explanation. Give it time and we'll figure this out too."

"Like Jamie's dreams!" Max looked away. I knew I had touched a sensitive point. "Six weeks," I declared, "and four dreams, all almost exactly alike. Counting mine, five dreams. It's easier for you, Max, you have Freud and I don't."

"But we both have Luke," Max said.

On some level, I wanted to take issue with his claim, but didn't.

"Moving right along," Max continued, shifting his body as part of his announcement to change subjects, "Deedee is still crusading. She gives me these lectures on why I should move in, implying but never directly, that if I don't become a boarder, it's not going to be in my best interest."

I winced. "Are you serious?"

"Actually, it doesn't bother me. I'm not the fearful type." He ruffled his forehead. The wrinkles extended back across his huge shiny crown. "Part of her pitch," Max continued, "is about how those living in the house—like Collis, Claire, Dan and the others—are given special preference . . . special knowledge. When she gets wound up, she's slick . . . real slick."

"You could cut it off," I suggested.

"I don't know if I want to," Max replied, as if thinking aloud. "Last weekend, supposedly, they all spent hours looking directly into the midday sun, and instead of hurting their eyes, it healed them. Claire told me she didn't need her reading glasses any more. All this under Luke's guidance." He stared at his plate.

"You're not finished, Max, are you?"

"No. I guess not," he responded, his voice strained. "Deedee was very tired last night, kind of babbling on and on. Then a couple of times—and I'm convinced she wasn't aware of it—instead of referring to him as Luke, she called him . . . God."

That comment ended the conversation for both of us. Max couldn't help but think of the letter from Celine's friend. Rather than sharing his thought with me, he remained silent on the entire issue. Hatshepsut—royal name: Christiana. Every time he recalled the smashed faces of her statues, he thought of Luke's eyes, especially the luminous blue one.

In the street in front of the restaurant, we hugged each other robustly.

"You take care," I said before turning away.

"I want you to know," Max volunteered, "no matter what happens, I'll always be there for you and Jamie."

I stopped in my tracks and searched my friend's face. His eyes glistened. For a moment, all my skepticism and impatience disappeared. "I love you, Max."

32

The taxi jolted down Seventh Avenue—a stop-start, zigzag excursion through mid-Manhattan. Oblivious to the activity outside, I focused my thoughts on Luke. I had tried to phone him for two hours. Rather than deny my impulse, I elected to visit him without giving notice.

Suddenly the windows of the cab framed a wall of stone, catapulting me into another dimension of perception. The sounds of cars and horns disappeared. I gaped at a middle-aged businessman, forced up against the stone wall. The man flattened his body along the hard surface, trying desperately to dig in with his fingers in an attempt to protect himself from some unseen force. His lips stretched over his teeth. His eyes widened in shock.

I tried to move away from the image, pulling my arms into my chest. Nevertheless, every detail in the wall made an indelible impression on my mind. I searched the man's contorted face for meaning; nothing surfaced.

The driver shouted, "You sick or somethin', fella?" His voice seeped through the fog.

"Huh?" I responded to the face in the rear view mirror.

"I asked you if you were sick," the driver repeated.

"No. I'm fine, just fine," I said. Still confused, I let my thoughts drift to Jamie. Her expression in the morning indicated that she had had another dream. Her refusal to discuss it added to the wall of silence growing between us. Her laconic two-sentence commentary about Terry's departure still haunted me. Did her surprise exit have any connection with Luke? And Max—loving, wonderful Max. *"I want you to know, no matter what happens, I'll always be there for you and Jamie."* No matter what happens. No matter what happens. I couldn't silence the echo. Was that Max's prelude to moving in? Or did he anticipate something that I could not see? Why did everyone seem so damned inscrutable? Something separated me from everyone I loved. Only my relationship with Rachel remained pure.

Instead of going directly to the loft, I asked the driver to let me off in front of Toby's. An almost empty restaurant greeted my light-footed entrance. The scattered late-morning faces were unfamiliar.

I sat at the first table, sipping a drink listlessly, stalling, rehearsing the questions I would ask. I peered out the front window for distraction. Laughter across the street caught my attention. Two men, who had been unloading sacks of powdered cement from a dump truck, sat on a parked car drinking beer and shouting at passing women.

Withdrawing into myself, I anticipated another verbal tennis match with Luke. He would speak in metaphors, be evasive . . . maybe even dishonest. I knew I would have to find a rationale to convince him to give me specific, concrete responses. The visions, which came more rapidly than ever before, had to be sorted out. Rachel's life, Jamie's life, perhaps even my own life, hung in the balance. Stopping the internal whirlwind, I chuckled at my dramatics.

An uncanny image intruded in the midst of this mind game. "Not again," I mumbled. Nevertheless two nuns and the strange little man who had once stroked my fur collar appeared. I spat the juice all over the table. I gaped at the unlikely trio. They were real! At that very moment, they were actually passing in front of the restaurant.

I charged into the street about two hundred feet behind them, then matched my pace to theirs. The sisters glided gracefully along the sidewalk, their hands buried in their habits. In contrast, the little man between them bounced unevenly as he walked. His head bobbed up and down, seemingly disconnected from his body. Easily distracted, he surveyed every store window he passed. The antique shop with the red neon sign captured his fancy. Stretching his neck to observe it more closely, he almost tripped. The sisters took his arms and gently led him along.

A small dog ran up to the childlike man, barking wildly at his feet. He knelt down to stroke it, cocking his head in a way that reminded me of Luke. As he rose to his feet, the nuns again took charge. I suppressed my impulse to intercept them.

Every muscle in my body tightened when I realized the three of them had turned into Luke's street. I continued to follow. I pictured the nuns' faces, wondering whether they were indeed the same women I'd seen before. One sister wrapped her hand forcefully around the man's arm. Their pace quickened. As they moved more rapidly, one nun slowly twisted her head over her left shoulder and looked directly into my startled eyes. Her black patch and bony nose offset the delicate wire-rimmed glasses. I froze. Without expression or the slightest hint of surprise, the lady turned her head and continued her promenade. Her self-assurance and directness unnerved me. Regaining my composure, I followed the receding figures again.

Although I had anticipated it, when I witnessed their entrance into Luke's building, I grew anxious. Halting at the front door, I listened for the usual clicks I associated with the elevator. As I waited, I indicted myself for this insane escapade, yet refused to abandon my pursuit.

My fantasies about these nuns had clouded my trust in Luke for months. Despite the risk of offending him, I had to either substantiate or dissolve the gnawing doubts.

Once the elevator doors closed, I entered the hallway. The freshly painted ceiling had plaster chips hanging from it. Austere and uninviting. My finger pressed the large plastic button. Twenty seconds passed. A minute passed.

Putting my ear against the elevator door, I listened for the motor's whine. Silence. They're stalling it, I told myself. They're holding the damned machine so I can't get up.

Spinning in place, I scanned the hallway, hunting for the staircase. Running to the steel door, I grabbed the silver knob and drew the door wide open. I reached for the railing and began my ascent. Initially, my legs stretched over two and three steps at a time. My toes gripped the steps instinctively in my shoes. Panting heavily, I reached the third floor and leaned against the wall, winded. I gave myself twenty seconds, then pushed off again and trudged up three more flights. Finally, at one point, I stopped completely. My head whirled; my fingertips tingled uncomfortably. Taking another deep breath, I forced myself up another last flight.

When I exited the stairwell on Luke's floor, I noticed a carton holding the elevator door open. Just as I had suspected. Suddenly Collis and Dan appeared in the hall, carrying cardboard boxes. They looked surprised when they saw me.

"You look terrible," Dan observed.

"What are you doing with the elevator?" I asked breathlessly.

Realizing that I had made the journey by foot up the stairs, Collis said apologetically, "I'm sorry. We thought we were just going to tie up the lift for a couple of minutes. We're loading books. Luke wanted these donated to St. Paul's."

"Oh," I said, not fully accepting their explanation. I brushed past them and entered the loft, hesitating while I knocked on the opened door. Rudy appeared, grinning his welcome.

"Come. Come in," Rudy said. "We weren't expecting you, but it's a nice surprise." He hugged me firmly.

"Well," I fumbled, "I . . . well, I tried to call, but the phone has been constantly busy."

"Not busy," Rudy admitted, laughing mischievously, "just off the hook."

"Anyway, I was hoping Luke would be available."

"He's busy now. But why don't you hang out for a while and I'll tell him you're here."

"Thanks," I replied. The warmth of Rudy's reception contrasted sharply with my feelings of distrust. I scanned the living room to alter my focus. I stared at the empty chairs, filling them with members of the group . . . companions on what was once a loving pilgrimage. The circle of friends had become a clique of strangers. The flowerpot sitting on the mantel, the same pot that I once believed moved without physical aid, attracted my attention. This time, I noticed a small box behind it. Opening it, I discovered a nylon fishing line. Then for the first time, I saw a small hook attached to the base of the pot.

"Ah, Peter," Rudy said, entering the room. "I see you're holding part of Collis's little magic kit. Everyone wants to help Luke, but he doesn't need it."

I looked at Rudy. "Then you're saying you know about this." He nodded his head affirmatively. "And Luke—he knows about it, too."

"Of course." Rudy smiled. "Luke knows about everything."

"Explain to me why he'd permit it."

"He doesn't. Nor does he prohibit it. He makes requests, but he doesn't control those who attend the classes. Or were you drawing a different conclusion?"

The two of us peered directly into each other's eyes. A stalemate. Rudy excused himself by dipping his head slightly. The flowerpot discovery reinforced every suspicion. Why hadn't I seen this before? Even now, as I scolded myself for being so gullible, Luke's words intruded, answering my question. "We see exactly what we want to see." I held my hands over my ears. I wanted to hear only my own voice. I couldn't let anything sidetrack me now.

Drifting into the kitchen, I listened attentively to every sound. I knew the nuns had to be somewhere in the loft. I knew the man with the child's face also had to be here. Deciding to penetrate farther into Luke's house, I moved toward the rear bathroom. Pausing at the staircase, I heard nothing. Then footsteps approached the upper landing. Very quickly I scurried down the hall quietly and entered the bathroom. I calculated the appropriate passage of time, flushed the unused toilet, and exited.

Ambling slowly back into the foyer, I met Rudy putting his coat on.

"Oh," Rudy said with some surprise, "I couldn't imagine what had happened to you."

"Just taking care of my more elemental needs."

"Luke said he'll try to see you . . . if you don't mind waiting around for a while."

"Fine. I've got plenty of time."

"Well, I'm off," Rudy said. "See you next Tuesday."

I contemplated the next class, wondering whether, indeed, I wanted to attend any more Tuesday nights.

The door banged shut as the elevator descended with Rudy, Collis and Dan aboard. Alone in this section of the loft, I continued to explore, traveling quickly through the remaining areas. All the rooms on this level were empty. Then I lingered once again at the staircase. My ears perked. Muffled sounds filtered through closed doors. Hesitantly, I started to climb the steps but terminated my endeavor midway. Rather than intrude any farther, I backed down and sat on the bottom step to overhear whatever I could from that location. A strange singsong voice became distinguishable, but the garbled talk from upstairs formed no recognizable words.

A chill rippled through me as I sensed someone staring at the back of my head. At first I froze, unwilling to confront the observer. But then, overcoming my initial discomfort, I turned around and looked directly up the staircase.

My eyes met Luke's smiling face.

"Come," he said, motioning with his head. I climbed the stairs, drawn by Luke's burning blue eye. It flared like a luminous torch. We embraced at the top of the landing. Luke's single-handed grip felt strong and binding as he balanced a bowl of soup carefully in his free hand. Feeling dishonest, I wanted to pull away, but instead I allowed the greeting to run its course.

"Rudy said you wanted to see me," Luke began.

"Yes."

"I'd like to be here for you, but I don't have the time today."

"Then when?" I pushed.

"Before class on Tuesday night," Luke replied with a smile. He turned to walk down the hall. I couldn't keep my eyes off him. Luke paused, pivoted around, and faced me again.

"There's more, isn't there?" he said.

"Yes," I answered.

"You could ask for what you want."

Embarrassed and suspecting that Luke knew my motivation, I struggled to push the words out of my mouth. "The . . . uh . . ." I exhaled, squelching a self-conscious laugh. "I thought two nuns and a curious man preceded me into your home. The man reminded me of you in some way." Luke did not respond but waited patiently for me to make my request.

"I really believe it's absolutely none of my business, but something inside, Luke, is pushing to find out. Are there two nuns and a strange man visiting you?"

Luke smiled. Extending his hand, he invited me to accompany him down the long and narrow corridor. As he veered around, his small bald spot seemed very pronounced—the perfect tonsure. He carried the bowl with both hands now, holding it delicately in front of him like a prayer book as he led the way. I felt hollow inside, as if my

doubts betrayed the love he had extended to me so freely.
The walls became entrapping. Was this little procession a
one-way trip?

As in the taxicab, the painted corridor unexpectedly
turned into massive brick walls. A young woman, her hair
flying in the wind, backed against the partition in a pose
similar to that of the businessman I had seen previously.
She, too, pushed against the bricks, fighting an unnamed
terror. Her mouth opened wide with a silent scream. Rubbing my eyes, I tried to follow Luke through the fog of my
vision. Then, to my left, against another wall, a mother and
child appeared . . . huddled near the floor. The woman's
arms wrapped around the little girl as her eyes riveted on
some moving object. I knelt down, wanting to help, losing
myself in my impression. I soon realized that neither the
mother nor the child could see me. Rising, I closed my
eyes. The walls of bricks and recoiling figures remained.
They grew even more vivid under my lids, and remained
even after I opened my eyes again.

Luke stood directly in front of me. He passed his hand
between his face and mine. The vision dissolved. I stared at
him, dumbfounded. Luke turned and led the way to a
closed door. We entered the room together. The younger
nun sat alone in a red love seat, her black habit draped
over the soft pillow like an eighteenth-century painting. In
the corner, the one with the eye patch stared at me uncom-
promisingly, her arms folded in front of her. The little man
stood by the window, wearing a half-completed jacket.

Deedee flitted around him, pulling and adjusting seams.
She puckered her lips when she saw me. Pointing to the
garment, she said, "Like my handiwork? Bet you never
thought I possessed such talents."

Extending his hand toward the one-eyed nun, Luke said,
"This is Sister Catherine, whom I believe you know . . . well,
you've seen each other often enough on the streets, I
understand." I felt exposed, realizing this woman and Luke

had discussed our fleeting encounters. I speculated that Luke even knew that I had followed them to his loft. I stared at Sister Catherine, wondering why her name sounded so familiar to me. Luke continued, "And this is Sister Agnes." I nodded to the seated nun. And then I knew. Sister Catherine and Sister Agnes! These were the same nuns that Cleo had referred to in her letter. I had finally found the connection and the conspiracy that Jamie's friend had tried to warn us about before her incarceration.

"Sisters, this is Peter Halsted," Luke said. They murmured their hellos.

After placing the soup bowl on the table, Luke took my hand and moved cautiously in the direction of the retarded man, who grinned comically at us. Luke touched his arm, then directed me to do the same. A sure, tactile salute. The man's eyes swept our faces, beaming brightly in a not altogether unfamiliar way. His joyful smile mirrored Luke's face during a trance.

"This is Simon," Luke volunteered. "He's my brother." The introduction shocked me. I turned to Deedee for confirmation. She giggled and nodded her head affirmatively. The nuns smiled, eyeing the retarded man maternally. "Good, Simon," Sister Agnes hummed reassuringly. Was it possible? I asked myself, my mind riddled with questions. All these months. All the wasted time and energy. Had I made something sinister out of what I simply did not understand? Or had this been a decoy, engineered purposely to confuse me? Cleo! Cleo had to be the key. Luke's voice drew my attention back to the room.

Directing himself to his brother, he spoke slowly, enunciating his words with exaggerated care. "Simon, this—is—my—friend." Luke slapped his chest to illustrate his point. "My friend. Now—your—friend—too."

His brother shook his head up and down. Luke indicated for him to be seated as he retrieved the bowl from the table. Very skillfully, he filled the spoon, cooled the contents with his own breath, then fed the man whose face reflected a mirror image of his own. "Good," Luke said, but Simon's eyes were blank as he consumed the liquid. Within seconds, he banged on Luke's knee furiously. Another spoonful was the quick response. When some soup trickled from the side of Simon's mouth, Luke wiped it delicately with a napkin. The other man smiled. He cooed like an infant. No one else in the room existed for me except these two brothers, bound so closely by their obvious caring for each other.

I backed away self-consciously like an intruder having interrupted an act of love. My suspicions seemed particularly cheap yet some of them survived even this life-affirming scene. Deedee slipped her hand into mine. "Come, Peter, I'll go down with you."

As we entered the living room, Deedee wrapped her arms around me. "Hey, you cheated me out of my hug upstairs," she said. I embraced her lightly, then disengaged. Deedee laughed, flipping my lapel. "You looked so silly up there, so shocked."

"Who are the two nuns?" I asked, ignoring her observation.

"They're Sisters of Mercy from St. Paul's on First Avenue. It's a residential home for severely retarded adults . . . well, at least the rectory is. Ah, I see I've hit pay dirt," she observed as my eyebrows furrowed. "That's right, the same St. Paul's where your friend Cleo was admitted. Small world, huh?" Enjoying the unspoken tension, Deedee withheld further comment for a few seconds, then reassessed her game. "I'm sorry, Peter, I didn't mean to play with you. Part of St. Paul's is a city psychiatric facility, but the rectory is reserved for people like Simon. When Jamie told me about what happened to her friend, I told Luke. He asked Sister Catherine and Sister Agnes to look in on her and try to help as much as possible."

Everything fell into place . . . almost too neatly for my

sensibilities. "I see," I answered.

"Do you? You know Luke really tries for you. Like Simon, you're something special to him, but I don't know why."

Her statement made me self-conscious. Special? If Luke only knew my thoughts. "Deedee, have they helped Simon?"

"Well, yes, in their way. As you saw, he doesn't talk nor can he really handle even simple tasks. The sisters take care of him and many others. It's really a beautiful place and he's very happy there."

"Simon and Luke look so alike," I added.

"They should. They're twins . . . not fraternal twins, identical twins. Rudy told me that because of Luke's rather unique talents, one doctor figured that when the egg separated, Luke received more than his fair share, leaving Simon hopelessly deprived." She laughed; then her face took on a very serious expression. "People will say anything to explain Luke away."

"Another question: How come he never talks about his brother?"

"I don't know for sure," she admitted, shrugging her shoulders. "Luke's very protective of him. Maybe that has something to do with it." She paused, pushing her nose into her face with her finger. "And then again," she teased, "maybe brother Simon is an angel of God." Just as she was about to approach me again, she noticed the wall clock. "Well, I have to go now," Deedee said, taking only a moment to throw me a kiss and then disappearing up the stairs.

I left the loft stunned. Whom could I trust? Luke? Deedee? The nuns? Or should I reconsider Cleo's warning? I toyed with all the questions as I hailed a cab, never noticing the taxi that had parked along the curb.

Max waited in the cab until my taxi turned on Prince Street and disappeared from view. He completed another

entry into his recently acquired diary, jotting down his
newest impressions: first the businessman and then the
mother and child, which came to him in the same fashion
as the other previous images. He had no doubt that they
coincided, again, with mine.

The parallel premonitions had to reflect his own uncon-
scious desire to solidify a position with Jamie, he surmised.
He had been trained to watch for such behavior in his
patients, and therefore found it difficult to ignore the same
possibilities in himself. Should he tell Luke? Somebody?
Anybody? He didn't want to withhold, yet he knew he
would remain silent. Too often he had watched his patients
entangle others needlessly in their own wild fantasies. He
loved Jamie too much to fuel the hysteria she had experienced in her dreams. The horse, at best, had to be a
curiosity. Had Celine never spooked him with her vision of
his so-called spirit guide being a four-legged animal, he
knew he would never have become so possessed with what
had to be a startling coincidence . . . Jamie's dream horse
and a real horse—both spotted black and white, both having watch-eyes.

As for Theadora, he assumed the power of suggestion
could have easily set the stage for a fanciful scenario. The
queen-pharaoh. A destroyed statue of Christ with a watch-
eye. He shook his head, easing himself out of the taxi. Sanity and logic would prevail, he told himself.

The driver helped him unload four suitcases and several
boxes onto the sidewalk. Then Rudy appeared. He hugged
Max exuberantly before carrying the cartons into the building.

A little sign taped to the door of his designated room
said, "Welcome home." Deedee and Claire helped him
unpack. Max placed portraits of his daughters on the
bureau. He stared at them without feeling his usual twinge
of loneliness. He removed the plastic red rose from his
pocket and deposited it on the wood surface. Dan visited

briefly, congratulating the new arrival on his move.

Later, as Max cleared the desk, he realized the top drawer had been locked. Searching for Rudy, he encountered Luke on his way to a session, "You'll find Rudy in my room," Luke said softly, answering Max before he had a chance to verbalize his question. He stared at the small rotund man, who continued on his way casually. He would have to get used to such things, he counseled himself.

The door was ajar, yet Max knocked before entering.

"Come in," Rudy called. "You don't have to be so formal. This is also your house now."

Max nodded, then explained about the desk drawer. As Rudy searched for a key, Max surveyed Luke's room for the first time. In many respects, it was not much different from his own. A bed, a bureau, a desk, some books, an ashtray filled with cigarette butts and a few empty cans of cream soda. Suddenly Max lost his breath as he noticed a photograph of a black and white spotted horse on the night table. He moved directly toward it. There was no mistake. The animal had a piercing blue eye. Calming himself, he asked, "Whose horse?"

"Used to be Luke's," Rudy answered, unruffled. "That's one of the heirlooms from his childhood in Pennsylvania. His parents had bought the creature for him as a youngster but had to sell it when Luke came to New York. I guess he's dead by now."

As Max ambled down the corridor toward his own room, he tried to remember the name of the stable where the horse with the watch-eye had been destroyed. Lever's. Leer's. Leary's. Leary's Livery on Eleventh. That's it!

"Find the horse and make friends with it before it's too late," Celine had counseled, "too late for someone you love." He reviewed the elements of Jamie's dream, the explicit threat to her and her child. This can't be happening, he told himself.

33

The matron slid the keys expertly into the latch of the huge steel door. Jamie peered through the wire mesh embedded in the glass window, searching for Cleo's familiar form. Hera, no longer draped in theatrical clothes, had dressed in basic blue for the hospital visit. She had agreed to accompany Jamie, wanting to lend additional support since Terry's abrupt exit. A baby-sitter stayed home with Rachel.

"Twenty minutes," the nurse repeated as the door clicked open.

As the two women entered the ward filled with more than forty inmates, many of whom were heavily sedated, Jamie located Cleo's bed, only to find it empty. Suddenly, a large form pushed through a group of women and lunged toward them. Hera gasped, backing away. Jamie laughed as her friend embraced her.

"God, I live for your visits," Cleo barked. "How's the little princess?"

"Fine. Wonderful. She misses you. We all do," Jamie said, using her fingers to brush the hair away from Cleo's face.

Cleo eyed her suspiciously, then noticed the woman beside her friend. Hera stood there, transfixed, her mouth wide open. She had not connected the names before, but Cleo had been the one she had seen in the back room of Luke's loft. Jamie nudged her.

"Uh, this is Hera, Cleo."

"Where did you dig her up?"

"Cleo!" blurted Jamie.

"Hello, Cleo," Hera said, ignoring the comment and try-ing to ignore her vivid memory.

"Well, hello there," she replied sarcastically. "Where'd you two lovelies meet?"

"We—"

Jamie cut her off. "We met at one of my concerts."

"What are you talking about?" Hera protested, missing Jamie's cue. "We go to Luke's class together."

Cleo's eyes popped. "Get her away from me," she shout-ed. "Another one of those fucking whoremongers."

"Cleo, it's okay, she's my friend."

Without any warning, Cleo pounced on Hera, who screamed. Several other patients in the ward also screamed. Another inmate, armed with a pillow, attacked one of the nurses. Jamie tried to restrain Cleo but couldn't. Someone threw a Scrabble game up in the air. Several women began to weep as the hysteria spread quickly through the ward. Suddenly, several attendants and an intern interceded. They slammed Cleo into the wall and injected a hypoder-mic into her arm, holding her until her strength faded. When they released her, she slid to the floor and began to sob.

Jamie sat beside her. She put her arms around her and held her as she would have held her own daughter, rocking gently back and forth.

"It's going to be okay, Cleo. You'll see."

"Jamie. Oh God. Jamie, please help me, please get me out of here. They all work for Luke, all of them. Please, Jamie, tell them to let me go home."

A nurse put her hand on Jamie's shoulder. "You'll have to leave now, miss."

"We just came. We were told twenty minutes."

"I don't care what you were told. I'm asking you to leave."

"She can't hurt anybody now. I'll help calm her down. I promise."

"I'm telling you to leave."

Jamie began to disengage, then changed her mind. "Twenty minutes, not a second less," she declared, turning her attention toward her friend. She hummed the lullaby Mary-O used to sing to her. Hera, trying to control the trembling in her body, watched from a distance.

An attendant came to the nurse's aid. He put his hand on Jamie's shoulder.

"Please," Jamie said, holding Cleo tightly in her arms. "Please take your hand off me."

The man tightened his grip. "I'm afraid you don't understand. You've been asked to leave."

The intern, who had sedated several of the other patients, overheard the last remark. "It's okay, Mike," he said, "she can stay."

"Somehow, I'm going to get you out of here," Jamie whispered to her friend. "But you must play their game for a little while longer. No more outbursts. Try to be quiet."

"O . . . okay, okay, Jame," Cleo said. "I'll . . . I'll . . . I'll . . ." She never completed the sentence. Crying like an infant, she squeezed Jamie as tight as she could, not wanting to ever let go.

In the corridor, Jamie shook her head, trying to explain the situation to Hera. "I'm sorry. She's a wonderful human being, she's just—"

"I have to tell you something," Hera blurted.

"Sure," Jamie replied.

"I've seen Cleo before. I don't know how to tell you this, but I saw her at Luke's, in the back room, and something very strange was happening."

Jamie stared at Hera. Cleo had been telling the truth all along. She made Hera tell her all the details she could remember, then she hugged Hera quickly. "I have to go now. Okay? I'll call you tonight. Thanks." She darted down the hallway.

"Wait, Jamie, I'll come with you," Hera said, sensing her destination.

"No. I have to do this myself." With her last word she disappeared behind the elevator doors. Jamie stopped in the hospital lobby only long enough to make a telephone call and inform Rudy she was on her way to see Luke.

When Deedee greeted her at the door, Jamie sighed in relief. She hugged her, then pulled away as she recalled Hera's story.

"Anything wrong?" Deedee asked.

"I want to speak to Luke. Did he get my message?"

"Yes. He's expecting you."

Jamie crossed her arms in front of her chest and walked into the living room. Rudy entered through the kitchen.

"Hello, Jamie," he said, putting his arms around her. She resisted his affection. He released her immediately and looked at her questioningly. Jamie turned away. Dan appeared at the hallway entrance and smiled brightly. He, too, gave her the traditional greeting.

"Can I get you something?" Rudy asked.

"No, thank you," she answered.

"Well, follow me then," Deedee said. Taking Jamie's hand, she guided her down the hallway.

When she realized that Dan had followed, Jamie stopped. "Where are we going?"

"What's the matter with you?" Deedee asked. "You want to see Luke, don't you?"

"Yes."

"Then, c'mon." She pointed to the ladder leading to the second-floor meditation room.

Deedee climbed up first and Jamie second; then Dan followed. They made their way through the narrow corridor into the secluded chamber. The only light in the black, insulated room came from a small candle. Luke was not there.

"Well, where is he?" Jamie asked.

"Be patient. He's finishing up a session." Deedee put her arm around her and guided her to a corner. "Here. We'll sit here together." Dan shut the door, then flopped down near the candle. They waited in silence. When Jamie felt Deedee rubbing her thigh, she stopped her hand. Suddenly, the door to the room opened again. Instead of Luke, Collis entered, clicking the latch shut behind him. A shiver shot up Jamie's back. She thought of Cleo locked in the ward. In a second, she was on her feet.

"Deedee, I came to see Luke. I'm going back downstairs."

The other woman stood up and approached Jamie. "Don't worry, you won't miss Luke. Maybe we can meditate together. Luke showed some of us a breathing exercise which helps to synchronize our heartbeats. It's intense."

"I don't want to play any games." She turned and moved toward the door.

Deedee slid sideways and positioned herself between Jamie and the exit.

"What are you doing?" Jamie asked.

"I know what you want. We'll make everything all right." Deedee moved closer. "Easy, honey, you seem so tense. Is anything wrong?"

Jamie stared at the other woman, disarmed by the warmth underlying the question. She considered asking about Cleo, but became distracted when Collis and Dan began to stand up. As Deedee put her arms out, Jamie backed away, turned and lunged toward the door. She unlatched the handle and flew through the opening. As she climbed down the ladder, she lost her balance and missed the last four rungs, falling on the floor. Hitting the floor, she began to cry. She then jumped to her feet and sprinted down the hall, oblivious to Max Sorenson, who sat in the den, fully engrossed in reading a book. In the foyer, she ran into Luke, who apparently had been carrying a tray of soda and tea into the living room.

"I've been waiting for you," he said, cocking his head quizzically to one side.

Jamie pushed him aside, throwing him off balance and knocking him and the drinks onto the carpet. As she fled through the front door, he called to her but to no avail. Max, startled by the urgency in Luke's voice, arrived in the foyer seconds later. He helped the rotund little man get back on his feet, then began gathering the broken teacups and soda cans from the floor.

34

I flipped my daughter into the air, laughing each time she giggled with delight. Placing her gently on the floor, I poked her belly, sending her scurrying across the room on all fours. I applauded Rachel, but my enthusiasm waned each time I looked at Jamie, who cleared the dinner table with a stone-faced expression. Why did I feel like we always came from opposite corners?

"Something wrong?" I asked. No answer. She avoided looking at me directly. "Jamie, you're like a whole different person tonight. You want to tell me about this new you?" I joked.

Her eyes reddened. "Not now," she said flatly.

I crossed the room and turned her toward me. I could feel her body tremble. "What's the matter?"

She pulled away and chased after Rachel, who had crawled into the living room. When she picked up the baby, her entire demeanor changed. A radiant smile greeted her daughter. "My sweet baby, Mama's going to put you in the playpen for a little while—yeah, I know, you're getting a little sleepy." She put Rachel down carefully, then placed her favorite teddy bear in her arms. The baby giggled. "Oh, God, I love when you laugh. Here, a pillow beside you and you're all set." Jamie kept stroking Rachel, as if she were unwilling to break the physical connection between her and her child. Her expression became somber, almost desperate. The joy evaporated.

When Jamie turned and saw me, I knew her anger had

been rekindled. I followed her into the living room. She picked up her coat and headed for the door.

"Jame, what's going on? Where are you going?"

"A walk. I need to walk."

"First tell me what's the matter."

"Stop telling me what I have to do," she shouted, "or what I should do. I want to be left alone . . . alone!" Her eyes filled with tears. I backed away. Jamie opened the door and exited. Five seconds later, she came back into the house and wrapped her arms around me. For the next five minutes, I held her tightly.

Once she relaxed, she disengaged and moved away from me. "Peter, I'm not going to sit down, okay?" I nodded my head. Jamie moved closer to me and stared directly into my eyes. "I don't want us to go to any more classes. I want a moratorium. No more Luke . . . at least for now."

"I don't understand."

Jamie turned and sighed. She told me about her visit with Cleo and about Hera's revelation.

"I also knew about her visit to Luke," I admitted.

"And you didn't tell me? How could you have done that?"

My explanation about my concern that she might misinterpret the information fell on deaf ears. Jamie insisted that she had a right to know.

"I'm sorry," I said quickly. "No more secrets. I promise."

Jamie's eyes fluttered nervously. Her voice dropped half an octave as she described her trip to Luke's with a needlepoint portrait of the minutes in the meditation room.

I couldn't respond. Perhaps Deedee only wanted to console her, I hypothesized.

Jamie stared at me sternly. "Deedee said she knew what I wanted. Do you know what I want, Peter?" I shook my head. "I want to be me," she declared. "And the funny thing is, I don't know what that means any more."

I approached my wife, but she backed away. "I love you,

Peter," she said, "but I need more space now."

"I just want to hug you. I want to help you feel safe. And, Jame, I want you to be you."

"You wanted me to take Luke's trip. You wanted company!"

"No," I fired back. "I wanted you to discover what . . . what seemed important then. Now, I don't know anymore."

"I wish I could blame you, but I can't. I can't even blame Luke. Terry was right. I have changed."

"You mean you spoke to her?" I asked.

"No. Not since that night. Oh, Peter, I lied to you about Terry. She told me why she left . . . because of Luke and me." She repeated Terry's fear of becoming victimized by one of her upcoming premonitions.

"Why didn't you tell me?"

"I was so mixed up . . . and I had sort of begun to believe in Luke—didn't want to tarnish his golden image. Wild, isn't it?" she mumbled. "Maybe I was just too stupid to know better."

I shook my head. I wanted to shout, not at Jamie but at Luke. Everything had gotten so out of hand. I wished we could have started all over again.

"I know this is going to be hard for you to understand," she said, "but I'm through building pedestals . . . for anyone—for Luke, even for you. I have to start to trust me now . . . what I see. Funny, but isn't that Luke's message after all?" She paused.

"I understand," I replied.

"No," she whispered. "I don't think you do. I can't let your lawyers handle Cleo's release any more. I'm going to do it myself." She sighed noisily. "And those dreams. Maybe Cleo was right . . . maybe if we get far enough away from Luke and all the craziness, they'll disappear. At least I can try, not only for me, but for Rachel. You do remember Rachel, don't you? We owe her more than all this insanity." Jamie covered her mouth with her hands momentarily, then freed herself to continue. "I'm back to what I asked for when we started talking. A complete break with the class and with Luke."

The firmness of her challenge surprised me. Everything about her—voice, eyes, body posture—exuded an uncommon strength and power. "Okay," I agreed finally. "Satisfied?" Jamie smiled cautiously. "I mean it," I assured her "...if that's what you want." Her face relaxed into a broad grin.

During the next hour, we played with Rachel until she actually fell asleep in the midst of a giggle. After putting the baby to bed, Jamie returned to the living room with her cello. As she practiced her scales, I sat on the floor beside the coffee table, sketching thumbnail designs for work. Despite my attempts to be totally absorbed in my work, I found myself distracted by the remaining tension between us. Not once did Jamie let her eyes drift from the exercise book. Her fingers scooted along the strings with such speed that they appeared blurred at times. Later, after she practiced a Bach piece, I applauded.

She laughed. "I'm not that good."

"Yes, you are."

My entire body relaxed now. I felt connected again. While she continued practicing, I began to scratch out a large sketch with a charcoal stick. Instead of forcing the lines, I allowed my hand to move freely, almost doodling across the page with broad strokes. A friend of ours, a sculptor, talked often about finding the form in the stone he chiseled rather than imposing a shape on it. I wondered whether I could do the same in a two-dimensional medium.

The word *allow* popped into my mind. As I released my hand, it moved as if the thought process had been transferred to my fingertips. Rather than doing the drawing, I observed myself doing the drawing. I could feel a surge of excitement as I completed the piece. Not a useful method to design corporate logos, I concluded, although I was rather pleased with the balance of seemingly abstract shapes and sharp lines.

I leaned back against the couch, putting some distance between me and the drawing. Then I saw it. I couldn't believe my eyes. To the left, near the top, I had sketched a wheel, a wheel with spokes. Near it . . . an arm, my God, a baby's arm. The nausea came quickly as I bent over, scanning every aspect of the piece. In another section, to the right, the apparently abstract forms looked like the open mouth of a large animal . . . a horse, it had to be a horse. I looked up at Jamie and knew I had to break my promise. I had to see Luke again.

"Jame, come here. I want you to look at this drawing." She sat beside me. "Okay, do you see anything, um, concrete in it?" I asked.

"No," she responded.

"Keep looking," I said.

She squinted her eyes, as she had seen me do on many occasions, and surveyed the whole piece. Her finger pointed at the top lefthand corner. "Here, right here, a wheel."

So it was there. She could see it too. I tried to suppress my anxiety. "Anything else? Do you see anything else?"

Jamie kept staring at the piece. Finally, I pointed to the form near the wheel. She leaned closer. "Peter, that looks like an arm."

"What kind of arm?"

"I don't know."

"Look at it again. C'mon, what kind of arm do you see?"

"Well, I would guess a child's arm. Is that right?"

The words tripped off my tongue before I had a chance to filter my thoughts. I explained to her the entire process I went through in "allowing" my hand to make the sketch. When I showed her the horse's mouth, she stared at me.

"Right here. See it?"

"No. This time I don't. Peter, are you trying to scare me?"

"Of course not," I whispered. "But, Jame, this is like the other images. Wherever I turn, they're there. I have to see Luke, just one more time. Please understand. I have to put the pieces together, and Luke's the only one who can help me do that."

"You did this on purpose, didn't you?" She jumped up. "It's over, Peter, do you hear me?" Her voice tremored. "It's all over."

"But I have to know why all this is happening."

"Well, I don't," she said sadly. "I have me now . . . and I guess, Peter, you have Luke."

I watched Jamie leave the room. Then, for what seemed to be an endless expanse of time, I stared at the drawing. The images were so clear. Finally, I turned away and walked up to the dollhouse that I had given Jamie at the time of Rachel's birth. She had insisted we keep it in the living room on permanent display. The serenity of the three wooden replicas of us on the porch seemed incongruous, given the current turmoil in our home.

When I heard Jamie coming down the stairs, I whipped around. She had Rachel wrapped in a blanket and a tote bag flung over her shoulder. I couldn't believe my eyes.

"Jamie, you're not serious. You couldn't do this. I didn't realize . . ." She looked back at me with a soft but peculiar smile. "I love you, Peter; I know you didn't realize, but I *have to* do this. Maybe it's not that we need time away from Luke; maybe we need time away from each other so that you can . . . we can . . . both decide what's important to us."

"Don't be silly," I said. "I know what's important to me."

"Do you?"

Before I could answer her question, she walked over to the miniaturized replica of our home and extracted the figures of herself and the baby, then opened the front door to leave.

"Maybe, well, maybe it's time we all came out of the dollhouse," she said in a hushed voice.

The door slammed behind her as I said, "I won't go to Luke's any more." My words bounced off the walls of the empty foyer.

35

I had waited for the morning impatiently, pretending to sleep, even dozing occasionally, only to awake with a jolt as my hand swept the empty bed beside me. Finally, I slid off the mattress and wandered through the hallway into the kitchen. Everything remained in place: the note pad by the phone, the baby's bottles in the rack beside the sink, the sketch of Jamie tacked on the refrigerator door. I walked over to the table and dropped into a chair. My fingers stroked my wife's soft mohair sweater, draped casually over the nearby counter. I half expected Jamie to meander into the kitchen and slip into the waiting garment.

A rustling at the side door riveted my attention. My ears perked. My entire body tensed. I listened for the key to be inserted into the lock. A full minute passed before I realized that a branch from the maple looming over the driveway had brushed against the house in the wind. I rested my head against the hard surface of the oak table and whispered Jamie's name over and over again until my throat became parched.

The first ray of sunlight woke me. My back ached from being hunched awkwardly over the table. I stared at the empty sweater on the counter. The events of the previous evening replayed in my mind. It had really happened . . . and yet I checked the house just in case. I even climbed the stairs to the second floor and peeked into Rachel's room. The empty crib sent a cold shudder down my spine. I dressed mechanically and left for the office.

Although I sketched a rough design for the facade of a new airport terminal building, my thoughts lingered with my wife and child. Why had it been so important to see Luke that one more time? Maybe Jamie was right and I had induced myself psychologically to include the wheel, the baby's arm and the horse's mouth in the drawing as an excuse to see Luke again. Was there any possibility that I could put the pieces together myself? I began to draw the recurring fragments. I remembered the haggard face of the man with the top hat, his cheeks ravaged by weather and age. My fingers tracked the pencil across the pad in loose circular lines while I recalled my impression of a cowering mother and child huddled against a brick wall. My foot tapped a nervous rhythm on the floor as I thought of the businessman trying to escape some unseen force. Obsessively reproducing the visual impressions over and over again, I knew I was just going through the motions at my desk, intoxicated now by the very imagery I sought so desperately to shake loose.

Even the office acoustics, which generally stimulated their own unique brand of excitement, left me cold. I flipped the pencil across my drawing board, then paced the room. Jamie's voice preyed on my mind, echoing, "It's over, do you hear me? It's over." But I was increasingly aware that it was not over. In some ways, I suspected, it had just barely begun. "I have me now . . . and Peter, I guess you have Luke." That wasn't true, I wanted to tell her; I didn't have Luke any more.

Unable to concentrate, I joined my staff in the studio, involving myself in the mechanics of varied projects. A half hour elapsed. Back in my office, I fielded several phone calls, then returned reluctantly to my original task, trying to sketch ideas for a mural.

The paper before me appeared luminous suddenly. Squinting, I continued to draw for several seconds while readjusting the overhead lamp. My manipulation did not remedy the situation. The glare increased, making it almost impossible for me to look directly at the table. Suddenly, a strange crashing noise assaulted my ears. I heard several more crashes, all identical. "What is that?" As I said it, my eyes widened with awareness. "A garbage can . . . that's it! A garbage can falling and smashing." The new connection perplexed me even more. My breathing became labored. I grunted as I kicked the table over.

Finally released from the experience, I sat quietly in my own stupor. I eased back into the physical world. Trudging to the window, I braced my hands up against the frame. Bloodshot eyes absorbed a selective overview of the city. Everything appeared more vivid than usual. The angles of one building silhouetted against another seemed more pronounced, the people in the streets more defined.

Maire entered my office. The overturned table surprised her. "What happened?"

"Nothing," I answered without facing her.

"Well, I'm not too proud to pick it up," she said, approaching the table.

"Leave it!" I snapped. She froze in her tracks. Noting her reaction, I furrowed my forehead. "I'm—I'm sorry. Please, just leave it there for now."

Nodding, Maire asked, "Are you okay?"

"I'm fine," I said, "but I'd like to be alone now."

"Okay. Call if you need me, huh?" Hesitantly, she exited.

Alone again. Phantom images whizzed through my head. My body felt unfamiliar, heavy, encased in alien armor. An attempt to root myself in familiar thoughts of Jamie and Rachel failed miserably. A deep gnawing discomfort about their safety haunted me.

I dialed my home number. Perhaps Jamie had come back. The first ring went unanswered. They're upstairs, I speculated. The second and third ring . . . no response. Maybe they're in the backyard, I hoped. By the seventh ring I considered hanging up, but held on until the twelfth.

An empty house. I wanted to cry, but I cut the feeling off. Don't give in! Stay with it! Find them! I lifted the receiver again and dialed Max's office number. No answer. I tried Hera's home without success. I had never felt so isolated; everyone that mattered seemed beyond my reach . . . except, perhaps, Luke.

The fragments of images that I had catalogued remained unconnected. They made sense neither alone nor as a collection. Yet I knew they related to each other somehow. I had to see Luke one last time. I imagined putting my hand around his throat and squeezing, forcing him to give me the answers that I needed so desperately. No more games. I'd bargain with the devil if I had to . . . anything for Jamie and Rachel. Anything!

I dialed the phone and listened to the insistent ringing.

"Hello," a soft voice answered.

"Hello. Rudy?"

"Yes," he responded.

"It's Peter. I'd like to speak to Luke."

"I'm not sure that's possible," Rudy replied. "Wait a second. I'll check and see."

A minute crawled by. Sweat gathered between my skin and the receiver. My fingers began to numb. Contracting muscles in the back of my neck created a dull, pulsating ache. Footsteps echoed over the tiny amplifier in the other phone receiver.

"I'm glad you called," Luke said softly.

"I want to see you; I must see you."

"I know," he replied. "Come now."

As I left my office, I felt so utterly unfulfilled. Had Luke rejected my request, it would have been unacceptable. And yet, his apparent warmth, his "I know" willingness to see me served to unnerve me even more.

The silver hair parted down the middle, the railroad cap pushed to the back of his head and the pouch of chewing tobacco hanging from his belt made Mr. Leary of Leary's Livery look as if he just stepped out of an antique turn-of-the-century engraving.

"That one, laddy boy, you don't forget," he said to Max. "Curse the day I set my eyes on him." His fingers braided the edge of the whip expertly as he talked. "More devil than horse in that animal. Yes, sir! I musta been plumb nuts to fool with him. Ya hear lots of stories about a horse born with a watch-eye. Thought it was all hogwash." He shook his head sadly. "McGrady and Connelly. He trampled both of them."

"What happened afterward . . . to the horse?" Max asked, looking carefully at the faces of the old coachmen dressing in the tack room.

"Gone. Got rid of him."

"You mean he was destroyed?" Max queried.

"Doubt that, son. I guess you know the horse was supposed to be destroyed," Leary said cautiously. Max nodded. "Well, never killed one of God's creatures before and didn't intend to start with this one. Besides, the horse didn't understand what he did." He peered at Max before continuing. "Well, I'll take a chance and tell you, 'cause that horse would have to be dead by now or barely standing. Let's see, that's about seven years ago. One of my drivers retired and offered to take the horse with him, off the streets and away from people where he couldn't do more harm."

"Do you know where he was taken?"

"That one I couldn't answer. Somewhere upstate, I remember him saying."

"Is it possible that someone is still using the horse now to pull a carriage?"

Tim Leary laughed. "Not unless you believe in reincarnation. Listen, he'd have to be thirty, thirty-five years old. No horse I know lived that long and could still walk." He patted Max on the shoulder. "That horse ain't going to give anyone trouble any more. You got my word on that."

After thanking Mr. Leary for his cooperation, Max headed for the door, pausing to take one last look at the men in the tack room. "Do they need a license to drive?" he asked.

"Sure do. All fingerprinted and photographed like taxi-cab drivers."

"Well, thanks again," Max said as he exited. He stopped suddenly, then returned to the office. "The man who took the horse with the watch-eye, the retiring driver, what was his name?"

"Jude—a real ornery cuss."

The man must have returned with the horse, Max speculated. Retired, therefore no longer licensed. He remembered the picture of the black and white spotted animal on Luke's bureau. He knew he had to ask one more question. "Sorry, Mr. Leary, but where did you buy the horse? Would you have a record of that?"

"Don't need to," the old man volunteered. "I get all my horses from the same place . . . a dealer in Pennsylvania."

Max left the stable abruptly. His body shuddered. Pennsylvania. Leary could have said any other place in the world, but he didn't. Pennsylvania, where Luke had been raised with a horse of the exact same description, including the rare watch-eye. A counterforce, just like the legend prophesied. Max thought of the queen-pharaoh's beloved niece killed by the rampaging animal. He knew that he would no longer dismiss Jamie's dream as a product of fear.

He had to find a phone booth; he had to warn Jamie. He could not deny what he now thought he knew. He had to act as he should have done so many times before.

Suddenly, a series of crashing sounds assaulted his ears. The glare of the horse's intense blue eye hovered before him, then disappeared. He tried to match the noises with the other impressions he had had over the past several weeks. Max didn't want to be passive any more. He had done that with his own children and lost them. To do the same thing with Jamie was intolerable.

As he ran to the booth at the corner, he fished frantically in his pockets for change.

Max pushed the lever down and inserted a coin. He dialed Jamie's number, unaware that she had taken her daughter and left her treasured Victorian home. The phone rang and rang and rang, leaving Max Sorenson alone and isolated in a phone booth on Eleventh Avenue.

36

To have Luke greet me personally at the door marked an unusual occurrence. Immediately after entering, I had the distinct impression that the house had been emptied for my visit. When he embraced me, I did not reciprocate; hugging him somehow meant denying Jamie.

An eerie silence replaced the usual noises of shuffling feet and mumbled chatter in the loft. Luke ambled into the living room, inviting me to follow. Neither of us spoke. We sat down opposite each other. Luke's face broke into the familiar wide-eyed grin. He extended his hands, palms down, toward me.

I closed my eyes purposely, cutting the bond with Luke in order to rekindle my previous thoughts. I did not want to be consumed by his ritual or have my questions dismissed before I posed them. Springing to my feet, I moved to the other side of the room.

"Deedee, and I suspect Dan and Collis, lured Jamie up to the meditation room and scared the hell out of her when she was supposed to be seeing you. How could you have let them do it?"

"Jamie is as precious to me as she is to you," he answered. "Nobody did anything to her. She came here scared."

I knew he was right, but I wanted to hold onto my power. "And I guess you'd make the same claim about Cleo."

"Uh, huh," he murmured casually.

"And Collis' little flowerpot trick with a fishing line," I said impatiently. "You knew about that, too. A fraud . . . and yet you let him stay in this house, your house, and share your table."

"If a child is confused and he breaks a window," Luke said, "do you cut off his hand? Collis, and even Deedee, are here, in part, to recognize their weaknesses just as Jamie came to discover her strengths."

I could not argue with the new determination that I, myself, had witnessed in my wife. "We were trying to learn about love, Luke. What the hell happened?"

"We are still on that journey."

"No, you've sidetracked yourself and the others. Luke, do you know why I'm here?" I asked, getting to the point of my visit.

"Yes," said Luke.

"Tell me why!"

"Destiny."

"That's hardly a direct reply," I retorted. "Nail it down! God lives in the details. What do you know, if anything, about these images?"

Luke pulled on his beard thoughtfully. "You have made it happen. You have allowed yourself to be in touch with more than a single dimension. We all have that power."

"Sure, I believe that, but what does destiny have to do with it?"

He smiled broadly. "Everything . . . and nothing. Destiny is an illusion, call it hindsight." Luke paused, cocking his head to the right like a small child. "You take two people from different places in the world . . . they make thousands of decisions in their lives until, one day at one instant, they come together. Now after that moment, you could go back and plot all their decisions and movements on a graph to prove that what occurred was inevitable. And so it was. But that's hindsight. Had one person turned differently, made a phone call at the right time, delayed one appointment or overslept, the outcome would have been different. But few allow themselves an opportunity to change 'destiny.'"

"But the dreams, the visions—they don't make sense," I said.

"How could they? You have made an enemy out of your dreams and visions. Welcome the stranger and he becomes your friend . . . someone you can understand and know. That knowledge gives you the power to alter the future or . . . change destiny."

"Luke," I whispered, shaking my head. "Can't you hear yourself? Jesus, you sound like Moses on the mountain. Right now, right this minute, I'm worried, scared to death about Jamie and the baby." My voice quivered. "She left me, Luke." No response. "Well, aren't you going to say something?" I paused. "I'd trade it all—everything I have, everything I've learned—to have her and Rachel back. Even the migraines! I'd even take the migraines back." As Luke bent forward to speak, I rushed to comment. "No. Don't say it. I know already. We can't go back. I'm not trying to make points for me any more. I want to help Jamie for Jamie, for Rachel. Right now, this very instant, I sense something coming, but I can't put my finger on it."

"Accept who you are and what you see."

"But I do accept it," I insisted.

"Do you?" Luke asked. "You came once, asking to know all that I know, yet each time there is more to see, you turn away . . . as does Jamie, Max and everyone else in the class."

"That's not true," I argued.

Throwing your desk over in the office is a way of cutting yourself off. Put blinders on your eyes and the world suddenly appears confusing."

I had difficulty listening when I realized, once again, the scope of Luke's awareness. He picked up on my thoughts immediately.

"Come now, Peter, don't be so shocked. If you observe different muscle cells from different hearts under a microscope, each pulses to a separate rhythm. If moved closer together, but still not touching, their beats change, finally pulsing together in perfect synchronization. And when women become friends, good friends, close friends, their menstrual cycles often begin to coincide. Actually, women who are not friends will also experience the same phenomenon when in close proximity." He paused to light a cigarette. "So here, in this group, the one you chose to join, our cycles have begun to coincide as well. But instead of biological function, we're dealing with consciousness . . . yours, mine, Jamie's, Max's, everyone's. There's nothing mysterious about what I'm saying. Ask any young child. They can 'read' attitudes, internal states in other people, long before they understand words. And then, my friend, they're taught systematically to block that very process and to be realistic, to be an adult. And so here we stand, separate and alone and scared, as if we're alien to each other, denying the knowledge and awareness we share together."

The fact that his explanation made perfect sense disturbed me even more. Had I been blocking what I knew? Was it that simple? I paced around his seated figure. "Okay, Luke. Since you obviously know what I'm talking about, why can't you answer my questions directly? Tell me about the old man with the high hat. And the screaming people against the brick wall. And the other images, including my sketch, which I assume you know about, too."

"I'm not here to do that for you."

"Then why are you here? Is this some sort of game? You give some answers, withhold others. That keeps you in a power position," I charged, "forcing those in your classes to believe they need you for what you choose to withhold. My God, look at me right now."

"Have you ever asked yourself why you're here? Oh, I know what it meant to you in the beginning. But why are you here now?" He paused, waiting for the answer I didn't have. "During this journey together," he continued, "whatever you have come to know, you have given to yourself."

As I listened to Luke's comments, my impatience intensified. "You always throw it back at me, Luke. In a way, I applaud that. But you have to stand up and own what you do. It's easy to sit on the sidelines and philosophize. But the action is in the trenches, in the streets—that's where life unfolds. And that's where what we know counts . . . not here, not in some ivory tower." I felt myself softening. "I'm not going to try for a direct response from you any more, Luke. It's all becoming too dangerous." I moved toward the door.

Stroking his beard, Luke began to speak. "There are two ways one can read the weather. We can climb on the roof and give a visual accounting based on what our eyes tell us. Or, as many weather bureaus have done, we can use radar to extend our knowing beyond the range of normal perception. Is the purpose of the second system not evident? Knowing in advance about storms, floods, whatever, enlarges our power to respond, to intervene, to evacuate where necessary . . . to take better care of ourselves." He paused, again pulling his beard. "When the weatherman's prediction of a hurricane proves accurate, do we blame him for the storm?" Luke downed a slug of soda. "I guess many of us ignore or destroy the radar systems. But ask the farmer or sailor or even the mother who uses such knowledge productively. Is it dangerous or is it life-enhancing to have such information?"

Wavering, I caught myself nodding automatically as Luke concluded his analogy. "Definitely, life-enhancing," I responded. "But there is one catch. The weather people know how to read their radar bleeps . . . I don't."

"Do you want to?" Luke asked.

"Why else would I be here?" I replied. "The man with the top hat, the people against the brick wall, the overturned garbage cans, the wagon wheel—they may be radar signals, but I can't read them, Luke. They're coming onto my screen scrambled. So I'm asking for your help."

Luke peered into my eyes. "What comes through you is yours."

"And what comes *from* you is yours," I countered. "I'm willing to own my stuff—my visions, even my panic. What are you, my dear friend, willing to own?"

"That's not what this game is about," Luke answered. "It's about your willingness to see."

"Is that what all this is for you—a game? I think this is about opening your mind and heart, listening to yourself. I think this is about respect and straight talk. I think this is about making a difference in people's lives, not just talking about it. Listen, Luke, I love you, but I can't be a yo-yo on a string like Rudy or Dan or Collis . . . or even Max."

"Rudy, Dan and the others have their own paths as you have yours. Don't turn away now." In an uncharacteristic gesture, Luke reached out and held my arm firmly.

Opening the door to leave, I withdrew from his grasp and looked into his staring eye. I loved him for where he'd helped me come to on my journey. But now, I had to move beyond his counsel.

"You're not coming back, are you?" Luke asked.

I touched his arm gently, then left without answering.

37

When I returned to the studio, I couldn't concentrate on my work. The voices of those around me echoed through a fog. Even the pencil in my hand appeared distant and detached. I whipped the office door closed. A hollow sanctuary. Jamie. Jamie. Jamie. I repeated her name like a mantra. Rachel giggled at me through the static of my escalating tension. My head began to ache. Ripping the phone off the table, I jerked the dial with my finger. The endless ringing went unanswered. Of course no one was there. When would I face it? When would I accept it? Slamming the receiver down, I tracked an elliptical path around the drawing table. Destiny. That word whistled in my ears. Could my wife and child be moving toward some unspeakable destiny? Could I know it? Could I allow myself to know it? Again I grabbed the phone, buzzing Maire.

"Yes," came the quick response over the wire.

"Fran Zercon. *Z-E-R-C-O-N,* Walters and Associates. In Gramercy Park. That's Jamie's mother. See if my wife's there," I directed, hanging up in the middle of my last word. I switched the intercom on again. "Sorry for the abruptness."

"That's okay," Maire replied. "You said you didn't want me to give you your calls, but one from your friend sounded urgent."

"Max?"

"Uh, huh. He asked for you to call him as soon as you return."

Without comment, I hung up, then dialed Max's number, only to hear the recorded words of his answering machine.

As the meeting with Luke replayed in my mind, I massaged my temples. The pain hit my eyes, then traveled back along the top of my skull, affecting the tightened muscles in my neck: a full-blown migraine, my first in almost two years. The intercom signal intruded. "Yes. Yes," I said urgently.

"Sorry. No luck. But they did say Jamie had been there and her mother thought she had a rehearsal later this afternoon."

"Was she with Rachel?"

"I don't know . . . want me to check?"

"Please," I said.

"Just hold, I'll be back on the line in a second." Within a minute, she returned. "Yes, she's with Rachel. She also had her cello."

"A rehearsal," I blurted. "That's it. Could you find out if she knew where the rehearsal was to be held?"

"I asked. They didn't know."

I could barely focus on her words. "Thanks," I said, abandoning the phone.

The pain muddled my thinking. I knew I had to be clear for Jamie and for Rachel. I threw open the bottom drawer of my desk. My hands leafed through the papers and cards frantically. Finally, I pulled the drawer off its runners and emptied the contents all over the floor. No pillbox. I grabbed the handle of the second drawer and overturned it on the floor as well. I kicked my foot through the boxes of pen points, staples and Magic Markers. Nothing. It had been two years since I had used any painkillers, two years since I had hidden an extra vial of capsules in the office. The pain began to interfere with my vision as the vise of the migraine tightened.

Suddenly, I jumped from the chair and scrambled to the

closet. I ran my fingers along the top shelf and located a plastic container. Withdrawing three capsules, I walked rapidly toward the bathroom. As I dumped the pills into my mouth, I caught a glimpse of myself in the mirror. I looked like a crazed junkie. The image shocked me. I spit the capsules back into my hand. Like a man stumbling through a drunken stupor, I moved slowly along the balcony until I reached my office—one hand still holding the water, the other forming a fist around the pills.

I had to try. There's no one left, no one to trust but me, I realized, as I dropped into my chair. Only me! I didn't quite understand how I could feel so trapped and liberated at the same time. Luke could no longer be my scapegoat or benefactor.

As I exhaled, I talked aloud. "Pain, you are my friend and, like my friend, I welcome you." The words bubbled from my throat naturally. The intensity of pressure in my head increased dramatically. I concentrated intently on the pain. Nothing existed but the migraine. The aching appeared to exceed the perimeter of my skull. I seemed to exist within it. Eventually, I discarded the last shred of resistance. Was I dying? I didn't even fight that notion. Though dizzy and blind with pain, I began to process the sensation differently than ever before. I had disconnected, let go. I became aware of myself separate from the pain. Suddenly, my body relaxed. The pills and small cup of water, which had been clutched in my hands, dropped to the floor. Simultaneously, the migraine began to dissipate. Within a minute, it disappeared completely. It worked. I had done it . . . by myself.

As I rose from the chair, I brought my wife and child into my mind's eye, loving them from afar. I concentrated as I never had before. I asked for God's help. I reached into the stormy sea in my mind, trying to locate them. Suddenly, a new image flashed before me: a clock, an ornate relic from the early 1900s, stood on its own stand beside the curb of a busy street. Black numbers set on a white field marked the passage of time. The clock, encased in heavy metal and painted green with decorative gold trim, had a stately air. Seven feet behind it, a massive cement pot held a small tree. I concentrated squarely on my vision, memorizing each detail until it finally disappeared.

Something about the clock and its setting seemed familiar, but I could not identify the location. Seizing a pen, I sketched my impression. The lines of the clock fell together easily; the curb and young potted tree moved into place. Inexplicably, my hand outlined an awning in the background. I stared at the drawing. I had no recollection of an awning.

Detailing the sketch, I began to depict the hands on the clock. Without thinking, I placed the little hand just above the five with the big hand drawn to face the nine: 4:45. I checked my watch to note the time: 4:05. Inhaling a deep breath, I lingered for an instant with my thoughts of Jamie and Rachel. Their presence haunted my every movement.

Charging out of my office, I stopped on the balcony and counted sixteen heads in the studio. I ran down the stairs and began to show the sketch to members of my staff, asking each if they could identify the location. Their conflicting answers created a comic and unrevealing montage. Battery Park. Forty-second Street Library. The clock in front of the Municipal Building on Centre Street. The Cloisters. An undisclosed location in Central Park. Entrance to the Waldorf. I realized suddenly that I was doing it again: asking others to supply me with my answers, not trusting myself to know. Abandoning the guessing game, I sprinted up the stairs, slammed closed the door to my office and stood alone in my own sweat. A blank! Zero!

Pressing the intercom, I said to Maire, "Every five minutes, I want you to try my home, just in case; then try Max Sorenson and also Hera's number. Call Jamie's mother again to find out if she's heard from her. And, Maire, tell

Mrs. Zercon that if her daughter does call, have her stay exactly where she is until I get there. Let me know immediately if you find out anything. Otherwise, no calls now." I released the lever.

I beckoned to the universe, inviting it to supply me with another vision. Within seconds, another new image filled my mind. A bronze statue of a soldier on a massive horse being led by a beautiful, winged angel. The man's cape spread like the sail of a schooner catching the late afternoon wind. The vision faded away. Concentrating on the horseman's weather-eroded exterior, I contemplated the huge pedestal on which it must have been mounted. I pictured various locations around the city where I remembered statues. Finally, I gave up my inept attempts. I knew guessing wouldn't work.

There would be more, I assured myself, standing alone before the billboard that decorated one entire wall of my office. The maiden from my favorite poster gazed at me with her watch-eye. Her face dominated the room. I found myself drawn to her compulsively.

Then my vision clouded. Suddenly, I saw the running figure of Jamie, her face frozen in terror as she crossed a blurred landscape. Oh, God, no, I shouted deep inside. My hands trembled as I checked my watch: 4:36. Nine minutes left. Nine minutes to what? A clock . . . but where? I knew something was hurtling toward my wife and child from the future, something I could not see.

Pressing my palms over my eyes, I reviewed my fleeting impression of Jamie. I tried to freeze the background, but the forms melted into abstractions of color. Let it go, I counseled myself, giving up my need to control the impression. At that very moment, an internal wall collapsed. Images flooded my mind. Four flags hanging from the facade of an elegant building. Taxis parked along a wide avenue. Three portable bookstalls stationed in the front of a stone wall. An antique music box, its handle turned by an old man. A naked maiden guiding a soldier atop the elaborate fountain of the Grand Army Plaza. Two canopied entrances to the Pierre. The freestanding antique clock beneath an awning with the distinctive inscription of the Sherry Netherland Hotel. A Sabrett frankfurter stand parked under a horseman's statue at Sixtieth and Fifth Avenue.

I raced out of my office, my feet crashing on the old wooden staircase and ricocheting like gunshots. Heads turned in the studio as the momentum of my form rattled even the most focused worker. Maire gasped as I roared past. Colleen jumped from her table and shouted to me, but I couldn't understand her words. I knocked over two drawing tables in my path, exiting finally through the front door. I sprinted into the street, jumped into my car and sped recklessly into the cluttered stream of traffic.

In front of a fruit market on Seventh Avenue, Max Sorenson dropped his packages in the middle of the sidewalk and began to run. The puzzle fell together for him at the same moment it had fallen together for me.

Acting concurrently, each of us moved alone, not knowing about the other. Desperately, we both raced to intercede.

With Rachel slung across her chest, Jamie, accompanied by Hera, arrived at the museum's recital center at the specified time only to learn that the rehearsal had been shifted to two hours later. Rather than linger in the large, somber auditorium and wait for the other members of the string ensemble, they decided to leave the cello in the ticket office and walk to Central Park.

They strolled around the large lake at the southern tip of this huge oasis in the city's midst. Huge, monolithic skyscrapers on Fifty-seventh Street and along Fifth Avenue hovered over the treetops like brooding mountain peaks.

The sun, disappearing behind an office building, bathed the park in its last moment of daylight. The two women avoided talking. It had been that way all day, ever since Jamie had arrived the night before and moved in with Hera. Talking about it made the separation more real for her. Although she had no regrets about her decision, she wanted a quiet time for her and her daughter. Hera had tried to convince her to see Max for therapy, to resume their former client-patient relationship, even if only for one session. But Jamie insisted that Max had become too close to me and much too close to Luke to help her. She argued that she could help herself and depend on herself.

As they began to climb the slope toward the street, Jamie cuddled her daughter protectively from the wind, which began to tunnel through the streets. She turned back momentarily and noticed the mist gathering over the lake, obliterating the paths, the park benches and the lampposts from her view. Something about what she saw seemed familiar and disturbing.

"Anything wrong?" Hera asked, noticing the peculiar way she clutched the baby's carrier as she stared back into the park.

"Oh," Jamie said, startled. "Nothing. C'mon, we should be getting back for the rehearsal."

As they proceeded to climb up the grassy hill, Jamie scanned the towering walls of cement and glass that faced her. Admiring the old charm of the Sherry Netherland with its marble trim, she consulted the antique clock that stood before it: 4:42. When they arrived at street level, the baby began to whimper.

"Of course." Jamie smiled, rubbing her daughter's belly. "You're hungry and I left your bottle in the cello case." Her eyes scanned the numerous vendors by the curb. Nothing suitable, she thought, until she noticed a stand selling fresh orange juice across the street. "Great," she mumbled, pointing to the sign decorated with pictures of oranges as she guided Hera toward the corner. They passed three portable bookstalls and an old man cranking a giant music box. Behind him, a host of pigeons landed on the statue of William Tecumseh Sherman, a caped horseman guided by the naked angel of life. In the distance, people gathered to watch a magician perform by the fountains of the Grand Army Plaza.

"Here," Jamie said, removing the sling from across her chest and depositing Rachel gently into her friend's open arms. "You stay here with Rach and I'll be back in a second." Hera held up the baby's hand and had her wave good-bye to her mother, who joined the crowd waiting for a green light at the corner.

When the traffic signal changed, the crowd, en masse, scurried into the street. A woman, burdened with at least five shopping bags, muttered through layers of make-up as she hurried past Jamie. She left a heavy scent of jasmine in her wake.

Once on the other side of the street, Jamie stopped again. She looked back at Hera, who sat on a bench facing traffic with little Rachel in her lap. Satisfied, she continued walking to the small stand. A young man was hawking his natural products: orange juice and fresh strawberries. Jamie ordered the juice for the baby and a small box of berries for her and Hera. As she turned back toward Fifth Avenue, she couldn't help but stare at the strawberries in her hand. Everything appeared so incredibly familiar to her today. Jamie stepped to the curb.

A huge bus, caked with mud, sputtered and backfired several times as it passed, leaving huge puffs of smoke behind it. In the small clearing behind clouds of exhaust, Jamie looked back at Hera and her child in her lap. For the first time she noticed the bright green plaid skirt that her friend wore. A second pocket of billowing fumes obscured her view. Then she heard that awful, familiar sound . . . the pounding of hooves against hard pavement. "Oh, God, no!" she screamed as she dropped the berries, the same kind, she realized suddenly, that she had picked on the mountainside in her dreams. Hysteria farther up the street sent the crowd at the corner scrambling back to the sidewalk. "Rachel," Jamie hollered, pushing against the fleeing horde of panic-stricken pedestrians that prevented her from crossing the street. "Rachel, Rachel!" she screamed again and again.

An enormous horse, pulling a sight-seeing carriage, rampaged down the avenue. Overturning trash baskets crashed onto the sidewalks, spitting their contents into the street. People hugged the brick walls of the buildings. A woman grabbed her young child and huddled in front of the Pierre. As the crowd dispersed, Jamie clung to a traffic sign in order not to lose her footing, then lunged back into the street. A man slammed into her, knocking her to the pavement. When he tried to help her to her feet and bring her to safety, she fought him. "Hera, run!" Jamie yelled as she watched her friend leap off the bench and trip over the edge of the curb. The baby rolled out of her arms into the street, directly into the path of the oncoming carriage.

Horrified, Jamie broke loose from the stranger, knowing already that she was too late. Changing direction, she ran toward the charging animal instead of toward her own child. "Me. Me. Me." The words erupted from her throat with each step she took nearer the crazed horse. Jamie saw the fiery glint of its frenzied watch-eye and thought of Luke. The image almost paralyzed her as she arrived at a point blocking the horse's path to her baby.

People shouted at her, but she couldn't hear. The wind danced in her clothing as she stood inert. The horse's hooves slapped a macabre cadence on the black macadam, echoing like thunder in the walled canyons of the city. A foaming lather of white perspiration ringed the upper portion of the animal's muscular body. The horse and its carriage kept coming and coming and coming. The gap narrowed, but Jamie didn't move.

At that moment Max rounded the corner between Jamie and the rampaging horse. Hera, frozen on the ground, screamed his name as he ran past her and threw his arms into the air in an attempt to wave off the animal and the carriage.

A second later, at a point sixty feet south of Max's intrusion, I swerved my car onto Fifth Avenue, just having jumped a high curb to avoid fleeing pedestrians. When I realized that the horse-drawn coach, no more than thirty feet in front of me, headed out of control for a distant sidewalk crowded with onlookers, I veered my vehicle into its path, breaking the animal's momentum and forcing it to stop.

I threw the door open, leaped into the street and spun around, mortified by the crowd that gathered just north of my point of entry into the avenue. I ran blindly toward the stunned group, my eyes flooded with tears, my body numbed. I shouted the names of my wife and child. People moved aside, sensing my urgency and my connection to the incident that they had all witnessed. When the last man stepped out of my path, I saw what I believed I would never see again: Jamie, alive, kneeling on the ground, hugging a very animated baby.

"Peter, oh, Peter," she murmured, recognizing my approaching form and extending her arm toward me.

I grabbed my wife and child, dropping to my knees on the ground. In that instant, I saw the inert figure of Max lying on the black macadam. Although I wanted to touch Jamie and Rachel all over to assure myself of their very existence, I couldn't. I looked up at Hera, who stood in front of the crowd, her eyes fixed on Max.

I reached out to touch my friend, but then, at that precise moment, my body felt limp, as if I were about to faint. I experienced myself suddenly outside of my body, a sensation not unlike the one Jamie had mentioned having in her dream. From my elevated position, I watched an abbreviated rerun of the incident.

Jamie stood at a food stand, completing her purchase of orange juice and strawberries, then glided to the corner. I caught a glimpse of Max racing toward the intersection from several blocks away.

Fifth Avenue filled with screams and darting bodies. Hoofbeats clamored against the pavement. As I watched the people scramble for their lives, street signs and garbage cans were tossed mercilessly aside by the runaway horse and carriage. I saw a withered old coachman leaning forward off his seat in a desperate attempt to recapture the reins he had dropped. Jamie darted into the street but was thrown to the pavement after colliding with a man. As he helped her to her feet, she fought him, shouting to Hera, who held Rachel in her lap. I also saw Hera lurch from the bench, trip and fall, losing her grip on the baby, who then rolled into the street. Breaking the man's hold, Jamie lunged forward, putting her own body between the charging horse and the fallen body of her daughter.

At that moment, Max turned the corner. For an instant, he paused and looked directly up at me as if he knew I watched from above. He waved a small red rose. As he turned, arms outstretched to alter the animal's course, his body collided with the fourteen-hundred-pound animal, causing it to turn away from Jamie and the baby lying in the street directly behind her. The impact catapulted Max into the air. He dropped limply to the pavement.

Without warning, my perspective shifted. Beside Jamie again, and still bent forward, I lifted Max's wrist ever so slightly and searched for a pulse. Nothing. I shifted my fingers, finally catching a good, strong beat. I pressed my face to the pavement next to his.

"Max," I whispered.

Suddenly one eye opened. It stared blankly at me. The emptiness of the expression frightened me.

"It's me, Max. Peter."

The eye shifted its focus and peered at my face . . . still no recognition. Finally, his other eye opened. He squinted as if trying to focus. Then Max Sorenson winked.

"You fabulous fool." I sighed.

"Oh, thank God," Jamie said.

Slowly, Max tried to raise himself.

"Don't," I warned, "just in case something's broken." I brushed some dirt off his face. "Thanks, ol' buddy."

Jamie leaned over and kissed Max. They stared at each other.

A police officer intruded. "An ambulance is on the way. Just rest easy where you are."

An old man in the costume of a turn-of-the-century coachman pushed his way through the crowd. He held a tall, black whip. A plastic flower pinned to his lapel highlighted a cardboard nameplate, identifying him as Jude. He begged forgiveness from all of us. Jamie looked at the old man in awe. She recognized him as the coachman whose life she had saved in a taxi ride with her mother.

In the distance, she noticed several other policemen holding the bridle of the runaway horse, a black and white spotted animal with a penetrating watch-eye . . . the horse from her dreams.

I stared at the animal, too, then turned back to the old man. "It's okay," I said, wanting to free him from responsibility for what had just occurred. We had all been participants.

As I turned back to Max, I noticed him relax his clenched fist, revealing a red plastic rose. We both stared at it. Max grinned, then dropped the imitation flower into my hand. "I don't need this any more," he whispered.

Jamie touched it. The red rose. Now she remembered the fleeting figure of Max in one of her dreams. While the horse charged her, he had peeked out from behind a boulder and waved; a red rose hung from his mouth.

"It was all there, Peter," she said softly.

"I know," I murmured, wrapping my arm around her and Rachel and holding them tightly to me. I stared at the ornament in my hand.

As we waited for the ambulance, it became apparent that Max had not been seriously injured. I glanced around at the crowd that had gathered and encircled us, then looked back at Jamie, Rachel and Max. I could feel my heart opening in a way it never had before. Suddenly, I realized that neither I nor any of us standing in that windy city street was alone. Whether we acknowledge it or not, we all hold hands . . . together.

A Final Reflection

Often, I have heard people say that we must always heed the advice of others, especially experts, in order to know how to act and what to value . . . that to listen to our own voices over that of a physician, a scientist, a politician, a teacher or whomever is to take a risky position. Although the input of others can be extraordinarily useful and meaningful, the greatest risk, ultimately, is not trusting and not following our instincts and intuition.

Across the bridge of time, I think of those days with Luke more than a quarter of a century ago. Time had sweetened those memories, allowing me to recreate some of those events with such a vivid paintbrush. Years later, when I heard about Luke's death, I pondered the enigma of his elusive soul. I can still recall standing in that street, feeling deeply grateful for his fleeting presence in my life but knowing, at the same time, to move on. On that fateful day, I finally gave the voice inside a proper hearing. My wife and I would go our own way, digging deeper inside—ever on an inward-bound adventure that would allow us, one day, to hold and behold ourselves and others with an even greater sense of reverence and love.

The path sometimes is clear, sometimes cloudy... but always there is a path. The more comfortable and self-trusting we become, the more obvious our path becomes.

SUGGESTED READING
Other Books by Barry Neil Kaufman

During our travels throughout the world, people ask us continually for support materials regarding our work with individuals, couples, groups, businesses and families with special-needs children. Our answer is similar to what we share with those individuals who attend any of the programs offered at our learning center, The Option Institute: the core of what we teach is attitude—making self-acceptance, personal empowerment, happiness and love tangible and useful . . . to deal successfully with a relationship or career challenge, top cope with an illness, to help a child facing difficult challenges or simply to put new vigor into our everyday lives. Unhappiness is not inevitable. We have been systematically taught to use discomfort and distress as a strategy to take care of ourselves. We can un-teach ourselves . . . and begin again. But first, we have a choice to make — to become students of what we want and make such personal change a priority in our lives.

The path is neither long, difficult nor painful. Although we, ourselves, are still very much students of what we teach, there are now written materials as well as audio tapes to help people on this journey.

Happiness Is A Choice: Not only presents a simple blueprint to empower the decision to be happy (create inner ease, comfort and peace-of-mind) but also shares six shortcuts to happiness, each of which opens a doorway into an open-hearted state of mind. This book contains the best of twenty years experience working with tens of thousands of people — synthesized into an easily digested, step-by-step journey to self-acceptance and empowerment. [Note: This book and the other books listed below were written by Barry Neil Kaufman. There is another book with the same title, unrelated to Barry Neil Kaufman's work. Mr. Kaufman's book is published by Fawcett Columbine (Ballantine Books/Random House).]

Son-Rise: The Miracle Continues: The original classic best-seller, ***Son-Rise***, was made into an award-winning NBC television special which has been viewed by 300 million people worldwide. This new book presents not only the expanded and updated journal of Barry and Samahria Kaufman's successful efforts to reach their "unreachable" once-autistic son and heal him but goes beyond to include the inspiring stories of five other families, from among the hundreds of families helped by the Kaufmans, who used the same loving approach to heal their own very special children. Give this book to anyone you know who has a special child or who wants to find a whole new loving and effective way to parent or to live their own life. Published by H.J. Kramer.

To Love Is To Be Happy With: Details the practical and powerful Option Process®, a simple dialogue format used to replace beliefs which inhibit us with beliefs which will liberate us to become happy, loving and empowered. This has become our cornerstone book and manual in helping people redesign their attitudes and their lives. Published by Fawcett Crest (Ballantine Books/Random House).

Giant Steps: Illustrates ten intimate and uplifting portraits of the Kaufmans' transformative dialogue and mentoring process in action. In this book, the reader holds hands with young people on special journeys who learn to break through their pain and triumph even in the face of challenge and crisis. Published by Fawcett Crest (Ballantine Books/Random House).

A Miracle To Believe In: Shares a most revealing portrait of Barry and Samahria Kaufman's working and healing lifestyle before they established their world-renowned learning center. This book gives an in-depth picture of their family and the group of daring volunteers who came together to love a special child back to life. It also provides a blueprint for work with children, adolescents, or adults with special problems. Published by Fawcett Crest (Ballantine Books/Random House)

A Sacred Dying: This moving account of death's transcendence through love is a valuable resource and learning tool for therapists and an inspiration to anyone confronting the ultimate challenge...the death of a loved one. This book details the account of a family that learns to lift the veil of fear and silence. The story follows one young man's struggle as he deals with the impending death of his mother. With the help of the author's guidance and friendship, this young man learns to accept and then embrace what is happening...ultimately teaching his entire family how to go beyond pain to find a new and special way to celebrate life and each other. Published by Epic Century Publishers.

Out-Smarting Your Karma And Other PreOrdained Conditions: The thinking person's book of insight and humor. Simple and thought-provoking sayings that cut through the clutter of confusion and allow us, in a moment of time, to reframe our vision and worldview. Accompanied by delightful drawings, this enchanting book will clear your mind, touch your heart and inspire your spirit. Published by Epic Century Publishers.

These books are available at local bookstores and libraries and can be ordered by mail through Option Indigo Press. *Special Sales:* All books are available at special discounts for organizations, premiums, fundraising and for educational use.

Audiotapes include *The 12 Tape Option Process® Lecture Series, The Keys to Option Mentoring, Body Vital/Stress Free Living, The Empowered Leader, No Fault/No Risk Parenting* — all by Barry Neil Kaufman. *Special Children/Special Solutions* by Samahria Lyte Kaufman. Videotapes include *Everyone Can Be Happy, Making Love Last, Beyond the Limits* with Barry Neil Kaufman, and others. All audio and video tapes, as well as the above books, can be ordered by mail. For a free catalog and ordering information, call or write:

Option Indigo Press
2080 S. Undermountain Rd., Sheffield, MA 01257
1-800-562-7171

About the Author

Barry Neil Kaufman, along with his wife, Samahria Lyte Kaufman, teaches a uniquely self-accepting and empowering process (The Option Process®) that also has educational and therapeutic applications. They are co-founders/ co-directors of The Option Institute and Fellowship (P.O. Box 1180-FS, 2080 South Undermountain Road, Sheffield, MA 01257-9643, (413-229-2100). The Institute offers personal growth workshops for individuals, couples, families and groups as well as individual counseling services. Workshops range from week-end and week-long exploratory sessions to eight-week intensives. Custom designed corporate training programs for businesses and specialized seminars for helping professionals are also available. In the years since its founding, The Option Institute has served as a beacon of hope and possibility for thousands of people from across the United States as well as for individuals from many other countries.

Additionally, the Kaufmans present motivational talks at conferences, guide workshops and seminars, lecture at universities, and appear in mass media throughout the country. As a result of their innovative and successful program, The Son-Rise Program®, which they developed for their once-autistic son, the Kaufmans also counsel and instruct families wanting to create home-based, child-centered teaching programs for their own special needs children.

Mr. Kaufman has written ten books, co-authored two screenplays with his wife (winning the Christopher Award twice and the Humanitas Prize). In his landmark book, *Happiness Is A Choice,* he pulls together the best of over twenty-five years' experience working with thousands of individuals and presents a blueprint of simple concrete methods to empower the decision to be happy.

His first book, *Son-Rise*, which details his family's inspiring journey to heal their once-autistic child, was dramatized as an NBC television movie. His subsequent books include *Giant Steps, To Love Is To Be Happy With, A Miracle To Believe In, The Book of Wows and Ughs!, A Sacred Dying, Outsmarting Your Karma And Other PreOrdained Conditions* and *Son-Rise: The Miracle Continues.*

For more information about The Option Institute,
call 1-800-71-HAPPY (1-800-714-2779)
E-mail: happiness@option.org
http://www.option.org